Telemorphosis

Theory in the Era of Climate Change

VOLUME 1

Edited by Tom Cohen

OPEN HUMANITIES PRESS

An imprint of MPublishing – University of Michigan Library, Ann Arbor

2012

First edition published by OPEN HUMANITIES PRESS 2012

Freely available online at http://hdl.handle.net/2027/spo.10539563.0001.001

ISBN-10 1-60785-237-3

ISBN-13 978-1-60785-237-7

OPEN HUMANITIES PRESS is an international, scholar-led open access publishing collective whose mission is to make leading works of contemporary critical thought freely available worldwide. Books published under the OPEN HUMANITIES PRESS imprint at MPublishing are produced through a unique partnership between OHP's editorial board and the University of Michigan Library, which provides a library-based managing and production support infrastructure to facilitate scholars to publish leading research in book form.

MPublishing
www.publishing.umich.edu

OPEN HUMANITIES PRESS
www.openhumanitiespress.org

Contents

List of Figures

"Earth's Shipping Lanes and Road Networks"

Acknowledgements

This volume was generated from a series of symposia sponsored by the *Institute on Critical Climate Change*, at the University at Albany. Co-founded by myself and Henry Sussman, then of the University of Buffalo (initially *IC3* was a cross-SUNY initiative), it was created to pose the question of how the 21st century horizons of accelerating "climate change" and eco-catastrophe alters critical languages inherited from 20th century agendas. It posed this question in what is increasingly apparent as the twighlight of the "humanities" in the public university, *IC3* queried implicitly after the future of critical aims and pedagogy. Few of *IC3's* events would have been possible without the energy and imaginative input of Mary Valentis. We are also especially grateful to Vice-President William Hedberg of the University at Albany for his interest and support, without which our efforts would not have been possible. I also thank Dean Elga Wulfert of the College of Arts and Sciences at Albany and Mike Hill, Chair of English, for their continued support during a period of institutional transitions. The broader project is indebted to the energetic collaboration of Professor Wang Fengzhen, who helped to extend this conversation to our Chinese colleagues. Finally, I thank Jason Maxwell, whose superb editorial skills, care, and assistance in preparing the volume for press were key to its production.

Introduction

Murmurations—"Climate Change" and the Defacement of Theory

Tom Cohen

> *The point is, today everyone can see that the system is deeply unjust and careening out of control. Unfettered greed has trashed the global economy. And we are trashing the natural world. We are overfishing our oceans, polluting our water with fracking and deepwater drilling, turning to the dirtiest forms of energy on the planet, like the Alberta tar sands. The atmosphere can't absorb the amount of carbon we are putting into it, creating dangerous warming. The new normal is serial disasters: economic and ecological.*
>
> – Naomi Klein, "The fight against climate change is down to us—the 99%" [2011]

> *Carbon pollution and over-use of Earth's natural resources have become so critical that, on current trends, we will need a second planet to meet our needs by 2030, the WWF said on Wednesday.*
>
> – Agence France-Presse, "Time to find a second Earth, WWF says" [2010]

1.

Warnings regarding the planet earth's imminent depletion of reserves or "life as we know it" arrive today more as routine tweets than events that might give us pause, particularly as the current wars over global "sovereign debt" and economic "crises" swamp attention. The intensifying specter of megadebt—at a time of "peak everything" (peak water, peak oil, peak humans)—dumped into a future despoiled of reserves and earning capacity has a specific relation to this white-out—the "economical" and "ecological" tandem shifts all attention to the first term (or first "eco"). In a post-global present consolidating what is routinely remarked as a neo-feudal order, the titanic shift of hyperwealth to the corporatist few (the so-called 1%) sets the stage for a shift to control societies anticipating social disruption and the implications of "Occupy" style eruptions—concerning which the U.S. congress hastily passed new unconstitutional rules to apprehend citizens or take down websites. The Ponzi scheme logics of twenty-first century earthscapes portray an array of time-bubbles, catastrophic deferrals, telecratic capture, and a voracious *present* that seems to practice a sort of tempophagy on itself corresponding with its structural premise of hyper-consumption and perpetual "growth. The supposed urgencies of threatened economic and monetary "collapse" occlude and defer any attention to the imperatives of the biosphere, but this apparent pause or deferral of attention covers over an irreversible mutation. A new phase of *unsustainability* appears in which a faux *status quo ante* appears to will to sustain itself as long as possible and at whatever cost; the event of the twenty-first century is *that there will be no event, that no crisis will disturb the expansion of consumption beyond all supposed limits or peaks.* In such an environment other materialities emerge, reference systems default, and the legacies of anthropo-narcissm go into overdrive in mechanical ways. Supposedly advanced or post-theory theory is no exception—claiming on the one hand ever more verdant comings together of redemptive communities, and discretely restoring many phenomenological tropes that 20th century thought had displaced. This has been characterized as an unfolding *eco-eco* disaster—a complex at once *economic* and *ecological*.[1] The logics of the double *oikos* appear, today, caught in a self-feeding default.

The present volume, in diverse ways, reclaims a certain violence that has seemed occluded or anaesthetized (it is a "present," after all, palpably beyond "tipping points" yet shy of their fully arrived implications—hence the pop proliferation of "zombie" metaphors: zombie banks, zombie politics, zombie "theory"). It departs from a problem inherent in the "eco" as a metaphoric complex, that of the home (*oikos*), and the suicidal fashion in which this supposed proper ground recuperates itself from a nonexistent position. The figure of an ecology that is ours and that must be saved precludes us from confronting the displacement and dispossession which conditions all production, including the production of homelands. Memory regimes have insistently, silently and anonymously prolonged and defended the construct of "homeland security" (both in its political sense, and in the epistemological sense of being secure in our modes of cognition), but these systems of security have in fact accelerated the vortices of ecocatastrophic imaginaries.

If a double logic of *eco-eco* disaster overlaps with the epoch in deep time geologists now refer to as the "anthropocene," what critical re-orientations, today, contest what has been characterized as a collective blind or psychotic foreclosure? Nor can one place the blame at the feet alone of an accidental and evil '1%' of corporate culture alone, since an old style revolutionary model does not emerge from this exitless network of systems. More interesting is the way that 'theory', with its nostalgic agendas for a properly political world of genuine praxis or feeling has been complicit in its fashion. How might one read the implicit, unseen collaboration that critical agendas coming out of twentieth century master-texts unwittingly maintained with the accelerated trajectories in question? The mesmerizing fixation with cultural histories, the ethics of "others," the enhancement of subjectivities, "human rights" and institutions of power not only partook of this occlusion but 'we theorists' have deferred addressing biospheric collapse, mass extinction events, or the implications of resource wars and "population" culling. It is our sense of justified propriety—our defense of cultures, affects, bodies and others—that allows us to remain secure in our homeland, unaware of all the ruses that maintain that spurious home.

The rapacious *present* places the hidden metaphoric levers of the eco or *oikos* in an unsustainable exponential curve, compounding megadebt upon itself, and consuming futures in what has been portrayed as a sort of psychotic trance—what Hillis Miller calls, in this volume, a suicidal "auto-co-immunity" track.[2] Yet the "Sovereign debt crisis" corresponds to a *credibility* crisis as well. The latter applies not only to the political classes of the post-democratic klepto-telecracies of the West but seems to taint the critical concepts, agendas, and terms received from twentieth-century itineraries that accompanied the last decades and that persist as currency. Far from opening beyond the propriety of the *oikos* theories of affect, living labor and critical legacies have doubled down on their investments, created guilds as reluctant as Wall St. to give up cognitive capital. All the while there is attention paid to 'saving' the humanities or a critical industry that might be extended for a while longer (as if with "sovereignty" itself). Bruno Latour [2010] presumes to call this recent and ongoing episode the "Modernist parenthesis" of thought. In his conjecture, the very pre-occupation with human on human histories, culturalism, archivism, and the institutions of power were complicit with a larger blind that, in his view, the ecological crisis belatedly discloses.[3]

At the moment of writing it is common to point to the 2011 "occupy" movement, viral and cloud-like, as the Bartlebyesque counter to a totalization of the systems of this control. Bartleby has become the figure for a rejection of end-fixated production. Were one able to speak of an *occupy* movement applied to critical concepts and twentieth century derived idioms one might imagine a call to occupy critical theory and conceptual networks—but with what interruption of received programs ("Sovereign debt"), what alternative materialities, what purported "ethics" involving commodified futures (and the structure of debt), what mnemotechnics, and with resistance to what power, if it is the *oikos* itself, the metaphoric chimera and its capture of late anthropocene imaginaries that is at issue? This is one of the implications of what this volume terms *telemorphosis*, the intricacy by which referential regimes, memory, and reading, participate in these twenty-first century disclosures. The occupy motif, at the moment, sets itself against a totalization or experience of foreclosure—political, mediacratic, financial, cognitive. Various strategies appearing in this volume involve what could equally be called a *disoccupy* logic or meme.

Such a logic of *disoccupation* assumes that the domain in question is already saturated, occupied in the militarist sense by a program that, unwittingly, persists in the acceleration of destruction and takeover. Critical thought of recent decades would have walked hand in hand with the current foreclosures. The explication of ecocatastrophic logics, accordingly, are not found in Foucault nor, surprisingly, Derrida. Timothy Morton's *Ecology without Nature* is one such effort at disoccupation—seeking to void the two terms of the title, and in the process disrupt the "revised organicisms" of contemporary critical schools which, he argues, have managed to lapse into sophisticated pre-critical modes not unrelated to a more general inertia.

The meme of *disoccupation* resonates, for instance, with what Robert Markley in this volume proposes as a practice of "disidentification," and is implied by Timothy Clark's tracking of a "derangement of scale" in the perpetual cognitive disjunctures that come up against the ecocatastrophic present. One would *disoccupy* the figure of subjectivity, refusing not only the comforting commodifications of "the other" in cultural theory, but also the later moral appeals to other redemptive beings, such as the animal (as Joanna Zylinska argues with regard to post-humanism and its "animal studies"). What might be disoccupied would be the metaphorics of the home, even where the latter would sustain itself today in cherished terms like trauma, affect, alterity, embodiment, or even culture.

Yet a refusal of supposed redemptive 'outsides' to capitalism does not lead to a place of critical purity beyond the implied moralism of 'occupy' but the return of, and orientation to, a violence before which no model of sovereignty can be sustained.

To imagine that one might disoccupy by refusing all the supposed redemptive 'outsides' to capitalism is not to find a place of critical purity beyond the moralism of 'occupy.' Occupation is never simply takeover and appropriation, but always involves destruction of what it claims. The viral migration of the "occupy" motif involves a premise of disoccupation covertly. In the present volume this takes different forms. If one is now beyond tipping points in a zone of irreversibility, what corresponds to this as a critical injunction? Catherine Malabou sets aside the entire way the figure of trauma and the "always already" have organized time. Claire Colebrook affirms, rather than accepting as tragic, *extinction* as a point of departure for thought, which can be used to work against the organicist ideologies of the present (such as sexual difference). Martin McQuillan shifts the referential spectrum of discourse to "other materialities" in the hypothesis of a post-carbon thought, while Robert Markley tracks the influx of geological times that displace human narrative matrices. Bernard Stiegler voids the biopolitical model, which he sees as exceeded by "the third limit of Capitalism" (when it impinges on the biosphere). From that point of excess he strategizes a counter-stroke to the capture of attention by telecratic circuits, initiating a *noopolitics*. Joana Zylinska disoccupies, to continue this motif, the covert model of soft "otherness" by which animal studies has invented itself as an anthropo-colonianism. Like posthumanism generally, Zylinska argues, animal studies sustains its subjectal hegemonies. Hillis Miller locates a source for the ecocatastrophic imaginary in the blind insistence of "organicist" models of reading that sustain the comforts of the *oikos*. Against this hermeneutics of security Miller posits an "ecotechnics" that is at once machinal and linguistically based (where language is not communicative, but literal and inscriptive in a manner exemplified by Kafka's Odradek). Justin Read displaces any biopolitical model, again, by relinquishing trauma, the *oikos*, survival and interiorities of any manner, instead describing the circulation of data (or the "unicity") from which the only remaining political gesture would be oriented to the ecocatastrophic. Jason Groves shifts the referential screen from, again, a human-centered index to the viral textualism of (alien) species invasion, the global rewriting of bio-geographies. Mike Hill transitions to the alteration of atmospherics under the imaginary of climate war technologies in a new horizon of invisible wars (and wars on visibility), which today include not only nanotechnologies but also the "autogenic" turning of wars without discrete (national) enemies into suicidal rages against the "homeland"—a sort of, again, auto-occupation that is accelerating.

2.

If it is possible to note that theory's retrieval of human and animal otherness against the horrors of capitalism is akin to political deferrals of the future for the sake of saving the present, then we might ask what might open the reactive self-bound logics beyond homeland security? What has been absent to date is any shared or possible *climate change imaginary*—or a critical matrix. The problem is that the *other materialities* that constitute the forces of climate change would pulverize whatever informs "imaginaries" in general, which have always been tropological systems. When a recent critical query asks, for example, how to define "a political subject of climate change" the authors focus on how the "climate crisis shapes particular subjectivities," properly putting any rhetoric of "crisis" itself to the side as appropriable. The problem lies in the premise of defining a "political subject" or *subjectivities* to begin with: "Unsurprisingly, much of the current discourse on climate change oscillates between these two poles: most dramatically, between imminent catastrophe and the prospect of renewal; between unimaginable humanitarian disaster and the promise of a green-tech revolution. As such the climate crisis regularly calls forth regimes of risk" [Dibley and Neilson 2010: 144]. This Janus-faced algorithm, the "political subject of climate change" (147), arrives as a form of cognitive disjuncture: "these two images. . . are alternative figures of the subjectivity of ecological crisis. They are complimentary. . . . something like a dialectical image of the subjectivity of climate change" (146). On the one hand, this theoretical intervention is typical of the cognitive reflex toward pre-emption of the worst in arguments focused on mitigation, on sustainability, and on various "environmental" agendas—despite none of these answering to what science would demand. Sustainability has been angled to "sustain" the level of comfort and acquisition that the economy of "growth" demands. On the other hand, there is a reflex of occlusion. This straining for a "subjectivity" that would account for a political feature of this new landscape comes up with two mutually canceling algorithms: a desperate sense of imminent crisis and end, alongside a hope of something as lulling as 'subjectivity'. As a number of essays in the volume imply, one might proceed otherwise: depart or begin from a subject without subjectivity (Catherine Malabou), or an exteriority without interior (Justin Read).

The *aporia* of an era of climate change are structurally different from those that devolved on the torsions of Western mestphysics. They are not the aporia explored by Derrida around the figure of *hospitality*, taken as an endless refolding that keeps in place, while exposing, a perpetuated and lingering logics that defers the *inhospitable*. (One mode of deconstruction as solicitation involves shaking the house or structure within which one finds oneself, and this circuit might itself be disturbed by a refusal to occupy.) As Masao Myoshi [2001] first suggested, the logics of extinction compromise the aims of an emancipatory future along with all else. Any project of "formal democracy" runs up not only against the twenty-first century post-democratic telecracies that render that episode of 90's thought transparently inscribed in the neo-liberal fantasy (or pro-paganda) it would appropriate back for the then bruised "Left." But it also faces the transparency by which market democracy not only appears a Potemkin figure itself but, in fact, guarantees planetary ruin by the de-mographic requirements of cars alone for any emerging middle class of India and China (as Arundhati Roy argues).[4] Any focus on global popula-tion control runs up against feminist progressivism [Hedges 2009; Hart-man 2009]; post-colonial narratives that would restoratively mime the promise of 90's neo-liberalism of a world of market democracy would require three planets of resource materiel to allow dispossessed others to reach our levels of prosperity. The profound 90's investment in the "otherness of the other," an other who would be recognized, communed with, raised into the *polis*, and colonized, appears today as a stubborn ar-chaism and, perhaps, as an epochal *error*, that maintained the sovereign trace of subjective mastery. It would seem that both metaphysics and its deconstruction jointly participated in what is now disclosing itself as the "anthropocene"—an epoch of self-affirmation into which Enlightenment ideologemes have played, as Dipesh Chakrabarty analyzes in the term "freedom."[5] The impasse between today's spellbound and rapacious pres-ent and supposed future generations, the rupture of any imagined moral contract to or recognition of same, has been in circulation for a while.

The present volume of essays focuses on this under-examined question: how do mnemotechics, conceptual regimes, and *reading*—a certain un-bounded textualization that exceeds any determination of writing—par-ticipate in or accelerate the mutations that extend, today, from financial systems to the biosphere? The volume gives this a name, *telemorphosis*.

There is a curious parallel between the total occlusion of ecoca-tastrophic logic during the present economic "crisis" and the ways "post theory" criticism recirculates today. Some of this seems transparent. What names itself the *post-human* tends to re-secure a "humanism" that was never there to begin with. If the *Übermensch* once gestured to a rec-ognition of the human species as profoundly life-denying, its nervous programs and tribal identities to be exceeded, the current post-human-ism affirms the future-closing possibility that 'we' might extend our lives without limit. It has shifted from an early Nietzschean premise—exceed-ing anthropo-narcissism—to Kurzweil's projection to make the organism synbiotic and amortal. The post-human is man who has escaped organic limits, thus prolonging a certain *present* (or individual life) indefinitely: a capitalization of duration. In addition to this extension of bodily life, 'high' theory has recreated global man: Hardt and Negri's premise of a "multitude" renovates Catholic male imaginaries; systems theorists oscillate within the most organicist of tropes (mother Gaia); "new media" theorists return to phenomenological premises from the very logics that would suspend such; and figures of embodiments circulate routinely. There is a parallel, here, to the efforts to prop up, again and again, the "Wall St." banks by a perpetually deferred megadebt leveraged against disappearing resources.

But some examples of this rich prehistory and its default investments to a suddenly reset referential horizon:

Judith Butler's *Precarious Life* [2005] redressed the defaced "other" of *the terrorist* by appealing to the category of a forbidden grieving. She relies not only on a model of *mourning, but also of affirming that which is lost and dehumanized in selective grieving.* The essay in question is marked by its occasion, which is a defense of humanistic studies today as a discipline that shapes a higher enlightenment of alterity—an ethical defense in an academic environment in which the utility of such fields is under budgetary review. The matter of ethics calls forth Levinas and the topos of face. Butler deploys these figures to ask whether "the humanities have lost their moral authority" in a post-"9/11" rhetorical horizon. In a manner akin to the rhetorical intent of the Bush "war on terror" (supposedly horizonless in time and geography, yet already retired and replaced with the economic "crisis"), Butler goes for the bait of interrogating the terrorist face or otherness:

> The human is not identified with what is represented but neither is it identified with the unrepresentable; it is, rather, that which limits the success of any representational practice. The face is not "effaced" in this failure of representation, but is constituted in that very possibility. Something altogether different happens, however, when the face operates in the service of a personification that claims to "capture" the human being in question. [Butler 2005: 144–5]

The essay is interested in the divide across which the human is constructed: "I am referring not only to humans not regarded as humans, and thus to a restrictive conception of the human that is based upon their exclusion" (128). And here is precisely a negotiated back-loop to a more humane order: "If the humanities has a future as cultural criticism, and cultural criticism has a task at the present moment, it is no doubt to return us to the human where we do not expect to find it, in its frailty and at the limits of its capacity to make sense" (151). But it may be that the humanities does not have a future (in this way). The commodity of "cultural criticism" offers itself incoherently—and does so with the premise that its ethical value lies in a reconciliation of *peaceable* others. Yet, it is still and precisely the artificed image of a human "other" with whom "we" would empathically commune that involves a foreclosure in the very way the "social" or "we" has been fashioned. Is not the premise of *mourning* itself the problem?

If, on the one hand, a residual humanism cannot stop re-inscribing itself in a familial *oikos* or boundedness, it would be neither helpful nor accurate to reject all theory with some accusation of humanist recidivism. The point, rather, is that it was never there to begin with in the stabilizing memes appealed to. There have always been counter-gestures towards inhuman and multi-scalar logics beyond the face, even if these attempts to escape anthropocentrism are met by simultaneous resistance. An instance would be the coupling of Braudel with Deleuzian dynamism and systems theory in Manuel De Landa's *A Thousand Years of Nonlinear History*. Despite being published in 1997, this magisterial study has no awareness at its closing of the horizons of ecocatastrophe or climate change. De Landa refers to organic and non-organic forms of shifting "bio-mass" that pass between terrestrial organizations. The writing insistently allows no *anthropocentric* perspective to emerge in tracking three parallel histories of the "Geological," the "Biological," and the "Linguistic." Despite addressing what it calls a comparative socio-linguistics, it nevertheless has no conception of *mnemonics* or rhetorical and perceptual regimes participating in or shaping the feedback loops. It leaves out, as does Butler's retention of Levinasian "others" for the amelioration of social recognition, what is here termed *telemorphosis*:

> Over the millennia, it is the flow of bio-mass through food
> webs, as well as the flow of genes through generations, that
> matters, not the bodies and species that emerge from these
> flows. . . . This book has concerned itself with a historical
> survey of these flows of 'stuff,' as well as with the hardenings
> themselves, since once they emerge they react back on the
> flows to constrain them in a variety of ways. (259)

At the far end of where "cultural studies" began, De Landa abandons
the narrative of "capitalism" altogether, which now has no discrete outside or discrete other: "What use is there in making this move, if we are
to crown the whole exercise with a return to the great master concept,
the great homogenization involved in the notion of a 'capitalist system'?"
(267). De Landa identifies with an agency that shapes itself through "cat-
alytic loops" and lateral migrations—miming a limit of systems theory
and its descriptive capture by organicist metaphors: "much as a given
material may solidify in alternative ways (as ice or snowflakes, as crystal
or glass), so humanity liquefied and later solidified in different norms"
(6).[6] De Landa's history culminates in a post-binarized order in which,
nevertheless, the problem of reference returns: "We still have to deal with
the world of referents, with the thousands of routinized organizations
that have accumulated over the years" (273). De Landa repeats here a
blindness of theory 'after theory': if theory is an enclosure within human
textualism, then—yes—one needs to exit. But that does not mean that
departure would allow one to occupy a new space of referents: the referent—as climate change discloses—is lost, fragmented, dispersed, always
futural and always exceeding our calculative and referential captures. And
it mutates. It is common to note an exponential *acceleration* of temporal
vectors in which the perceptual and cognitive regimes we have at our disposal are increasingly incapable of *experiencing* the mutations and changes that mark our climate. That is to say: we have consumed, theorized,
sanctified, justified and moralized ourself with such speed and frenzy that
we have sped by and failed to witness the cataclysmic geology that is rupturing (or ought to be rupturing) the present.[7]

3.

One would need to situate the ephemeral non-phrase "climate change" beyond all the variations on empathic alterity. For the 'other' like all supposedly redemptive outsides has been long commodified, and can be disturbed only by an asubjectal non-alterity that exceeds modernity and its smug formation of a critical 'we.' The ethical attention to otherness relies on the same metaphorics of the home and hospitality that can only play on the borders of the bounded. To track the ways in which our cognitive regimes and their critical sophistications have participated in this acceleration one might be alert to the ways in which our semantic reaction-formations, recuperations, redemption narratives, and re-humanizations maintain themselves as rhetorical regimes tied to these loops of foreclosure. Mnemotechnic circuits operate outside of the fables of alphabeticism or human archivism (to say nothing of a specifically Western or pseudo-monotheist "era of the book"), and actively pervade the production of life forms (DNA, RNA, photosynthesis, cell formation, and so on). Rather than something like text being sequestered from the orders of the political and now a geomorphic *real*—as, says, systems theory may assume—text would more helpfully refer to something like *asystematic* forces: not logics of exchange, production, circulation and order but disarticulation and dispersal. If text is rejected as some form of linguistic or idealistic capture then this is only if there has not been a full enough emphasis on the "non-human" conceit of language (Benjamin). Here, semiosis precedes rather than is added on to *bios* (so-called "biosemiosis"). There is no animal who opens the world through speech; in the beginning is the mark or inscription, which we retroactively domesticate as that which served to open up our home.

Given more, or different times, one might suggest that a sort of affirmative perspective emerges:

First: the twentieth century preoccupation with human on human justice might be interrupted, with incompatible referentials arriving that would operate beyond archival memory and social history.

Second, what we call the "political" would migrate from an exclusively social category (Aristotle), as it has been defined in relation to the *polity*, to a cognitive or epistemographic zone.

Third, the era of the Book and its attendant nihilisms (alphabeticist monotheism) would appear as a dossier in the trajectory of telemorphic practices and memory regimes.

Fourth, rather than segregate *textual* premises from the "real" world according to referential regimes and theotropes, the notion of text would intensify the sense of multiscalar and inhuman logics all operating in an open field that would be better referred to as an (a)*biosemiosis*, or nano-inscriptive process.

Finally, in the "anthropocene era," writing practices might be apprehended in their interweave with carbon and hydro-carbon accelerations, from a position *beyond mourning* and the automatisms of personification, or "identification."

What emerges in the above postulates is that a *hermeneutic* reflex and semantic ritual might be repositioned. We would not only locate reactive processes of meaning in the sphere of textual criticism but discern a broader tendency towards the foreclosure of forces of the future. A certain reading practice—or returning to the proper (or the other) from which one might draw credit—would be akin to cannibalizing a fantasmatic past for the sake of an unreal future. The financial system in its current vortices, in which global currency collapse is constantly threatened, resembles the "unsustainability" of resource consumption and global heating. And each echoes with the current cognitive trances—"unsustainable," yet extending *themselves* credit ("quantitative easing"). To think that the modern question of power ought to be one of mourning and sovereignty—or of questioning how we lost an originary openness and fell into systemic closure, or how we failed to recognize some genuine others—precludes facing up to the fact that misrecognition, violent dispersal, decentred and inhuman forces have produced the mourned other and the sovereign as a lure that closes down confrontation with disappearing "futures." At issue is not just moving "beyond" the fetishization of mourning (get over it!) but parrying this steel trap relapse that, as in the model of the *organicism* analyzed by Hillis Miller ("it's everywhere"), fuels the acceleration. One returns to a putative domain of very small things: inscriptions, nano-settings, memory regimes, perceptual settings.

The contemporary trends of today's theory "after theory" often circle back to pre-critical premises. And they share a curious trait, aside from mourning 20th century master texts. Without disjuncture, the "new" model of networks and holistic circuitry that binds humanity and effortlessly traverses otherness and inter-species communications is the oddest replica of the previous organicisms whose suspension was the beginning of "theory" as such.[8] One is left with the impression that, as Žižek remonstrates of "the critical Left" during the 'naughts [Žižek 2009], recent critical pre-occupations discretely collaborate with the accelerations we are witnessing today.

4.

Bruno Latour, as observed above, offered a curious fable in which he identifies what he calls the "Modernist parenthesis" as the default mode of thought that accompanied the disclosure of an ecocatastrophic horizon. The twentieth century focus on "critique" that would be transfixed with reading and rewriting its own chaotic histories would have walked hand in hand with the unfolding impasse to terrestrial life. Latour's "Modernist parenthesis" includes the very project of *critique* and a pre-occupation with the past at the expense of addressing the past's now exponentially accelerated consequences. Latour—whose speculation departs from a painfully *Gaiesque* reading of the film *Avatar*—proposes that, as part of any reset today, the term *materiality* ought to be retired as part of a faux binary. He also recommends jettisoning the term "future", which he would replace with the ratcheted down and humbled term "prospects."

The label "*Modernist* parenthesis" is an intriguing trope. It resonates with a term like the "anthropocene" that can only, it implies, be pronounced in a future past tense which the speaker *would* inhabit. What might reading be if we were already looking back at our present, from a future that we cannot yet allow? Latour seems unaware to what degree he inscribes himself in this specular construction, both by his use of the retro-organicism of the Gaia metaphor and his premise, a signature of the "modernist" gameboard, of announcing a temporal break and new beginning, the revolutionary hypothesis of his imagined "parenthesis." It is thus reluctantly that he finds his way back to a canonical twentieth century text, the "tired. . . trope" of Benjamin's Angel of History to make his point:

> I want to argue that there might have been some misunderstanding, during the Modernist parenthesis, about the very direction of the flow of time. I have this strange fantasy that the modernist hero never actually looked toward the future but always to the past, the archaic past that he was fleeing in terror. [. . .] I don't wish to embrace Walter Benjamin's tired "Angel of History" trope, but there is something right in the position he attributed to the angel: it looks backward and not ahead. "Where we see the appearance of a chain of events, he sees one single catastrophe, which unceasingly piles rubble on top of rubble and hurls it before his feet." But contrary to Benjamin's interpretation, the Modern who, like the angel, is flying backward is actually not seeing the destruction; He is generating it in his flight since it occurs behind His back! It is only recently, by a sudden conversion, a metanoia of sorts, that He has suddenly realized how much catastrophe His development has left behind him. The ecological crisis is nothing but the sudden turning around of someone who had actually never before looked into the future, so busy was He extricating Himself from a horrible past. There is something Oedipal in this hero fleeing His past so fiercely that He cannot realize—except too late—that it is precisely His flight that has created the destruction He was trying to avoid in the first place. [Latour 2010: 485–6]

This default appeal to Oedipus is perhaps too quick. Latour creatively misreads the "tired. . . trope" of an Angel who is, in Benjamin's text, already something of a charlatan. The Angel is thoroughly impotent, aware of the scam of what the undead masses expect of him (to make them whole). "He" can't give the undead masses and debris of history, turned toward him, what they want but lingers, as if wanting to, until he is simply torn away by what is called a "storm from the future." This last angel is but the ragdoll of a certain *angelicism*—not just the costumed human face (with wings) imposed on the sign as messenger, here of no message, but the entire will to redemption narratives that his very form signifies. The text reads differently if one focuses on the word in Benjamin's text, "storm," which is repeated three times as the subject of three declarative sentences. It is a climactic term and subsequently indexed to what *Thesis XVIII* invokes as the aeons of organic life on earth within which human time appears as fractional seconds (an "anthropocene" perspective). Benjamin's so-called Angel of History is in fact a vaudevillian figure and not the avatar of the hero, the materialist historiographer. He embodies and destroys both the angelicism of an utopist Marxian and the theotropes of a Cabbalist—the two specular idioms which the *Theses* fuses in order to cancel one another out. The description of the Angel is so abdicating, deceptive, and suicidal (one can imagine him diving for a cigarette as he looks at the masses) that it nullifies, in advance, the project of materialistic historiography. It also cancels any "*weak* messianism"—or any messianism whatsoever. The Angel is shown as a con, held to his post by his expectant readership who still wants to be made whole. It will never be clear whether the Angel only thinks this is what is wanted of him, or if the undead masses think he wants them to want this. He is the last trace of anthropopism, dolled up as a human figure to mediate chance. When he is torn away by the "storm" he removes the anthropo-narcissm of angelicism, the lure of giving matter a human form, face and, in this case, betraying bird wings. He is the last personification of a human face plastered on an imaginary other, already a wire-framed incandescent in Klee's graphic deconstruction. He mimes and is dismissed as the sort of "weak messianism" that Benjamin elsewhere pretends to evoke—and which Derrida will return to, and try to use to keep a rhetoric of the future open (the trope of an impossible "democracy to come"). In this way, the Derrida of *Specters of Marx* regresses from Benjamin's destructive project by restituting the phrase "weak messianism." Derrida's omission of ecocatastrophic logics from his otherwise compendious agenda—for instance, nowhere to be found in *Specters'* "ten plagues" of the new world order—echoes elsewhere in an archival limit he seemed to require for "deconstruction" to rhetorically stage itself.

It is not that Benjamin's Angel trope is about fixation on the past—as archive, trace, histories of power, identity formations, narratives of justice, inscriptions—and hence ritual or time management. It is that "He" thinks that's what his readers seek in him, and he both gestures toward wanting to oblige (with, say, weak messianism?) and effectively gets out of dodge. Benjamin's Angel is given to us as a sort of con: knowing what his readership needs and hires him for (since "He" is the messenger of no revelation and reports to no god, is nothing but *sign* itself), He wants to help but is violently blown away. This lure of redemptive history is about *angelicism* tout court, its reflex or façade, the compulsion to reconstitute and to be reassured (even sanctified). The *trompe l'oeil* points not only to where this faux Angel is in costume as the last anthropomorphic form and *face*. (He looks human, is more or less male traditionally). It also points to the disappearance of the pretended mediation of an otherwise void sign (angel as messenger, as hermeneut). It gives the lie to a certain pretense to ethics, and to cognitive moralisms, and indicates a participation of angelicism in a more radical evil of which it is, adamantly, structurally, and violently unaware.

The impulse toward *angelicism* pervades the recycling of twentieth century critical idioms in sophisticated variations. And this systemic relapse, like the *Nachkonstruction* of an *oikos* whose non-existence would accelerate its militarized defense, itself appears to further a suicidal arc. This new angelicism, like what Timothy Morton [2007] calls "revised organicisms," merits suspicion. It is opportunistic to note where various critical traditions of return and redemption mingle. In a conversation between Lauren Berlant and Michael Hardt on "love" as a political agency at a conference titled "On the Commons; or, Believing-Feeling-Acting Together" we can read yet one more variant of an appeal to an angel that would make us and our past whole. Let us ignore that the commons in question for Hardt and Berlant is not water, oil, or food but the "transformative" zone of a new social "relationality" of liberal souls. "Love" here retains the soft debris and promise of a Christological meme. If for Hardt love "makes central the role of affect within the political sphere," for Berlant a more aggressive claim erupts:

> Another way to think about your metaphor, Michael, is that in order to make a muscle you have to rip your tendons. I often talk about love as one of the few places where people actually admit they want to become different. And so it's like change without trauma, but it's not change without instability. It's

> change without guarantees, without knowing what the other
> side of it is, because it's entering into relationality. The thing I
> like about love as a concept for the possibility of the social, is
> that love always means non-sovereignty. Love is always about
> violating your own attachment to your intentionality, without
> being anti-intentional. [Davis and Sarlin 2011]

Perhaps the metaphorical faux pas about "tendons" being ripped is a
clue to the skeletal argument (this is not, literally not, the way to build
muscle). What one witnesses is the effect of doubling down in the idiom
of commitment ("change without trauma"?), a closing off, as academics
of a certain age and temperament murmur, narcissistically, about *affect*.
One has found a new name for the oscillation that retains a sovereignty
of intentionality under a shifted algorithm: "Love is always about violat-
ing your own attachment to your intentionality, without being anti-inten-
tional." Sometimes, as we hear, it's just not about *us*, even where self-love
is called the commons and projects a socio-union, or *jouissance*, beyond
the confines of a dubious "collective" individualism. Perhaps this is one
marker of an end of a cycle, this fusion of critical and culturalist idioms,
returning to a redeeming origin—this time as "farce." This sort of eddy
appears as the comfort spa for what could be called academic theory's
"Lehman moment."

5.

What is interesting in the horizons converging at present is not how a certain *irreversibility* impacts or is excluded still by telecracies and cognitive
regimes. Nor is the main point of interest how sophisticated critical agendas have discretely served an agenda of institutional inertia—especially
in the guise of critique. What is interesting is not the shape this will take,
the variable catastrophes that are calculable or envisioned. What should
be interesting is a logic of foreclosure or *psychosis* that has become, in
part, normatized, accommodated or confirmed by corporate media.[9] This
psychosis takes the form of excluding, occluding, or denying what is fully
in the open and palpable, whether in science or before one's eyes.

Latour assumes that a "Modernist parenthesis" erred by its assiduous
focus on rereading the past otherwise, but he misses the target of Ben-

jamin's cartoon. It is not attention to the past but rather angelicism that constitutes a violent hermeneutic relapse. Perhaps an example of Latour's paralyzing 'parenthesis' would be Derrida's injunction against thinking the "future" in order to keep open the incalculable and the "to come." In fact, the current plunge in economic and societal "prospects"—lost "sovereignty," debt enslavement, banker occupation, collapse of reserves, and so on—is not premised on an undue focus on the past but is all about alternative time-lines. In this respect Latour's "prospects" run into the same capture of futures that occurs in the market, whether manipulated from above to defer reckoning (the "too big to fail" logic) or bet against. Calculations about future events, the forward narratives that flood media and alternative journalism, suggest a time in which the commodification of the "past" has flipped forward—marking both past and future as fantasmatic projections. One is not, so to speak, nor have we been, outside of "literary" constructions, least of all when we say something like *system* or *reserves*. What is called the market, now technically rogue in the sense that it serves as a façade of manipulations to play for time, is all about bets on future circumstance. Expanded to commodified futures and *derivatives*, and credit default swaps; wired through ingenious and self-imploding "financial instruments"—said market parallels the global despoilment of future reserves and times (generations).

It would be indulgent to run through variations of this. Some are familiar: the consolidation of a new form of totalitarianism and internal security apparatuses; new climate war technologies (applied internally) testing the "full spectrum dominance" protocols that the Pentagon retains as its post-imperial template (which Mike Hill explores in this volume). Some are becoming visible: untimed prognoses of biospheric collapse (marine food chains), extreme weather disasters (mega-drought, flooding, fracking induced quakes). Others hover at the edge of recognizability: mass extinction events, the mathematics of global population "culling." These nonetheless, like hydo-carbons and oil itself, literally shape visibility and invisibility—no oil, no hyper-industrial techno-culture, no photography as we know it, no cinema, no global transport. Is there an imperative, as Martin McQuillan suggests, to rethink the histories of writing and cognition in relation to carbon and hydrocarbon culture explicity—and to do so not only in relation to human mnemo-technologies? When Claire

Colebrook converts extinction from a tragic taboo to an affirmative perspective she deflates the semantic boundedness that any angelicism has always sought to save. The problem is not that the past draws human narcissism toward it in the latter's critical revisionism and deconstructions; the problem is that the more active "other temporalities" intervene, the more the artefacted present appears spellbound.

6.

Certain threads appear across these essays in the aftermath of this residual angelicism, and the retreat of face:[10]

Time. Robert Markley requires for any thinking of ecocatastrophic exigencies a displacement of "human" temporalities with the geological. This model to be displaced adheres to all culturalist templates and shows itself in the regressive symptom of any argument for "sustainability" at present: "Sustainability ultimately refers to an idealized homeostasis between humankind and environment that never existed except in the sense that robust ecological systems could remain unaffected by low-density populations of humans chasing a few bison hither and yon." Instead, "climatological time produces interference patterns that provoke complex and self-generating modes of *disidentification.*" This "disidentification" is applied to the problem of other modes of textualization and reading. By appearing indexed to temporalities into which human technics and life-effects are embedded, "the idea of climatological time paradoxically transcends and deconstructs a long philosophical and rhetorical tradition that contrasts *kronos* (chronological time) to *kairos* (the opportune moment, the "right" time, or, as in contemporary Greek, the weather)."

Ecotechnics. Hillis Miller exploits this default in the metaphorics of the *oikos* or home to note several things through a reading of Kafka's curious verbal pet-thing, Odradek living outside and under the house. In a ranging speculation on the state of contemporary imaginaries confronted with the machinal inevitabilities now released by politics and material processes (rising oceans, say), Miller traces how ecotechnics both constructs itself and—since it does so by a technic that contradicts the premise of an interior shelter—generates an "auto-co-immunity" spiral, or suicidal movement. In reflecting how this works he marks where an endlessly recurrent *organicization* of and in thought, a certain way of reading literary effects, has all along furthered the destruction of an earth it had romanticized improperly—with notions like nature, body, sustainability, or even the figure of Gaia herself in systems theory. Miller turns from Kafka's positioning of language in its most pre-letteral formations as (with Benjamin or de Man) to the non-human. From this, non-human reading of *Odradek* Miller passes to a critique of contemporary America. Miller's US is less an evil exception and more the poster-child for a zombie acceleration and suicidal "auto-co-immunity" complex. As Miller speculates on the rising sea levels from his home on the Maine coast: "The earth is not a super-organism. It is not an organism at all. It is best understood as an extremely complex machine that is capable of going autodestructively berserk, at least from the limited perspective of human needs. Global warming will bring about wide-spread species extinction. It will flood our low-lying islands, our coastal plains, and whatever towns, cities, and houses are on them." That is, it implies *avant la lettre* a dispossession of metaphor.

Care. Bernard Stiegler draws out the problem of a third limit of Capitalism that encroaches on the biosphere. Stiegler makes a pharmocological call for the reconfiguration of "care" and the dispersal of the "short-time" and telecratic degradations of libidinal economies which anaesthetize and infantilize the present: "The third limit of capitalism is not only the destruction of the reserves of fossil fuel, but the limit constituted by the drive to destruction of all objects in general by consumption, in so far as they have become objects of drives, and not objects of desire and attention—the psychotechnological organisation of consumption provoking the destruction of attention in all its forms, on the psychic level as well as the collective level." Stiegler's strategy shifts from any biopolitical imaginary to a field in which psychopower as the blind capture of attention might be countered by "waging war against speculation, but also against modes of life founded on the short term, of which the most every-day example is the organisation of society by a marketing systematically exploiting drives by destroying libido as that which evinces the capability of sustainable investment." Stiegler's shift to a thought of technicity without reserve, echoed in other essays in this volume, shifts the grounds of the political to "a *noopolitics* susceptible of reversing and overcoming the deadly logic of psychopower... where economizing means taking care."

Unicity. Justin Read tours the logics of a telecratic global polis in which binaries have been suspended, biopolitical premises displaced, and a mode of pure exteriorization reigns amidst subjects without subjectivity: "the Unicity is the line at which the world reaches absolute network integration, the mutual embedding of seemingly diverse informational networks into a complex systematic singularity." The topography of this "unicity" and virtual telepolis displaces what had been called public space into a *circuitry* of data formations and the recyclable memes of production or consumption without explicit reference, and before which the only politics possible would be elicited by eco-catastrophic and zoo-political tacts or ruptures: "By including all into a singular oneness, the Unicity functions only in terms of absolute exteriority. Everyone and everything is always already 'outside.' ...This absolute exteriority alters how we must think of power and relations to power. Once everything is on the outside, there can be no such thing as *transcendence*, at least not as some metaphysical Being that inheres in physical matter."

Scale. If not only critical theory but the geopolitical imaginary seems to be in cognitive hiatus before the logics of climate change, Timothy Clark recalls us to the problem of any metrics, or "scale," that cognitive regimes face. While not unrelated to broader forms of anesthesia or denial, he finds a "derangement of scale" between cognitive affect and the material effects evoked, which continually eludes any stable metric. This derangement arrives as a network of disjunctures: "Here a barely calculable nonhuman agency brings about a general but unfocused sense of delegitimation and uncertainty, a confusion of previously clear arenas of action or concepts of equity; boundaries between the scientific and the political become newly uncertain, the distinction between the state and civil society less clear, and once normal procedures and modes of understanding begin to resemble dubious modes of political, ethical and intellectual containment."

Sexual (In)difference. If Stiegler infers that the prospect of impacting or altering the *biosphere* arrives as a "lucky" point of reconfiguration for thought, Claire Colebrook takes the taboo premise of human disappearance—the limit implication of so-called "anthropogenic" global warming—as a point of departure. She finds that the affirmation rather than occlusion of extinction opens logics that had been, and are, occluded in the regime of organicism. The affirmation of extinction as a logic, rather than being somehow pessimistic, opens thinking beyond the mourning of sexual difference, which had "always operated as a moralism in theories of life." Writing against ecofeminism as itself a discretely regressive practice, she finds the dominance and ideology of sexual difference to have been an organicist ideology which finds itself suspended before the thinking of extinction: "it is precisely because of a certain clinging to bounded sexual difference and a fear of individual extinction, that the human species is now forced to confront a species extinction that will open it up to the extinction of the sexual difference of kinds."

Non-species Invasion. If *ecotechnics* names a non-existence of the eco as "nature," "home," or interior, Jason Groves opens a genre variation in which the present is read from the perspective of ex-species logics. Underlying the disarticulation of human modernity that climate change represents behind the façade of globalization, Groves tracks the terrestrial transfer and eco-invasions of alien species that operate as real world disarticulations of contemporary human life and its *geographism*. This border-destroying transfer operates, in its bio-contaminations, as a form of real-work textualism outside the purview of anthropic perception, and without face: "The liquidation of the continental scheme, registered by the geographers as a 'crisis in conceptualization,' is in fact occurring robustly outside of a conceptual horizon."

Bio-ethics, otherwise. Joanna Zylinska adds an entire other dimension to ex-species thoughts with a discrete demolition of current critical practices and their soft circulation within retro-humanist motifs rebranded, in the texts she examines, as the "post-human." She turns, specifically, to animal studies. At issue implicitly is the trend by which the "post-human" as trope has been deflated and domesticated from its once Nietzschean premise to speculation of cuddly cyborgs and pets. In this way, the "post-human" itself has posited (and then inhabited) a human definitional that never existed to begin with, and has done so repeatedly. In the tendency for "animal studies" to choose as its exemplary *other* (and sometime erotic partner) mammalian pets with names, or companion species, one encounters the sort of faux other that updates 90s multiculturalism to supposed intra-species communication. This act of "extension" persists within the recuperations of human mastery. In reversing this template of the inclusion and recognition of others she not only posits a a "bio-ethics, otherwise" which would have to account for microbes, viruses, and distinctly uncuddly life-effects, but also a bio-ethics that departs from a conception of "life": "not just a dog, a cat or a horse from the family of befriended or domestic animals, but rather a parasite, bacteria or fungus?" If so-called animal studies relapses by "extending" the model of empathetic others from the subaltern, to the animal, *three fundamental blind spots* [mark] the intermeshed trajectories of thought in animal studies: 1—The humanist blind spot, 2—The technicist blind spot, where much work goes into recognizing the animal's anima, i.e. its "subjectivity," with the animal becoming an extension of the human. 3—The violentist blind spot, where violence is posited as the enemy of ethics."

Post-Trauma. Catherine Malabou demands an abrupt departure from the way anteriority and mnemonics have been organized. She analyses the way trauma has been circulated with the temporal injunction of the "always already:" it is assumed that we must inhabit a site of guilty loss. From this assumption that we are always already at loss, always already traumatized, an entire structure of repetition compulsion and mnemonics ensues. Reversing this bad conscience would entail an abrupt departure not only from the residual strictures of psychoanalysis—here, the fetishization of trauma as a fetish of subjectivity maintenance—but those of post-structuralist orthodoxy themselves. Refusing the Lacanian (and Derridean) demand that the "always already" re-inscribes everything in an organization of sheer anteriority, she posits a thought beyond the "always already" through a normativity of what is called the post-traumatic (a metaphor for which is PTSD). This shift would issue in a subject without subjectivity. This creative destruction of the traumatized subject opens a different chrono-politics and materiality beyond mourning and perpetual re-inscription: "the post-traumatized subject disconnects the structure of the *always already*. The post-traumatized subject is the never more of the always already. We propose to entertain a fourth dimension, a dimension that might be called the material. . . . If destruction has always already happened, if there is something as a transcendental destruction, then destruction is indestructible. What if the always already might explode? What if the always already were self-destructive and able to disappear as the so-called fundamental law of the psyche?"

Ecologies of War. Mike Hill shifts the scene further into technologies of the contemporary war machine as it redefines itself as climate change war. Hill argues that not only have the terms of atmospherics been telemorphically redefined (with new conceptions of the "aerial"), but also that the protocols of combat have shifted against the human soldier altogether. The premises for conflict and resource wars shift from the geographical wars of enemy states (enemy *others* as in the past) into a self-devolving and indefinite system that exceeds any human reference and redefines what is in the kill-chain. This *autogenic* system is turned against its innovators, and itself, and becomes the condition for its own advance. In this newly self-armed zoosphere: "machine vision re-works our spatial bearings and enables the weaponization of temporality itself."

Post-Carbon Thought. Opening further the relation of writing to the hydrocarbon era of energy, Martin McQuillan invokes the specter of a "carbon thought" which traverses both rhetorical and material register. Carbon is indicative of what he invokes as "other materialities." Focusing on both the hyperbolic energy consumption that marks the late *anthropocene* and the trajectory of writing as a carbon-indexed technology that has redefined the artefaction of "life" itself, McQuillan formulates a new energetics in which script and fuel emanate from forces of the past that are stored and spent for a non-renewable, and therefore accelerating, future. The thought of carbon or the possibility of a post-carbon thought is probed as an alternate way to think against the present (the befuddled, ravenous time of "peak everything"). McQuillan conjures this in relation to any possible poetics of *oil.* For it is oil that has always been figured as waste and source, as residual black and viscous storage of disarticulated past organic "life," a sheer anteriority and storage system of black sunlight cycled over aeons, sucked, that will be transposed (into energy, technics, light, fuel). Through this active history in question one encounters "the theo-thanto-carbo-economy" that both persists in writing forms and must be deconstructed by them in a far more urgent manner than has been opened by the legacies of, say, deconstruction in the familial and auto-immune paralysis one finds it in today: "Writing philosophy about carbon, like making film about oil, is one of those tasks that must inevitably inhabit the positions of the theo-thanto-carbo-economy but somehow render those positions plastic by reading the deposits emitted by the economy in order to rearrange them according to a new logic and criteriology."

Health. Eduardo Cadava and I turn, here, to what might be a mere Satyr play within this dossier: a critical blog addressing a recent episode in post-democratic America's current hallucinology. Interrupting the creation and undermining of "Obama-care" at a certain juncture, Cadava and I interrogate what the 'ill' is that cannot be cured in a system that is afflicted with a sort of zombie "democracy" and that is also marked by systemic occlusion of climate change from its media and political discourse. We in turn explore how small political destructions preclude an American political imaginary from finding anything like its own social (or historial) prescriptions.

Notes

1.   The present volume grew out of a series of symposia focused on critical theory in an era of climate change, hosted by the *Institute on Critical Climate Change*, a project devised by myself and Henry Sussman and executed by the creative efforts of Mary Valentis, a full partner in the enterprise (http://www.criticalclimatechange.com/). The companion volume to this effort is edited by Henry Sussman and published as *Impasses of the Post-Global: Theory in an Era of Climate Change* II (series on *Critical Climate Change*, Open Humanities Press).

2.   Since the economic "crisis" has eclipsed any possible attention to the ecological "crisis," and since the trope of *crisis* itself operates as a rhetorical diversion (like, in Naomi Klein's reading, "shock"), the occlusion today of the latter represents more than a victory for corporate media in America, where "climate" cannot be mentioned in a presidential election. This occlusion is acknowledged as "global" or systemic, as the global discussions and farcical outcomes of Copenhagen, Cancun and Durban make clear repeatedly [Wente 2011; Thornton 2011]. Naomi Klein's recent shift from the analytic of "shock" as a planned tool of militarized expropriation to "climate change" as the "biggest crisis of all" runs up against the impasse. That is, of imagining it as an organizing other for social activism [Klein 2011]. Diverting from her influential analysis of the uses of predatory "shock" Klein marks a "new normal" in which "serial disasters" appear as unexceptional or naturalized (in the epigraph opening this introduction).

3. It is an interesting marker of the global "credit crisis" when the lords of finance meet at Davos to speculate on alternatives to the rogue "capitalism" they have been produced by—while consolidating a neo-feudal order of debt slave societies. At the heart of climate change denial is a toxic mix of short term memory formations (telemarketing, algorhythmic trading), corporate propaganda, and an odd rhetorical cocktail of theological defiance and defensive humanism in which the trigger is the word "anthropogenic," provoking a speciesist rejection of *blame* (it wasn't *us*, and its premise is a hoax to force eco-socialism, and so on).

4. This is the argument of Arundhati Roy in "Is there life after democracy?" (2009), calculating the implications of China and India's middle class all acquiring cars alone. The premise of liberationist or post-colonial critique mimes, with its restorations of universal subjectivity, the neo-liberal promise of a world of American consumers.

5. Referencing a speciesist crisis that "cannot be reduced to a story of capitalism" (Chakraharty 2009: 221), Dipesh Chakraharty elaborates a "universal" unification of man displacing cultural identifies not out of a positive but a "negative universal history": "climate change poses for us a question of a human collectivity, an us, pointing to a figure of the universal that escapes our capacity to experience the world. It is more like a universal that arises from a shared sense of a catastrophe. It calls for a global approach to politics without the myth of a global identity, for, unlike a Hegelian universal, it cannot subsume particularities. We may provisionally call it a 'negative universal history'" (222).

6. De Landa glosses: "It is important, however, not to confuse the need for caution in our explorations of the nonlinear possibilities of (economic, linguistic, biological) reality, and the concomitant abandonment of utopian euphoria, with despair, resentment, or nihilism. . . . And while these views do indeed invoke the 'death of man,' it is only the death of the 'man' of the old 'manifest destinies,' not the death of humanity and its potential for destratification" (273).

7. To index such a perspective is not to accede to a discourse of crisis or apocalypse, but the obverse; nor has it anything to do with mourning. The *anthropocene* marks processes that are entirely banal, of the mud (as Timothy Morton avers). Rather than having relinquished textualization for the real world of social relation and historical narratives, for the "political" and institutional power, it seems post-theory made a wrong turn from which it has difficulty pulling away. What seems readable today is rather the multi-planed orders of a sort of bio-textualization without limit—not one bounded or defined by human writing or technologies of human memory alone.

8. In fact, one might read the "late Derrida" upside-down, not as a movement beyond his early exanthropic violence but as the retracing of what a

pre-Derridean narrative leading to, or paused, before that would have been. One could read these pre-occupations and their rhetorical compromises as a strategy to embed his project within the canonical academic community in a way not easily erased. But the result has been a post-Derridean "deconstruction" that pretends it exists as a continuity with or in possession of a certain capital to be tended and given orthodoxy, an inability to depart from what is not in Derrida's text (climate change, say) or to recuperate its threads gradually (deconstructive "ethics"?)—that is, an auto-immune phase. One could say that Derida had always had two columns at work, the exanthropic and that entering humanistic discourses and circulating there, and that the second has come, rather predictably, to dominate just as the first, eclipsed, may be called for. The turning point would seem to be when Derrida, no doubt trying to counter the implosion of de Man and the way that was aimed against "deconstruction" in America, would risk such hyperbole, to rally the troops, as "deconstruction" is justice.

9. The turning away from "climate change" as a public discussion or one pursued by states has been confirmed during the global economic crisis—which has supplanted the "war on terror" meme in this regard. That has taken the form of *deferring* any address as if until the economic situation permits by providing extra public resources [Harvey 2011; Wente 2011], or the foreclosure enforced by corporate media and financial capture of "political" discourse [Thornton 2011].

10. The present essays are introduced as indexed to a single covering topos (*Time, Care, War*, and so on). The approach is the residue of an earlier proposal by Henry Sussman to compose a broader "atlas" to critical climate change, which I retain very loosely for the overview it provides. The premise was to examine what alterations and ruptures occur within those chosen *topoi* when they are placed in contact with the emerging twenty-first century logics in which the calculi of mass extinction events and resource depletion overtakes and the socio-historical projects and deconstructive aims of twentieth century criticism.

Works Cited

Agence France-Presse. "Time to find a second Earth, WWF says." 2010 October 13. <http://www.rawstory.com/rs/2010/10/time-find-earth-wwf/>.

Benjamin, Walter. "Theses on the Philosophy of History," in *Illuminations*, translated by Harry Zohn, introduction by Hannah Arendt. New York: Random House, 1969.

Butler, Judith. *Precarious Life: The Powers of Mourning and Violence*. London: Verso, 2005.

Chakrabarty, Dipesh. "The Climate of History: Four Theses." *Critical Inquiry* 35.2 (Winter 2009): 197–222.

Clark, Timothy. "Towards a Deconstructive Environmental Criticism." *Oxford Literary Review* 30.1 (2008): 44–68.

Cohen, Tom, Claire Colebrook, and J. Hillis Miller. *Theory and the Disappearing Future: On de Man, on Benjamin.* Routledge: London, 2011.

Davis, Heather and Paige Sarlin. "No One is Sovereign in Love: A Conversation Between Lauren Berlant and Michael Hardt,"*amour* no. 18.http://nomorepotlucks.org/editorial/amour-no-18

Derrida, Jacques. *Specters of Marx: The State of the Debt, the Work of Mourning, and the New International.* Trans. Peggy Kamuf. London: Routledge, 1994.

Dibley, Ben and Brett Neilson. "Climate Crisis and the Actuarial Imaginary: The War on Global Warming." *New Formations* 69 (Spring 2010): 144–159.

Harvey, Fiona. "Rich nations 'give up' on new climate treaty until 2020," *guardian.co.uk*, Sunday 20 November 2011 15.54 EST.http://www.guardian.co.uk/environment/2011/nov/20/rich-nations-give-up-climate-treaty?INTCMP=SRCH

Hartmann, Betsy. "Rebuttal to Chris Hedges: Stop the Tired Overpopulation Hysteria." 14 March 2009. Web. <http://www.alternet.org/environment/131400/rebuttal_to_chris_hedges:_stop_the_tired_overpopulation_hysteria/>.

Hedges, Chris. "Are We Breeding Ourselves to Extinction?" 11 March 2009. Web. <http://www.alternet.org/story/130843/>.

Klein, Naomi. "My Fear is that Climate Change is the Biggest Crisis of All": Naomi Klein Warns Global Warming Could Be Exploited by Capitalism and Militarism. Democracy Now! March 9, 2011. http://www.democracynow.org/2011/3/9/my_fear_is_that_climate_change

---. "The fight against climate change is down to us – the 99%." *The Guardian*, Friday 7 October 2011.http://www.guardian.co.uk/commentisfree/2011/oct/07/fight-climate-change-99/print

Latour, Bruno. "An Attempt at a 'Compositional Manifesto." *New Literary Hitstory 41* (Summer 2010): 471–490.

Myoshi, Masao. "Turn to the Planet: Literature, Diversity, and Totality." *Comparative Literature* 53.4 (2001): 283–297.

Morton, Timothy. *Ecology Without Nature: Rethinking Environmental Aesthetics.* Cambridge: Harvard University Press, 2007.

Roy, Arundhati. "Is there life after democracy?" Dawn.com. 5 July 2009. September 7, 2009. <http://www.dawn.com/wps/wcm/connect/dawn-content-library/dawn/ news/world/06-is-there-life-after-democracy-rs-07/>.

Thornton, James. "Are Climate Change Reporters an Endangered Species?" HuffingtonPost, Dec. 25, 2011 http://www.huffingtonpost.com/james-thornton/are-climate-change-report_b_1160147.html?view=print&comm_ref=false

Townsend, Mark and Paul Harris. "Now the Pentagon tells Bush: climate change will destroy us." The Observer. 22 February 2004. Web. <http://www.asiaing.com/pentagon-climate-report.html>.

Wente, Margaret. "Climate theatre of the absurd." *The Globe and Mail*, Dec. 13, 2011.http://www.theglobeandmail.com/news/opinions/margaret-wente/climate-theatre-of-the-absurd/article2268504/

Žižek, Slavoj. *First as Tragedy, Then as Farce*. London: Verso, 2009.

---. *Living in the End Times*. London: Verso, 2011.

---. "Nature and its Discontents." *SubStance* 37.3 (2008): 37–72.

Chapter 1

Time

Time, History, and Sustainability

Robert Markley

Critical climate change invariably poses questions about time or, more precisely, different registers of time: experiential or embodied time, historical time, and climatological time. Each of these registers resists hard and fast definition, in part because climatological time—accessible through and mediated by a range of complex technologies—complicates and disrupts the connections among personal identity, history, and narrative that Paul Ricoeur, for one, identifies as constituting the phenomenological and historical perceptions of time. Climatological time has emerged from a complex genealogy of symbolic economies that mark the limits and continuing crises of representation.[1] Consider the implicit but entangled registers of time in Henry Wadsworth Longfellow's 1847 "Evangeline." At the beginning of the poem, Longfellow asks his readers to imagine the landscape of Acadia on the east coast of Canada:

> *THIS is the forest primeval. The murmuring pines and the hemlocks,*
> *Bearded with moss, and in garments green, indistinct in the twilight,*
> *Stand like Druids of eld, with voices sad and prophetic (5).*

Although cast in the imagery of prehistory, this "primeval" forest, is inhabited primarily by memories of—or a deep nostalgia for—a vanished and yet thoroughly humanized past that has been absorbed into, yet remains constitutive of, the landscape. Longfellow's repetition of his opening half-line signals an implied recognition of the dialectic relations between human acts and acts of nature that define Nature.[2] The "for-

est primeval" becomes coeval with, and indivisible from, an anthropocentric world:

> *This is the forest primeval; but where are the hearts that beneath it*
> *Leaped like the roe, when he hears in the woodland the voice of*
> *   the huntsman?*
> *Where is the thatch-roofed village, the home of Acadian farmers,—*
> *Men whose lives glided on like rivers that water the woodlands,*
> *Darkened by shadows of earth, but reflecting an image of heaven?*
> *Waste are those pleasant farms, and the farmers forever departed!*
> *Scattered like dust and leaves, when the mighty blasts of October*
> *Seize them, and whirl them aloft, and sprinkle them far o'er*
> *   the ocean. (6)*

The opening of "Evangeline" throws into relief fundamental tensions
among three notions of time: embodied time (the lives of the villagers),
historical time (the "pleasant farms" and farmers who have been "Scattered like dust and leaves"), and climatological time—the sense of a natural world of wind and oceans that marks the limits of narrative and the
bounds of the anthropocentric "primeval." The tensions in Longfellow's
poem reveal the contested discourses, memories, and conceptual models
that we term "Nature," but the forest that Longfellow asks us to imagine
is "primeval" only from the bounded perspective of experience, memory,
and recorded history. Ten thousand years ago, during the Younger Dryas,
Longfellow's Acadia lay under more than a mile of glacial ice, and the east
coast of the Canadian Atlantic was uninhabited and, in effect, uninhabitable.[3] In this respect, the climatological time that haunts Longfellow's
poem, yet resists representation, informs the very traditions—literary,
political, scientific, ecological, moral, and socioeconomic—that allow
us to make sense of global climate change and the critical apparatus that
makes possible considerations of our historical moment.

In this essay, I outline a brief history of the registers of time and explore
some of the ways in which the complex tensions among embodied, historical, and climatological time underlie contemporary understandings
of and commitments to sustainability. Sustainability, I argue, is a function
of particular ways of conceiving of time, and therefore the different reg-

isters of time that I discuss both produce and are reinscribed by invocations of sustainability as an ethics, a policy goal, and an environmentalist rallying cry. Embodied time, historical time, and climatological time are mutually constitutive as well as culturally and historically inflected, and it would take several full-length studies to examine critically the ways in which different cultures have tried to negotiate among them. In focusing on aspects of western literary traditions, I trace the ways in which time remains embedded in history, culture, and technology; it is not an abstract and objective measurement of duration, but a dynamic set of relations mediated by technoscientific understandings of climatic variability and climatic change. In this respect, as I argue below, the idea of climatological time paradoxically transcends and deconstructs a long philosophical and rhetorical tradition that contrasts *kronos* (chronological time) to *kairos* (the opportune moment, the "right" time, or, as in contemporary Greek, the weather).[4] In complex ways, an understanding of climatological time complicates a straightforward political response to the crisis of global warming in the twenty-first century.

The familiar catch-phrases that invoke "the world our grandchildren will inherit" or urge us to "save the earth for future generations" reveal the extent to which sustainability is indebted to conceptions of embodied time, that is, to individual experiences of wind, heat, cold, rain, drought, and the thousand climatic shocks that flesh is heir to. Reinscribing a conception of time that dates back to the Old Testament, sustainability evokes a succession of individual lifetimes—an unbroken sequence of embodied experiences from the past and into the future that presupposes sociocultural evolution taking place against the backdrop of the timeless present of an abiding Nature. Troubling this quasi-biblical vision of succession and a socio-genetic inheritance of moral authority, property rights, social responsibility, and racial, ethnic, and religious identities is a fundamental question: what exactly is being sustained? Is it the stability of the planetary ecosystem (and its numberless subsystems) as a self-perpetuating, Gaiaesque whole? Or the productivity of the natural world so that technologies of resource extraction and practices of intensification allow selected populations to maintain, improve, and extend first-world standards of living? In an important sense, a sophisticated approach to this question invites an exploration of a critical archaeology of time. The work of literature mediates the intimations of sublime change—of climatological time—by restricting time to anthropogenic history. Contemporary rhetorics of sustainability draw on a rich legacy of images of ecological stability by re-envisioning the pastoral tradition—the eternal spring of the bucolic countryside—and the georgic, the strategies of intensification that allow for the endlessly increasing exploitation of resources. The roots of these genres in the classical world and their successive re-imaginings in Europe and the Americas suggest the extent to which notions of sustainability subsume and rework tensions that have characterized views of nature for literally thousands of years.

Judeo-Christian and Classical Traditions

The era in which Longfellow wrote—before Darwin but after the revolutions in geology that challenged (or allegorized) the Mosaic history of creation—had to contend with competing traditions of history and try to negotiate between biblical chronology and a nascent understanding of deep time.[5] Western conceptions of Nature have been shaped, to a significant extent, by the incommensurate traditions of Judeo-Christian and pagan views of the natural world, and remain caught between competing historiographic methods, narrative modes, and conceptual models: a Judeo-Christian perception of history as the mysterious unfolding of God's will and a pagan view of historical experience that resists teleological explanation.[6] In Genesis, humankind is exiled from Paradise because Eve and Adam sin. Their expulsion from the Garden into a world of labor and scarcity makes the fall of nature an effect of humankind's willful disobedience. In Book X of *Paradise Lost*, John Milton figures original sin as the fall from an eternal spring into the unstable climate patterns that characterized northwestern Europe during the Little Ice Age:

> *the Creator calling forth by name*
> *His mightie Angels gave them several charge,*
> *As sorted best with present things. The Sun*
> *Had first his precept so to move, so shine,*
> *As might affect the Earth with cold and heat*
> *Scarce tolerable, and from the North to call*

Decrepit Winter, from the South to bring
Solstitial summers heat. ...
Some say he bid his Angels turne ascanse
The Poles of Earth twice ten degrees and more
From the Suns Axle; they with labour push'd
Oblique the Centric Globe ...
... to bring in change
Of Seasons to each Clime; else had the Spring
Perpetual smil'd on Earth with vernant Flours,
Equal in Days and Nights ... (X: 649–56, 668–71, 678–80)

Milton describes an unpredictable and demonized nature as a mark of the fall not only into postlapsarian history but also into the extremes of the seasons: the Angels literally push the earth into its obliquity, the 24 degrees of deviation in its angle of rotation, and thus end the "Spring/ Perpetual" that Milton erroneously believes would be a consequence of a perpendicular rotational axis.[7] An idealized May or June day in the English countryside becomes emblematic of an unfallen nature.

As this passage from *Paradise Lost* implies, the Judeo-Christian understanding of historical time is implicated in the theology of sin, labor, and longed-for redemption; God's displeasure and favor thus are deeply bound up in a sacrificial economy that seeks to mitigate the effects of "Decrepit Winter" and "Solstitial summers heat." The account in Genesis of Cain and Abel measures the moral difference between their offerings by assuming that agricultural and livestock yields reflect the moral status of the giver. In Book XI of *Paradise Lost*, Milton contrasts the sacrifices of the "sweatie Reaper who brought/ First Fruits, the green Eare, and the yellow Sheaf,/ Uncull'd, as came to hand" to those of the "meek" shepherd, who sacrifices "the Firstlings of his Flock,/ Choicest and best" with "all due Rites perform'd." Although Cain, Milton declares, "was not sincere" and "inlie rag'd" that Abel's sacrifice was received favorably, the moral distinction rests on the fiction that the productivity of a fallen world will allow for the sacrifice of the "Choicest and best." In an important sense, such sacrifices are always devoted to a statistical inference of climatic stability—the predictability and abundance symbolized by Abel's offering. In an agro-pastoral culture, the point of sacrifice is to stabilize or maintain the climatic conditions that promote social cohesion and regularize the consumption of fruits, game and domesticated animals, cereals, fish, and so on: send rain, thaw the land for planting, end the drought, let the flood waters recede, bring back the elk or fish or bison. A sacrificial economy perceives and treats sin, transgression, and violation as both the cause and effect of the climatic instability—the earth off-kilter—that Milton imagines. Climatic change, therefore, characteristically is figured in terms of catastrophes that mark the limits of historical time, the irruption of God's wrath and vengeance.

Pagan myths, in contrast, emphasize the material prosperity of the Golden Age and suggest that virtue is, in effect, a by-product of an idealized existence of ease and plenty. They offer no clear-cut causal mechanism for the Fall from virtuous abundance to sinful scarcity. The fear of the gods and the desire to propitiate them consequently are bound up in a classical tradition that explains the fall of nature as contingent rather than irrevocable, without invoking an overarching metanarrative to explain climate change. Rather than yoking climatic change to human sin, the natural world and the history of human inhabitation frequently recede into mystery and a-causality.

In Book 15 of the *Metamorphoses*, Ovid gives to Pythagoras a long speech that places climatic change beyond the limits of history, an epiphenomenon in a universe of endless transformations:

> 'I, for one would believe that nothing continues the same
> for long. The Golden Age eventually changed to the Iron;
> and places also have often been subject to transformation.
> I've seen myself what was once the solidest stretch of earth
> Replaced by water and land formations supplanting the ocean.
> Shells can be seen on the ground some distance away from a shore,
> And ancient anchors have been discovered on mountain summits.
> Plains have been turned into valleys by rushing torrents in full spate;
> Flooding can likewise flatten a mountain to level ground.
> Marshes can dry into sand and arid deserts be watered
> to form great pools. New springs can gush at the bidding of Nature,
> while others will trickle to nothing. When earthquakes cause
>   an upheaval,

rivers have gushed from the ground or else dried up and subsided.

...

'Antissa, Pharos and Tyre, that famous Phoenician city,
were once surrounded by waves, but none is an island today.
In the time of its early inhabitants Leucas was part of the mainland,
Where now it is ringed by the sea. They also say that Messina
Was joined to Italian soil, till the sea abolished the common
Boundary and formed the strait which divides the isle from
  the mainland.
The Achaéan cities of Buris and Hélice are to be found,
If you look for them, under water. The sailors will still point out
The toppled buildings and walls beneath the floods that submerged
  them. (15: 258–72; 287–95)

For Ovid, the catastrophic changes that sever understanding from an inaccessible history of drowned cities and vanished passages are embedded within a belief in ceaseless change, including the transmigration of souls, rather than in the anthropogenic corruption of a prelapsarian Nature. In a broadly Lucretian universe, causation threatens to become, in the words of the eighteenth-century Newtonian Colin Maclaurin, "a lucky hit in a blind uproar" (4). For Ovid, climatic change resists the kind of theocentric explanation that Maclaurin demands and becomes instead the stuff of memories ("they say") or legends ("they also say"). Distanced from a sense of embodied time, it is marked only by mute artifacts, like anchors on mountain summits, that resist causal explanation. Ovid offers a non-anthropogenic view of the stochastic processes of the natural world that call attention to the limitations of historical representation as a measure of time. Rather than symbolizing a world rendered comprehensible by a sacrificial economy or a phenomenological identification of mind and world, anchors on mountaintops stand totemically for the limitations of premodern climatological knowledge, for the inability of humankind to comprehend fully the transformations of the earth.

Ovid's emphasis on his speaker's experience ("I've seen myself") points to the ways in which embodied time is written in terms of memory. In his study of meteorology in the late seventeenth and eighteenth centuries, Jan Golinski calls attention to the ways in which the nascent science of meteorology grappled with the poverty of its languages of observation and description. The author of the anonymous Worcestershire diary called his daily weather register "my Ephemeris or Historicall Remarques on vicissitudes of the weather, with a narrative of its course & Tracing it in its various winding meanders round ye year" but complained that "our Language is exceeding scanty & barren of words to use & express ye various notions I have of Weather &c" (19). This "scanty & barren" language restricts the ability to turn the daily experience of the weather into a theory of climate. Without a causal, scientific narrative to explain changes in the weather, such records drift toward the theocentric semiotics of catastrophe and apocalypse: the experience of embodied responses to the weather tends to be cast in providentialist terms. In his account of the devastating wind storm, a once in 500 years extra-tropical cyclone, that struck England and Wales in late 1703, Daniel Defoe describes his fears that as the storm approached, "the Night would be very tempestuous," he recognized, because "the Mercury [in his barometer] sunk lower than ever I had observ'd it on any Occasion whatsoever." But the plunging readings seemed so anomalous that they "made [him] suppose that the Tube had been handled and disturb'd by [his] Children" (24).[8] The full force of the storm dilates the time between midnight and dawn, both in distracting Defoe from his observations and in threatening to end both experiential and historical time: after midnight, he admits, his "Observations [of the barometer] ... are not regular enough to supply the Reader with a full Information, the Disorders of that Dreadful Night having found me other imployment, expecting every Moment when the House I was in would bury us all in its own Ruins" (25). This sense of impending destruction becomes an emblem of God's vengeance on England for its sins. Defoe sees time in dialectic and emblematic terms; his peril and salvation are also England's. In this sense, the gaps left by imperfect languages and unattended barometers mark the ruptures within history and experience that structure voluntarist theology: divine power always threatens to end *kronos*, chronological time, and to appropriate *kairos* as divine vengeance.

Beyond Anthropogenic Time

By the end of the eighteenth century, the "empty" time of mathematical simulation and climatological reconstruction paradoxically begins to assert its explanatory power by disembodying climate, that is, by treating climatic change not as the catastrophic irruption of divine judgment but as a non-anthropogenic time that transcends both individual and historical experience. At the end of the eighteenth century, climatological time emerges as a distinct ontological challenge to theocentric time in three interlocking sets of developments. All three sought to redefine the scientific basis for understanding deep time and, in the process, recast traditional conceptions of Nature. In the 1790s the nebular hypothesis of planetary formation advanced by Pierre Simon de Laplace, the argument for species extinction by Georges Cuvier, and the "discovery" of geological time by James Hutton transformed conceptions of climate by decoupling history from human experience and memory.

The nebular hypothesis anthropomorphized the life cycle of planets in terms of youth, maturity, old age, and heat-death, offering a model of climatic change as the consequence of irreversible, universal processes.[9] Laplace removed Newton's God from the mathematical equations that produced a compelling model of the origins, evolution, and fate of the solar system. Hutton's vision of geological time with "no vestige of a beginning,—no prospect of an end" presented a cyclical history of erosion and upheaval that continually reshaped the earth" (1:200). This continual reshaping both went beyond and challenged the theological catastrophism that ascribed evidence such as the drowned cities and toppled buildings to the vengeance of an awful God. Eighty years after Defoe had echoed a near-universal sentiment among early natural philosophers— "Nature plainly refers us beyond her Self, to the Mighty Hand of Infinite Power, the Author of Nature, and Original of all Causes" (2)—Hutton's geological history challenged perceptions of the reliability of experiential notions of duration, history, nature, and causality.[10] The earth itself threatened to become a sublime, ahuman environment. Cuvier's account of the extinction of fossilized species raised profound questions about the limits of Mosaic history and the ways in which past environments differed from present conditions.[11] The fascination with the skeletal remains of dinosaurs, giant sloths, and mastodons that gripped London,

Paris, Philadelphia, and New York in 1800 suggested that nature bred entire species that required primeval ecologies no human ever had seen. The emphasis throughout the nineteenth century on the savage violence of prehistoric carnivores indicates the extent to which it was difficult to imagine the ecological conditions that provided forage for gigantic species of plant-eaters.

Even before Darwin published *The Origin of Species*, then, scientific thought had begun to challenge the biblical monopoly on conceptions of history and had provoked competing models of climatological time, the creation and reshaping of the earth and its natural environment, and humankind's future. The fad in Victorian science fiction for end of the universe stories, many riffing on Mary Shelley's *The Last Man*, testifies to the ways in which the specter of species extinction could be reimagined on a massive, planetary scale. Extinction thus haunts the tendency in late eighteenth and early nineteenth-century science to chart, measure, and quantify both the natural world and the social regimes of economics and politics.[12] In this sense, the understanding of long-term change, of a climatological time that exists outside human experience, gestures paradoxically towards embracing and resisting the mathematically regular, aestheticized universe imagined by Laplace. A time that transcends and beggars human experience, however, can be conceived only differentially, paradoxically, in its relation to phenomenological perceptions of time and existence. If mathematical reductionism locks man and climate into intractable processes that lead to extinction, it also provokes redefinitions of ideas of divinity and therefore to the complex relationships of humankind to experience, Nature, and time.

Nineteenth-century transcendentalism suggests that the ruptures between microcosm and macrocosm, between humankind's experience of time and Nature's time, are produced by the self-generating alienation of custom or ideology, what William Blake called "mind forg'd manacles."[13] In his essay "Nature," Ralph Waldo Emerson recasts the threat of extinction within phenomenological notions of time, nature, and experience:

> the knowledge that we traverse the whole scale of being, from the centre to the poles of nature, and have some stake in every possibility, lends that sublime lustre to death, which philosophy and religion have too outwardly and literally striven to ex-

press in the popular doctrine of the immortality of the soul. The reality is more excellent than the report. Here is no ruin, no discontinuity, no spent ball. The divine circulations never rest nor linger. Nature is the incarnation of a thought, and turns to a thought again, as ice becomes water and gas. The world is mind precipitated, and the volatile essence is forever escaping again into the state of free thought. . . . That power which does not respect quantity, which makes the whole and the particle its equal channel, delegates its smile to the morning, and distils its essence into every drop of rain. Every moment instructs, and every object: for wisdom is infused into every form. (542)

In gesturing toward the reflexivity of microcosm and macrocosm, Emerson yokes Hutton's geological time or Laplace's universal time to experiential moments and perceptions that defy scientific reductionism. Human life, like the planet itself, is "no spent ball," but a web of complex, proliferating, and dynamic energies.[14] In contrast to Milton's view of seasonal change as a mark of the fall, Emerson locates "perfection" and "harmony" in individual days. He begins this essay by observing:

There are days which occur in this climate, at almost any season of the year, wherein the world reaches its perfection, when the air, the heavenly bodies, and the earth, make a harmony, as if nature would indulge her offspring; when, in these bleak upper sides of the planet, nothing is to desire that we have heard of the happiest latitudes, and we bask in the shining hours of Florida and Cuba; when everything that has life gives sign of satisfaction. . . . These halcyons may be looked for with a little more assurance in that pure October weather, which we distinguish by the name of the Indian Summer. The day, immeasurably long, sleeps over the broad hills and warm wide fields. To have lived through all its sunny hours, seems longevity enough. (540)

In contrast to nineteenth-century scientists struggling to explain the prospect of an earth succumbing to the heat-death ostensibly predicted by the second law of thermodynamics, Emerson finds time both focused and dilated, intimations of immortality distilled into the "sunny hours" of "pure October weather" that bring to the climate of northern New England the kind of "satisfaction" ostensibly experienced in the tropical sunshine of the Caribbean.[15] "Spring/Perptual" becomes a distillation of thought and experience, an imaginative transcendence of the often dank realities of the "bleak upper latitudes" of the planet. Emerson's "halcyons" locate embodied human experience within a matrix of "harmony," in which multiplying complexities produce greater intimations and emotive understandings of Nature as "the circumstance which dwarfs every other circumstance," an unalienated universal composed of, and generating, infinite experiences of "that power which does not respect quantity, which makes the whole and the particle its equal channel."

Transcendentalism thus can be seen as one response to the fundamental paradoxes posed by climatological time. Rather than a mathematicized universe that exists beyond the limits of perception and experience, and that can be imagined only in terms of the irrelevance or negation of embodied experience, the world becomes open to the interweaving of mind and matter. In Emerson's "Nature," the transcendental imperative that "does not respect quantity" encourages humankind to embrace the processes of an ongoing reintegration of self and environment natural rather than to succumb to the profound ontological as well as epistemological displacements of what Emerson terms "custom." To turn away from "our life of solemn trifles," humankind must recognize that Nature can be described only as a kind of double negative, a negation of a natural world already alienated by "the ambitious chatter of the schools [that] would persuade us to despise" material existence in favor of metaphysical abstractions. Nature's time therefore exists as the primeval negation of humankind's efforts to measure and institutionalize time: "Here no history, or church, or state, is interpolated on the divine sky and the immortal year." In an important sense, the threat to traditional structures of thought and belief posed by Laplace and Cuvier is subsumed by Emerson's encompassing change within an organic regeneration of both mind and climate—"We come to our own, and make friends with matter." Dynamic and unpredictable change is transformed into the energies of self-renewal.

Yet the ethics of individualism that Emerson typically is credited with (or accused of) promoting constitutes only one half of a dialectic in the nineteenth century. In *Late Victorian Holocausts*, Mike Davis charts the devastating human and environmental consequences of European imperialism and the hallucinogenic optimism that colonial proprietors could plough under complex ecologies throughout the underdeveloped world to grow cash crops (cotton, opium, tea, tobacco, and rice) for export to Europe and North America. Unrestrained imperial expansion and robber-baron capitalism trumpeted the view that the climates of India, Africa, and the Americas could be "improved" by large-scale, moncultural cultivation. This view of Nature as an infinite storehouse focuses less on what Marx calls exchange value than on the infinite elasticity of use-value: the belief that John Locke advanced in the *Two Treatises of Government* (1690) that the calculus of infinite productivity forms a consensual basis for individual and property rights—and property secures the basis of political and social identity.[16]

Locke invokes explicitly the classical ideal of a "golden age" when humanity, or at least specific populations, reaped the benefits of a beneficent Nature. In such a world of abundant resources and a stable climate, as he argues in his second treatise, labor offers the prospect of limitless productivity rather than marking, as it does in the Judeo-Christian tradition, humankind's banishment from Eden. "In the beginning," Locke declares, "all the World was *America*" (2, ¶ 49, 301)—that is, all the world was open to an unending exploitation guaranteed by the fecundity of the nature. In this formulation, labor is divorced from a material world of life-and-death calculations (when to plant, when to harvest, how much seed to conserve for next year's planting, whether to kill the cow to feed one's family during a harsh winter, and so forth) that defined agricultural existence during the Little Ice Age in much of early modern Europe.[17] By the later eighteenth century, neo-Lockean liberalism had turned bodies into reliable machines, capable of increasing their useful labor, and the land into a repository of potential value that could be mined, refashioned, and exploited without suffering any diminution in either extent or productivity.[18] By the nineteenth century, as Davis suggests, the Lockean argument that the fruits of one's labor theoretically cannot exceed a normative notion of physiological sufficiency had been corrupted into the conversion of humans into interchangeable units of labor, and the natural world becomes an *effect* of humankind's use. The time of the world thus becomes the time of capitalist calculation. In the long tradition of apocalyptic science fiction that emerges in the nineteenth century, it is precisely this world of humankind's dominion that, to quote H.G. Wells in *The War of the Worlds*, begins "losing coherency, losing shape and efficiency, guttering, softening, running at last in that swift liquefaction of the social body" (82). These apocalptic scenarios, the "Grotesque gleam of a time no history will ever fully describe!", invariably have ecological overtones because, in their playful cultural necrosis, they offer a way of imaginging a time after human history: the end of *kronos* and the aftermath of *kairos* (145).

Time and Fiction in the Age of Global Warming

The expanses of pre-human history that extend into the deep backward and abysm of time underscore the fact that climatological time, measured in millennia, exists beyond daily experiences of the weather, beyond the duration of individual lifetimes, beyond the accumulated memories of generations, and beyond the technologies of observation, inscription, and recording that characterize the rise of modern meteorology in the nineteenth century. The tensions between observation and speculation in meteorological sciences that Katharine Anderson describes in Victorian England foreshadow the contours of contemporary debates about global warming and its consequences. In the twenty-first century, we have come to understand climatological time as a dynamic and consensual knowledge about the interpretations of a wide range of proxy data: ice cores from Greenland, tree rings, sediment layers in mud and swamps, patterns of coral growth, and so on that can be analyzed to reveal signs of long-term variability based on specific chemical signatures, pollen samples, and gas bubbles trapped in ice.[19] In this respect, the cognitive understanding of climate has become a process of acclimating one's embodied experience to increasingly complex technologies and to the resulting displacements, in time and space, of observational and experiential authority. Climatological time is dynamic, shaped and recalibrated, as Bruno Latour suggests, by the networks, alliances, and assemblages that collect, transmit, verify, interpret, and disseminate data; that then reaffirm or modify assumptions and values about the natural world; and that continually negotiate the vexed relationship between seemingly individual, embodied experience and scientific knowledge.[20] A crucial effect of the technologies of climate science is that our experience has been refocused, or really recalibrated, to integrate into our lived experience consensual inferences from ratios of isotopes, compression of layers in ice cores, models of global circulation of water, atmospheric circulation, large-scale deforestation, and satellite images. In this respect, climatological time registers the complex theoretical and practical relationships between *qualitative* experience and *quantitative* knowledge, between human history and the earth's history. Recycling becomes, in one sense, a sacrificial rite to an ideal of sustainability.

The technologically-mediated, proxy observations of longterm climate change, then, force us to recalibrate to traditional notions of common sense, to the embodied and expansive times of Emerson's Nature. Even for scientists, policy-makers, environmental activists, and informed citizens who believe in anthropogenic global warming and are striving to promote whole-scale changes in modes of production and habits of consumption, the time-scales of climatic change cannot be experienced viscerally but only imagined. Phenomenologically, they are part of what Derrida calls, in a different context, the *"irreducible virtually of time and space"* (162). Scientific knowledge requires a willing suspension of experiential belief in the facticity, the experiential groundedness, of a world of familiar seasons, a continuous anthropocentric history, and the Lockean tendency to treat the natural world as a storehouse of infinite productivity.

In this respect, climatological time produces interference patterns that provoke complex and self-generating modes of *disidentification*: proxy data is both integrated into patterns of daily experience (recycling plastic bottles, buying energy-efficient cars) and sequestered from traditional behaviors (continuing to eat meat, despite the carbon footprint of meat production). In Bruno Latour's sense, we have never been, and cannot become modern, because we remain caught (and oscillate) between the dialectical impulses toward the purification of identities (the self-aware green ethicist) and the proliferation of hybrids (the conflicted, steak-eating Prius owner).[21] This is why, even as the literate public worldwide has been deluged with information (and misinformation) about global warming and its likely consequences, the effects of this media saturation paradoxically have reinforced as well as challenged longstanding views of humankind's relationship to nature. The managerial ethos of late twentieth and twenty-first century corporate culture that tends to treat climate change as a marketing opportunity is a descendent of the brutally insensitive optimism of neoclassical economics.

Given its geneaology, the ideal of sustainability that underlies most plans of collective action to address global warming risks reinscribing a Lockean vision of the inexhaustibility of natural resources into the idea of a preternaturally resilient ecology that exists outside of the dynamics of climatological time. The measure of several generations—of one or two extended human lifetimes—becomes the timescale of sustainability. In this regard, sustainability tends to be co-opted into a seemingly objective semiotics of mathematics and neoclassical—and neoliberal— economics, what Philip Mirowski calls "the very ideal of natural law[,] . . . the verification of a stable external world independent of our activity or inquiry" (75). This projection of stability from mathematics onto "a stable external" nature effectively treats complex and dynamic ecologies as constants rather than variables; the closer sustainability approaches a set of statistical inferences over decades or a century, the more it tends to remain complicit in exploitative ideologies of resource extraction and the political and administrative hierarchies, centralized bureaucracies, technologies of economic calculation and accounting, the policing of resources and populations, and distributive political economies that are required to manage finite resources.

That said, the paradoxes of disidentification can be captured, if not rationally comprehended, only in fictional projections of human experience. In an important sense, the phenomenological perception of climate now includes the simulations—the science fictions—of human experience as a probability calculus, as projections of the climatological future. Published a year before Hurricane Katrina devastated New Orleans, Kim Stanley Robinson's novel *Forty Signs of Rain* uncannily anticipates the sequence of natural disasters and political failures that devastated the city: Washington D. C. is hit by a perfect storm—a tropical storm surge coming up the Potomac, ten inches of rain in the Chesapeake watershed rushing down river, and a record high tide: the city floods. "[I]mages from the [flooded] Mall dominated the media," and viewers around the nation see "TV helicopters often interrupt[ing] their overviews to pluck people from rooftops. Rescues by boat were occurring all though the Southwest district and up the Anacostia Basin. Reagan Airport remained drowned, and there was no passable bridge over the Potomac" (352). Although the novel and its sequels, *Fifty Degrees Below* (2005) and *Sixty Days and Counting* (2007) focus on the ecological, scientific, political, and personal crises of the trilogy's main characters—from Beltway insiders, to bioclimatologists working at the National Science Foundation, to displaced Buddhist monks—Robinson's treatment of individuals and the world at large confronting the consequences of global warming is neither a "realistic" novel about climate change nor a near-future, "hard" science fiction novel, but a genre-bending exploration of the ethics and politics of existence at a time when neither eco-truisms, nor managerial strategizing, nor self-propelling fantasies of technological amelioration seem adequate. Robinson's trilogy offers an opportune way to think through the lived experience of character and climate in the early twenty-first century. His *Science in the Capitol* trilogy marks the intersection of the different registers of embodied, historical, and climatological time: the experience of surviving temperatures fifty degrees below zero after the Gulf Stream stalls; the fictional history of national politics and the politics of science over the course of two years as a new, progressive administration takes office; and the onrush of catastrophic changes—melting polar caps and drowning islands—that recur literally millions of years after the last period of comparable warmth. In this regard, Robinson invites his readers to experience imaginatively the processes that Ovid casts in the poetics of endless change: the drowned "Achaéan cities of Buris and Hélice" eerily foreshadow a fictional Washington and an all too real New Orleans.

Coda

Human beings seldom witness abrupt climate change in the course of a lifetime. Those who do historically face long odds on adapting to a natural world radically transformed. The prospect of rapid warming and the disastrous scenarios that Robinson envisions lead to profoundly different ways of conceiving the timescales of what we understand as the object of sustainability. Sustainability ultimately refers to an idealized homeostasis between humankind and environment that never existed except in the sense that robust ecological systems could remain unaffected by low-density populations of humans for climatologically brief periods of time, on the scale of centuries rather than millennia. Robust, in this respect, does not imply a moral, ethical, or sociocultural value judgment. Between 11,000 and 12,000 years ago, during the Younger Dryas, Western Europe was frozen tundra without much in the way of recognizable vegetation, colder and more forbidding than much of Siberia is today. Longfellow's forest primeval was millennia away from taking root, the coastline of Canada lying dozens if not hundreds of miles to the east because larger ice caps lowered sea levels by dozens of meters. Human populations huddled in scattered caves or clung to the Mediterranean littoral. Physiologically indistinguishable from any of us, Ice Age peoples produced intricate art and effective weapons. They did not flourish. There is overwhelming evidence that the most common biological response to severe climate change (of more than three degrees centigrade) is not to adapt but to die: populations crash, and, within the short, short reign of *homo sapiens*, bands of hunters and gatherers vanish, subsistence farmers fall prey to malnutrition, starvation, and disease, and empires fall.[22] When climate changes, people kill each other with greater frequency, population centers are abandoned, and centers of calculation do not hold. Systemic climatic change is no more or less characteristic of Gaia than the long summer of climatic calm that has existed for the last ten thousand years, unpredictable oscillations no less "natural" than ideals of sustainability. Longfellow ultimately gives way to Lucretius.

Notes

1. See Goux.

2. On the dialectical nature of landscape, see Crumley's "Historical Ecology: A Multidimensional Ecological Orientation" and "The Ecology of Conquest: Contrasting Agropastoral and Agricultural Societies' Adaptation to Climactic Change" and Ingerson.

3. See Burroughs.

4. See White.

5. See Rudwick's *Bursting the Limits of Time: The Reconstruction of Geohistory in the Age of Revolution* and *Worlds before Adam: The Reconstruction of Geohistory in the Age of Reform*.

6. See my "Summer's Lease: Shakespeare in the Little Ice Age."

7. Percy Bysshe Shelley makes a similar assumption in his poem *Queen Mab*; see Gidal.

8. I discuss this text at greater length in "'Casualties and Disasters': Defoe and the Interpretation of Climactic Instability."

9. See Numbers.

10. See my *Fallen Languages: Crises of Representation in Newtonian England, 1660–1740*, Bono, and Hellegers.

11. See Rudwick's *Bursting the Limits of Time* and *Worlds before Adam*. Also, see O'Connor.

12. See Porter and Mirowski.

13. William Blake, "London," 1794.

14. The literature on Emerson, Thoreau, and environmentalism is vast. See particularly Buell's *The Environmental Imagination* 219–251 and *Emerson*.

15. On thermodynamics, see Clarke.

16. See my "'Land enough in the World': Locke's Golden Age and the Infinite Extensions of 'Use'."

17. See Fagan.

18. See Tully, Pocock 22–30, Wood, Rapaczynski, Arneil 132–67, Carey, and Michael.

19. There are a number of good introductions to the history of climate change. See Lamb, Burroughs, Calvin, and Linden.

20. See Latour's *Science in Action: How to Follow Scientists through Society*.

21. See Latour's *We Have Never Been Modern*.

22. See Burroughs.

Works Cited

Anderson, Katharine. *Predicting the Weather: Victorians and the Science of Meteorology.* Chicago: University of Chicago Press, 2005.

Arneil, Barbara. *John Locke and America: The Defence of English Colonialism*. Oxford: Clarendon, 1996.

Bono, James. *The Word of God and the Languages of Man: Interpreting Nature in Early Modern Science, Ficino to Descartes*. Madison: University of Wisconsin Press, 1995.

Buell, Lawrence. *Emerson*. Cambridge, MA: Harvard University Press, 2004.

---. *The Environmental Imagination: Thoreau, Nature Writing, and the Formation of American Culture*. Cambridge, MA: Harvard University Press, 1995.

Burroughs, William J. *Climate Change in Prehistory: The End of the Reign of Chaos*. Cambridge: Cambridge University Press, 2005.

Calvin, William H. *A Brain for All Seasons: Human Evolution and Abrupt Climate Change*. Chicago University of Chicago Press, 2002.

Carey, Daniel. "Locke, Travel Literature, and the Natural History of Man." *Seventeenth Century*. 11 (1996): 259–80.

Clarke, Bruce. *Energy Forms: Allegory and Science in the Era of Classical Thermodynamics*. Ann Arbor: University of Michigan Press, 2001.

Crumley, Carole. "The Ecology of Conquest: Contrasting Agropastoral and Agricultural Societies' Adaptation to Climactic Change." *Historical Ecology: Cultural Knowledge and Changing Landscapes*. Ed. Crumley. Santa Fe: School of American Research Press, 1994. 183–201.

---. "Historical Ecology: A Multidimensional Ecological Orientation." *Historical Ecology: Cultural Knowledge and Changing Landscapes*. Ed. Crumley. Santa Fe: School of American Research Press, 1994. 1–11.

Davis, Mike. *Late Victorian Holocausts: El Niño Famines and the Making of the Third World*. London: Verso, 2001.

Defoe, Daniel. *The Storm*. London, 1704.

Derrida, Jacques. *Specters of Marx: The State of the Debt, the Work of Mourning, and the New International*. Trans. Peggy Kamuf. New York: Routledge, 1994.

Emerson, Ralph Waldo. "Nature." *Essays and Lectures*. Ed. Joel Porte. New York: Library of America, 1983.

Fagan, Brian. *The Long Summer: How Climate Changed Civilization*. New York: Basic Books, 2004.

Gidal, Eric. "'O happy Earth! reality of Heaven!': Melancholy and Utopia in Romantic Climatology." *Journal of Early Modern Cultural Studies*.8.2 (2008): 74–101.

Golinski, Jan. *British Weather and the Climate of Enlightenment.* Chicago: University of Chicago Press, 2007.

Goux, Jean-Joseph. *Symbolic Economies after Marx and Freud.* Trans. Jennifer Curtiss Gage. Ithaca: Cornell University Press, 1990.

Hellegers, Desiree. *Natural Philosophy, Poetry, and Gender in Seventeenth-Century England.* Norman: University of Oklahoma Press, 2000.

Hutton, James. *Theory of the Earth, with Proofs and Illustrations.* 2 vols. Edinburgh: Printed for Messers Cadell, Junior, Davies, and Creech, 1795.

Ingerson, Alice E. "Tracking and Testing the Nature-Culture Divide." *Historical Ecology: Cultural Knowledge and Changing Landscapes.* Ed. Carole Crumley. Santa Fe: School of American Research Press, 1994. 43–66.

Lamb, H. H. *Climate History and the Modern World.* 2nd Ed. New York: Routledge, 1995.

Latour, Bruno. *Science in Action: How to Follow Scientists through Society.* Cambridge, MA: Harvard University Press, 1987.

---. *We Have Never Been Modern.* Trans. Catherine Porter. Cambridge: Harvard University Press, 1993.

Linden, Eugene. *The Winds of Change: Climate, Weather, and the Destruction of Civilizations.* New York: Simon and Schuster, 2006.

Locke, John. *Two Treatises of Government.* Ed. Peter Laslett. Cambridge: Cambridge University Press, 1960.

Longfellow, Henry Wadsworth. *Evangeline, A Tale of Acadie.* 4th ed. Boston: William Ticknor, 1848.

Maclaurin, Colin. *An Account of Sir Isaac Newton's Philosophical Discoveries.* London, 1748.

Markley, Robert. "'Casualties and Disasters': Defoe and the Interpretation of Climactic Instability." *Journal of Early Modern Cultural Studies.* 8 (2008): 102–24.

---. *Fallen Languages: Crises of Representation in Newtonian England, 1660–1740.* Ithaca: Cornell University Press, 1993.

---. "'Land enough in the World': Locke's Golden Age and the Infinite Extensions of 'Use.'" *South Atlantic Quarterly.* 98 (1999): 817–37.

---. "Summer's Lease: Shakespeare in the Little Ice Age." *Early Modern Ecostudies: From Shakespeare to the Florentine Codex.* Ed. Karen Raber, Tom Hallock and Ivo Kamps. New York: Palgrave, 2008. 131–42.

Michael, Mark. "Locke's Second Treatise and the Literature of Colonization." *Interpretation.* 25 (1998): 407–27.

Milton, John. *Paradise Lost.* London: S. Simmons, 1674.

Mirowski, Philip. *More Heat than Light: Economics as Social Physics, Physics as Nature's Economies.* Cambridge: Cambridge University Press, 1989.

Numbers, Ronald. *Creation by Natural Law: Laplace's Nebular Hypothesis in American Thought.* Seattle: University of Washington Press, 1977.

O'Connor, Ralph. *The Earth on Show: Fossils and the Poetics of Popular Science, 1802–1856.* Chicago: University of Chicago Press, 2007.

Ovid. *The Metamorphoses.* Trans. David Raeburn. New York and London: Penguin, 2004.

Pocock, J. G. A. *Virtue, Commerce, and History: Essays on Political Thought and History, Chiefly in the Eighteenth Century.* Cambridge: Cambridge University Press, 1985.

Porter, Theodore. *Trust in Numbers: The Pursuit of Objectivity in Science and Public Life.* Princeton: Princeton University Press, 1996.

Rapaczynski, Andrzej. *Nature and Politics: Liberalism in the Philosophies of Hobbes, Locke, and Rousseau.* Ithaca: Cornell University Press, 1987.

Ricoeur, Paul. *Time and Narrative.* 3 vols. Trans. Kathleen McLaughlin and David Pellauer. Chicago: University of Chicago Press, 1984–1988.

Robinson, Kim Stanley. *Forty Signs of Rain.* New York: HarperCollins, 2004.

Rudwick, Martin S. J. *Bursting the Limits of Time: The Reconstruction of Geohistory in the Age of Revolution.* Chicago: University of Chicago Press, 2005.

---. *Worlds before Adam: The Reconstruction of Geohistory in the Age of Reform.* Chicago: University of Chicago Press, 2008.

Tully, James. *A Discourse on Property: John Locke and His Adversaries.* Cambridge: Cambridge University Press, 1980.

Wells, H. G. *The War of the Worlds.* Ed. David Y. Hughes and Harry M. Geduld. Bloomington: Indiana University Press, 1984.

White, Eric. *Kaironomia, or the Will to Invent.* Ithaca: Cornell University Press, 1987.

Wood, Ellen Meiskins. *The Pristine Culture of Capitalism: A Historical Essay on Old Regimes and Modern States.* London: Verso, 1991.

Chapter 2

Ecotechnics

Ecotechnological Odradek

J. Hillis Miller

Humanity [must] ... furnish the effort necessary in order to get accomplished ... the essential function of the universe, which is a machine for making gods.

– Henri Bergson

Our world is the world of the "technical," a world whose cosmos, nature, gods, entire system, is, in its inner joints, exposed as "technical": the world of an ecotechnical. The ecotechnical functions with technical apparatuses, to which our every part is connected. But what it makes are our bodies, which it brings into the world and links to the system, thereby creating our bodies as more visible, more proliferating, more polymorphic, more compressed, more "amassed" and "zoned" than ever before. Through the creation of bodies the ecotechnical has the sense that we vainly seek in the remains of the sky or the spirit.

– Jean-Luc Nancy, Corpus

[The universe] knits us in and it knits us out. It has knitted time space, pain, death, corruption, despair, and all the illusions—and nothing matters.

– Joseph Conrad, Letters to Cunninghame Graham

Technology as Model

"Eco" comes from the Greek word *oikos*, the house or home. The prefix "eco-" is used more broadly now to refer to the total environment within which one or another "living" creature "dwells." Each creature dwells in its "ecosystem." Included in that system are other circumambient creatures—viruses, bacteria, plants, and animals—but also the climate in the broad sense of the environment. The ecosystem also includes "technical apparatuses." I mean all those manmade teletechnological devices like television sets, iPhones, and computers connected to the Internet, into which our bodies are plugged.

I would add this to Nancy's formulation: The total environment more and more reveals itself to be "technological," that is, in one way or another machinelike. The "body" is, according to Nancy "linked" to its technological ecosystem in manifold ways, as a prosthesis of a prosthesis. That body, however, is more and more being shown also to function like a machine. It is a technical product of the ecotechnical. "The body" is a complex set of interlocking mechanisms that are self-generating, self-regulating, and self-reading sign systems. "There is no 'the' body," (*"il n'y a pas 'le' corps"*), in the sense of a unitary organism, says Jean-Luc Nancy (*Corpus* 104). These corporeal sign systems are the products of chance permutations extending over millions of years, such as those that have produced the human genome. These sign systems do not depend on human consciousnesses or on actions based on the choice of a voluntary code-reader in order to function. They just go on working and unworking.

This essay focuses on Kafka's uncanny little story, if it can be called a story, *"Die Sorge des Hausvaters"* ("The Worry of the Father of the Family") (1919). I use Kafka's 474 word text as a way of thinking what results from a shift from an organic unity model to a technological model as a paradigm for thinking in various domains. My essay might be called a thought experiment. "What would happen if . . . we used a technological model rather than an organic model to understand X?" Whether Kafka's text can be "used" as a way of thinking about this or about anything else, or whether anything at all can be done with *"Die Sorge des Hausvaters,"* remains to be seen. It does not go without saying.

Among the domains to be subjected to my thought experiment are languages, human and inhuman; sign systems generally; literature and literary criticism, along with literary theory; "life," "the body," the immune system, the endocrine system, the brain, consciousness, the unconscious, the self or "ego"; the atom-molecule-thing-virus-bacterium-vegetable-animal-human being sequence; societies, both human and inhuman, communities, nations, and cultures; history; the Internet and other such teletechnological assemblages (radio, telephone, television, cell-phones, iPhones, etc.); the global financial system; the environment, the weather, climate change; astrophysics from the Big Bang to whatever endless end the cosmos may reach. According to many scientists, the universe's expansion is apparently accelerating. Galaxies are gradually getting so far apart that ultimately no light or other signals will be able to get from one to any other. Talk about the Pascalian "silence of infinite spaces"! The iPhone will be of no use then.

The organic unity model has had a tenacious hold on thinking in the West from the Greeks and the Bible down to Heidegger and present-day eco-poets and extollers of "the body." We tend, moreover, to think of organisms as "animated" in one way or another. An organism is inhabited and held together by a soul (*anima*) or by some principle of life. Consciousness, mind, the ego, the soul animate human bodies, just as animals, trees, flowers, and the earth as a whole are alive, animated by an integrated principle of life, and just as dead letters, the materiality of language, the marks on the page, are animated by a meaning inherent in a collection of letters and spaces. As Martin Heidegger, notoriously, expresses this, "*Die Sprache spricht.*" Language speaks (210), as though it were animated by an *anima*. Another way to put this is to say that anthropomorphisms and prosopopoeias have been ubiquitous in our tradition as grounds for formulations in many domains. John Ruskin called these personifications "pathetic fallacies." The Book of Numbers in the Old Testament, for example, asserts that "If the Lord make a new thing, and the earth open her mouth, and swallow them up, with all that appertain unto them, and they go down quick into the pit; then ye shall understand that these men have provoked the Lord" (Num. 16:30). Isaiah, in a passage cited by Ruskin, asserts that "the mountains and the hills shall break forth before you into singing, and all the trees of the field shall clap their hands" (Isa. 55:12). Ruskin calls this a justifiable pathetic fallacy because it deals with God's power, that is, with something that is infinitely beyond human understanding and language. St. Paul speaks of the way "the whole creation groaneth and travaileth in pain" (Rom. 8:22), as though the creation were an animate creature. A living thing, whether vegetable, animal, or human, is to be distinguished from dead matter by its organic unity. Every part works with the others to make that living thing more than a mechanical assemblage of parts. The human ego or self we think of as organically unified. We tend to think of a "natural language" as an organic unity of words organized by an innate, universal, grammar and syntax, such as that imagined by Noam Chomsky. A good community is an organically unified set of assumptions and behaviors. History is made of transitions from one set of such assumptions and behaviors to the next, in a series of Foucauldian "epistemes," with inexplicable leaps between. Some of today's eco-poets, like many native peoples, imagine the earth as a quasi-personified "Pan-Gaia," Mother Earth. This lovely lady has human beings under her benevolent care, so we need not fear that climate change will harm us. Mama Earth would not let that happen. The "organic unity" model of a good poem or other literary work has had great force from the Romantics to the New Critics. If it is a good poem, it must be organically unified, with all its parts working harmoniously together to make a beautiful object like a flower or like the body of a graceful woman.

Martin Heidegger, in *The Fundamental Concepts of Metaphysics: World, Solitude, Finitude,* asserts that the stone is world-less, *weltlos,* the animal is poor in world, *weltarm,* whereas human beings are world-building, *weltbilden* (389–416; original 268–87). A "world" is implicitly a whole, once more an organic unity. We tend to assume that in one way or another technology names a human process of making out of parts assembled together something that is in some way useful, a prosthetic tool extending man's power and a product of his ingenuity, inventiveness, and manufacturing power. A technological artifact is not animated, though we tend to personify our machines, to refer to our automobiles, for example, as "she." *Techné* is opposed to *Physis,* just as subject is opposed to object. *Techné* is a skill manipulated by subjectivities and their bodies. Technology adds something to a nature thought of as already externally out there and as organic. Heidegger hated modern technological gadgets. He refused to use a typewriter. Only a man holding a pen can think, he thought, that is, do "what is called thinking." Human beings think with their pens. Heidegger saw the wholesale technologizing of Russia and the United States, and, through them, the technologizing of the whole world, as rapidly bringing true organic civilization, that is Greek and German culture, to an end.[1] "Only a God will save us," he said on the famous occasion of an interview with *Der Spiegel*. He would no doubt have found the present global triumph of teletechnology abominable. We tend, however, even to personify our computers and the Internet. We feel that there is a God in the machine. Our prosthetic gadgets think and work for themselves, not always along the lines we want them to work and think.

Such examples of the organic unity model could be multiplied indefinitely. They are everywhere. Who would dare to say of them what Ruskin says of one of his examples of the pathetic fallacy ("The spendthrift crocus, bursting through the mould/Naked and shivering, with his cup of gold"): "This is very beautiful, and yet very untrue" (par. 4).

The alternative techno-machinal model has also a long history going back at least to Leibniz, to the idea of a watchmaker God, to such eighteenth-century books as de la Mettrie's *L'homme machine*, and down to recent work that thinks of the human immune system as more machine-like than organic, or to the rejection of anthropomorphisms in thinking of the cosmos or of climate change. Our presupposed paradigm of the machine, however, has mutated over the last century from examples like the steam engine and the internal combustion engine to forms of technology that are embodied sign-systems or communications machines, like television, iPhones, and a computer connected to the Internet. Even automobiles these days are computerized. They are as much complex sign systems as they are gas-powered engines to turn the car's wheels. Before looking a little more closely at the strange features of the ecotechnological model, however, I turn to Kafka as an exemplary thinker/non-thinker of the inhumanly machinal.

Machinal Auto-Co-Immunity as Context:
Our Present State of Emergency

I do so, however, in a context. I am thinking not of the context of the important discussions between Walter Benjamin and Gershom Scholem, or between Benjamin and Berthold Brecht, on the question of whether Kafka is to be thought of as a mystic in the tradition of the Kabbalah or, on the contrary, as a faithful recorder of social conditions in pre-Holocaust Prague.[2] My context, rather, is our situation here in the United States and in the world today. Why and how should I read Kafka's *"Die Sorge des Hausvaters"* today, this moment, on November 4, 2011? It does not go without saying that reading this little text is at all useful and justifiable in our present state of emergency.

What is that emergency? The United States is engaged full-tilt in four radical forms of apparently unwitting "auto-co-immune" self-destruction, to borrow Jacques Derrida's neologism. The systems that should save and protect us are turning against ourselves.

One form of our suicidal folly is the refusal to move immediately to universal single-payer health care as the only way to keep health care costs from escalating further and further as a percentage of our GDP. That cost is already 16% of GDP, or even, according to some estimates, 20%, at least twice that of most European countries. This absurdity is bankrupting thousands when they get sick, killing tens of thousands of people every year who cannot afford health care, but also bankrupting the country, at the expense of making pharmaceutical companies and health insurance companies fathomlessly rich.

Another folly is the refusal to do anything serious to regulate the suicidal greed and risk-taking of banks and other financial institutions. Sub-prime mortgage-based credit default swaps and complex "derivatives" are the conspicuous example of this folly and greed. A minor consequence of the present "financial meltdown" is the dismantling of our educational system, especially public universities and especially the humanities. Our universities are in lock-step with finance capitalism. Harvard University lost about forty per cent of its endowment in the meltdown. Nothing has been done, for example raising taxes on the rich and large corporations, to ameliorate the outrageous discrepancy between the wealth of the top 1% and the remaining 99%. That 1% has survived the meltdown with increased income, wealth, and political power enabled through their manipulation of the media and "buying" of Congress.

A third form of auto-immune self-destruction is the refusal to withdraw from a disastrous war in Afghanistan, that "graveyard of empires." Complete troop withdrawal is now scheduled for 2014. I hope I can be pardoned for being skeptical about whether that promise will be kept. It depends on who is in charge at that point. If Alexander the Great, the British, and the Soviet Union could not conquer and pacify that country, we are unlikely to be able to do it, even with a draft, millions of troops, and the further destruction of our economy, though of course the industrial buildup for WWII actually pulled our economy out of a decade of depression. It put everyone to work making guns, ammunition, tanks, and planes that would be then destroyed on the battlefield, in a triumph of the military-industrial complex.

The fourth looming catastrophe is the worst. It makes the others look trivial. We are doing practically nothing to keep this catastrophe from happening. Humanly caused global climate change, all but a tiny majority of scientists tell us, is most likely already irreversible. It is even now leading to more violent hurricanes, typhoons, and wild fires, the transformation of the United States Southwest into an arid desert, polar ice melt, tundra defrosting, glacial melting in Greenland, and so on. The ice and permafrost melting is generating feedback mechanisms that are raising global temperatures to lethal levels. The disastrous consequences of all these suicidal actions were more or less unintentional, though after a certain point we should have been able to see what was happening. The mystery is why we did nothing until it was too late. The internal combustion engine, chemical agriculture, and coal-fired electricity plants seemed like really neat ideas. They seemed to be technological inventions whose implementation would lead to improved quality of life all around. In a similar way, it seems a neat idea to be able to talk to or "text" to anyone anywhere in the world on a cell phone, though the concomitant changes in community and society were not at first evident. I mean the way these telecommunication gadgets are producing a mutation in the human species. The medium is the maker, and one thing it makes is the nature and collective culture of the human beings who use a given medium.[3] Global climate change on the scale it is happening will lead to widespread species extinction, water wars, the inundation of coastal plains worldwide (Florida, India, Vietnam, Australia, the Northeastern United States, where I live, small Pacific island nations, etc.), and perhaps ultimately to the extinction of *homo sapiens*, those wise creatures.

It is a feature of all four of these interlocked systems that changes in them are the product of chance, of random acts that statistically add up to a pattern. These systems are explicable by chaos and catastrophe theory. This means that they are all subject to sudden catastrophic change when they reach a certain unpredictable tipping point, as in the sudden unforeseen, but foreseeable, collapse of the investment companies Bear Stearns and Lehman Brothers, and the insurance giant AIG. Those collapses triggered the recent worldwide "financial meltdown." Another famous example is the way the flap of a butterfly's wing in Guatemala can, we are told, trigger a destructive hurricane in the Gulf of Mexico.

I can understand the head in the sand resistance to thinking about these linked domains and then trying to do something about them. Human beings have a limitless capacity for denial, for kidding themselves. *Homo sapiens'* possession of sapience, however, suggests that we should at least have a look around as the water rises above our chins. How can we explain, if not stop, our penchant for self-destruction? Part of the problem of course is that we are not objective witnesses. We are ourselves part of these self-destructive processes, one element in interlocking stochastic system we only think we can control. I claim Kafka's text might help us confront what is happening. That is a big and problematic claim.

Odradek the Illegible

What makes the reader queasy about *"Die Sorge des Hausvaters"*? This slight seasickness is brought about by the way this text resists being read according to any of the comforting organic unity models. These models are so ingrained as to be taken for granted. That is the case in general with ideological prejudices.

The English reader's problems begin with the title and with the question of its translation, not to speak of the translation of the text itself. Stanley Corngold's admirable new translation of Kafka's stories translates *"Die Sorge des Hausvaters"* as "The Worry of the Father of the Family." Peter Fenves, the translator of Werner Hamacher's essay, gives "Cares" for *"Sorge"*: "Cares of a Family Man" (118). It is not entirely easy for an English speaker to get the hang of the nuances of the word *"Sorge,"* as it is used in German. My German/English dictionary gives a whole set of not entirely compatible meanings for "*Sorge*": "grief, sorrow; worry, apprehension, anxiety, care, trouble, uneasiness, concern." This list is followed by a diverse set of idiomatic phrases employing "*Sorge*," e.g. "*die Sorge ertränken*" or "*ersäufen*," to drown one's sorrows in drink, and "*keine Sorge*," "Don't worry," "Never fear." That is somewhat like what we say today: "No problem."

Readers of Heidegger will remember the quite specific use he makes in *Sein und Zeit* of "Sorge," as distinguished from "*besorgen*," "*Besorgnis*," "*Fürsorge*," and "*versorgen*," not to speak of "*Angst*." Macquarrie and Robinson translate "*Sorge*" as "care." Chapter Six of Section One of *Sein und Zeit* is called "*Die Sorge als Sein des Daseins*" ("Care as the Being of Dasein"), and "*Sorge*" is firmly distinguished from "*Angst*," anxiety. Earlier Heidegger distinguished, in the permutations of words in "*Sorge*," between "*Besorgnis*," the "concern" we have for things ready to hand, from "*Fürsorge*," the "solicitude" we have for other *Daseins*, in our primordial condition of "being with" other *Daseins*. Each is a different form of "*Sorge*," care. (*Being and Time* 227, 157–9; original 182, 121–2). Is what the "*Hausvater*" suffers "care," or "concern," or "anxiety," or just "worry"? Just what is he worried about? What are his cares? The text is not entirely clear about that, but we shall see what we shall see.

"*Hausvater*" brings its own problems. No straightforward English equivalent exists, since "the father of the family" does not carry the implication of patriarchal domination and responsibility within the house. The Greek word "*oikonomos*" meant manager of a household, from "*oikos*," house, and "*nomos*," managing, or lawgiving. "*Hausvater*" is a precise enough translation of "*oikonomos*." "Eco" as in "economy," or "ecology," or "ecotechnology" refers to the house in the extended sense of "environment." An "ecosystem," says the *American Heritage Dictionary*, is "an ecological community together with its physical environment, considered as a unit." The whole earth can be thought of as one large ecosystem that is now undergoing rapid climate change, or change in the house within which all earthlings dwell together in a global village. Jean-Luc Nancy's term "ecotechnological" suggests that the whole environment is to be thought of under the aegis of the technological. This is a pantechnologization into which we and our bodies are plugged as a flash memory stick is plugged into a computer's USB connection, ready to receive whatever information is downloaded into it.

I have not even yet quite finished with the title. Who assigned the title? Who is to be imagined as speaking it? Presumably Franz Kafka, the author, who gave a name to what he had written. He had a right to do that, as a *Textvater*. Who then speaks the text? Presumably the *Hausvater*, who says of Odradek authoritatively informed things like, "Sometimes he disappears for months at a time; he has probably moved into other houses; but then he inevitably returns to our house (*doch kehrt er dann unweigerlich wieder in unser Haus zurück*)" (73). Since both title and text seem to be spoken or written in versions of Kafka's characteristically neutral, deadpan voice, it is hard to know how much irony the title directs at the concern, care, sorrow, or worry of the house-father. Is Odradek really anything the *Hausvater* ought to worry about? The house-father perhaps has more serious things at hand that ought to generate concern. "*Sorge*," however the reader takes it, seems, at least at first, an excessive term for what Odradek might justifiably cause.

If my reader thinks I am paying too much attention to nitpicking questions of translation and semantics, the first paragraph of "*Die Sorge des Hausvaters*" is my model and justification. It does not yet describe Odradek. Rather it speculates, fruitlessly, about the word's etymology and meaning. I agree it is a strange word, but are not all proper names strange, singular, unique? Nevertheless, they all tend to have semantic meaning, as does my family name, "Miller," or my wife's given name, "Dorothy": "gift of God."

Before looking at what the text says about the word "Odradek," let me, in the interest of getting on with what might become an interminable reading, suggest a working hypothesis. I claim that the name "Odradek," the "thing" called Odradek, the text about Odradek, and the implied speaker(s) of the title and text have a common destructuring technological structure. "Structure" is not an entirely good word for what I am trying to describe, since it suggests a static assemblage. The oxymoron "destructuring structure" suggests not only that the assemblage in question is in a process of constant dynamic movement, but also that this movement is in one way or another a dismantling, I would even dare to say a deconstructuring.

The relation among the four odd deconstructuring structures I have identified is difficult to name. The relation is not metaphorical, nor allegorical, nor even exactly analogical. Perhaps one might say these structures are in resonance, or consonance, or *Stimmung*. The resonance, however, is not exactly a harmonious chiming. It is more a *"Klang."* All are dissonant versions of one another.

The best model I know to describe these strange structures is to say that they are all are extremely peculiar little machines, each one *sui generis*, unlike all the others except in being strangely and contradictorily machinelike. What is machine-like about these structures, and what is peculiar about them if we think of them as machines? Each is made of parts that are assembled or articulated to make something that *works*. It does something, like any good machine. Each is both machine-like and also a self-functioning sign-system. Each seems in some way the product of *techné*, of an art of know-how. Each, however, is in one way or another incomplete or fissured, fractured by a crack, or cracks. Moreover, each forbids rational description or explanation. Each seems to be lacking meaning and identifiable purpose. The maker, finally, of these little unworked or inoperative (*désoeuvrées*[4]) machines cannot be easily identified, nor can one imagine what weird intention motivated his (her? its?) exercise of a manufacturing technique. Each of these non-machinal machines has what Walter Benjamin, speaking of Kafka's parables and stories, called a "cloudy place," a place where reasonable understanding and interpretation fails.[5] Let me look at each of these unworked machines in turn, in their echoing disconsonance.

The first paragraph of *"Die Sorge des Hausvaters,"* strangely, discusses what contradictory things experts have had to say about the word or the name "Odradek." I say this is strange not only because a discussion of etymology is an odd way to begin a story or a confession, if it is either of these, but also because it is not at all evident how linguists have got hold of a word which appears to be a secret kept between Odradek and the *Hausvater*. Only now, it appears, is the father of the family revealing a secret that has been up to now apparently kept inside the house, so to speak. He conspicuously does not begin by saying, "I have submitted this name to linguists expert in etymologies, and here is what they say." Nevertheless, the word has apparently already been the subject of a lot of (fruitless) speculation. The *Hausvater*'s "cares" may have to do with his unsuccessful attempts to figure out, with the help of experts, what the word means. "No one," however, he says, "would occupy himself with such studies if there were not really a creature called Odradek." The *Hausvater* has Odradek in his care, at least during those times the strange animal-machine is roaming around the halls and stairways of his house or lurking in the attic. Therefore it is the house-father's care or *Sorge* to figure out what the creature's name means. Since Odradek, so far as I know, exists only in Kafka's text, I and other readers who have taken the word into their care are doing just what the *Hausvater* says no one in his or her right mind would do.

Nevertheless, linguists have got hold of the word somehow, says the *Hausvater.* Structural linguists and etymologists, we know, do not really care all that much about the existence or non-existence a word's referent. It is a word's putative meaning as an item in a network of differential relations to other words that interests them. Moreover, the linguists in this case disagree sharply. The speaker concludes, irrationally, from their inability to agree, that etymology is of no use in assigning meaning to the portentous sounding conglomeration of three syllables, "Odradek." "Some say," the little text begins, "that the word *Odradek* has roots in (*stamme aus*) the Slavic languages, and they attempt to demonstrate the formation (*Bildung*) of the word on that basis (*Grund*). Still others maintain that its roots are German, and that it is merely influenced by the Slavic" (72).

Somewhat unreasonably, the *Hausvater* concludes that this disagreement or uncertainty means that such researches are useless in finding a meaning for the word. Just because experts disagree, it seems to me, is no valid reason for giving up the search. "The uncertainty of both interpretations (*Deutungen*), however," says the text, "makes it reasonable to conclude that neither pertains, especially since neither of them enables you to find a meaning (*Sinn*) for the word" (72). I do not see how that uncertainty makes it reasonable to conclude any such thing. The *Hausvater*'s reasoning is as irrational as the word "Odradek." One or the other of the schools of linguists may be right. Nor does it rationally follow that trying out one or the other, or both, of the hypothesized roots might not reveal a plausible meaning for the word. What would forbid the word

"Odradek" from being a hybrid, like Kafka's disturbing kitten-lamb in "A Crossbreed," or like Kafka himself as a speaker of both German and Czech? "Odradek" may be a combination of Slavic and Germanic roots somewhat uneasily joined, with a fissure or fissures, perhaps a bottomless cloudy chasm,[6] opening up within the word, between its syllables or within them. Many such hybrid words do exist, for example in a polyglot or mongrel language like English.

What is at stake in this question of identifying meaning from etymons, however, as the reader will have noticed, is nothing less than the organic model as it dominates the traditional terminology of etymology, as in the term "word stem." The word "Odradek," experts claims, "has roots in" (*stamm aus*) either Slavic or German. One or the other of those languages is its "basis" (*Grund*). The word "Odradek" is rooted in the ground of either Slavic or German languages. The word has grown from them as a flower grows from its roots and stem.

The German word *Grund*, moreover, does not just mean "ground" in the "literal" sense of earth, garden soil. It is the German equivalent of the Greek *logos* or the Latin *ratio*. Latin *ratio* is afflilated with *radius* and *radix*, root, as in our English word "radish," an edible root. Heidegger's book about the principle of reason is called *Der Satz vom Grund*. He follows Schopenhauer in making this translation of the Latin phrase *principium rationis*. As a translation of the Latin formula, the Leibnizian idea that everything has its reason, that reason can be rendered to everything, *der Satz vom Grund* sounds extremely odd to an English-speaker's ear. "*Grund*" for "reason"? That is not reasonable. It does not make sense.

"Etymon" comes from Greek *etumos*, true, real. The branch of linguistics called "etymology" is the search for the true original word from which later words are derived, as flower from root. The organic model, in this case, carries with it the whole system of Western metaphysics as embodied in that complex word, *logos*, meaning word, mind, ratio, rhythm, substance, ground, reason, and so on. In casually repudiating a procedure of reasoning out the meaning of the word "Odradek" by way of tracing its stem back to its roots in a grounded etymon, Kafka's speaker is rejecting the claim of that whole branch of linguistics to be able to identify true meaning: "neither of them [the two hypothesized language roots: Slavic,

German] enables you to find a meaning for the word" ("*man auch mit keiner von ihnen einen Sinn des Wortes finden kann*") (72).

In spite of the speaker's firm prohibition, Kafka scholars from Max Brod to Werner Hamacher have not failed to take the bait. They have risen to the occasion. They have proposed all sorts of meanings for the separate syllables of the word "Odradek." These various meanings are to a considerable degree incompatible. Brod's essay containing his solution to the riddle of the word "Odradek" was already published in Kafka's lifetime. It presupposes Brod's characteristically religious reading of Kafka. Brod claims that the word "Odradek" contains "an entire scale of Slavic words meaning 'deserter' or 'apostate' . . . : deserter from the kind, *rod*; deserter from *Rat* (counsel), the divine decision about creation, *rada*." (qtd. in Hamacher 319). Brod puts this succinctly in another essay: "(Slavic etymology: having defected from counsel [*Rat*]—*rada* = Rat)" (Hamacher 319). Hamacher ironically wonders whether this reading of Odradek as meaning an apostate from the kind or *rod* says something about a man whose name was B*rod*. Wilhelm Emrich, in a book on Kafka of 1958, also cited by Hamacher, embroiders a bit on Brod's definition and secularizes it:

> In Czech [writes Emrich] . . . there is the verb *odraditi*, meaning to dissuade or deter someone from something. This word etymologically stems from the German (*rad* = *Rat*: advice, counsel, teaching). The subsequent Slavic "influence" is embodied in the prefix *od*, meaning *ab*, "off, away from," and in the suffix *ek*, indicating a diminutive. . . . Odradek . . . would therefore mean a small creature that dissuades someone from something, or rather, a creature that always dissuades in general. (qtd. in Hamacher 319–20)

That is all quite rational and clear. What Emrich says, however, does not jibe with what Brod says. For Brod, Odradek is in the condition of being an apostate. For Emrich, Odradek is someone who dissuades someone else from something. They cannot both be right. Moreover, neither Brod's meaning nor Emrich's is exemplified in the text itself. The *Hausvater*'s Odradek neither is shown to be an apostate from any faith, nor does he attempt to dissuade anyone, the *Hausvater* for example, from anything. Odradek just nimbly races up and down stairways, corridors, and halls, or lurks in the attic. These places are those inside/outside regions of a house or home that appear so often in Kafka's writings, for example as the locations of Joseph K.'s (almost) endlessly postponed trial in *The Trial*.

Werner Hamacher's own reading/non-reading of the word "Odradek" is by far the subtlest and most extensive I know. It goes on for pages. I cannot do justice to it here, but a sketch of what he says may be given. You must read Hamacher's essay for yourself. I identify three central features of what Hamacher says about "Odradek." 1) Hamacher is a distinguished master of what might be called paronomastics, the study of puns and wordplay, not the same as the science of word interpretation. Even the most apparently far-fetched associations are grist for Hamacher's mill, hay for his making. Hamacher makes a lot of hay. 2) The result is an amazing series of more or less contradictory words that Hamacher finds buried in "Odradek." If William Carlos Williams says a poem is "a small (or large) machine made of words" (256), Hamacher sees in "Odradek" one of those little unworked machines I am claiming is a new paradigm for thinking in many realms. The series Hamacher generates is like a forever incomplete set of variations on a few given sounds, like music by John Cage, John Adams, or Philip Glass, like a certain form of postmodern generative poetry, that by Georges Perec, John Cage, the Oulipo group,[7] or like some apparently mad sequence of superimposed words and phrases in *Finnegans Wake*,[8] or like the ones and zeroes in a computer file stored in the hard disk's random access memory, or like the just over three billions of DNA Base pairs in the human genome. The human genome is a huge set of permutations accumulated over millions of years, many of them meaningless or without apparent function. They are variations on a handful of basic letters naming chemical agglomerations. 3) Hamacher repeatedly insists that the upshot of this paronomastic investigation is not to identify the meaning, however complex, of the word "Odradek," but to confirm its lack of meaning or its paradoxical meaning as asserting that it is outside any meaning, that it means meaninglessness. Most etymologists agree that the first syllable, "od," is a privative, and that the last syllable, "ek," is a diminutive. The problem is the seemingly limitless plurivocity of the syllable "rad":

Any interpretation of "Odradek" that lays claim to certainty, conclusiveness, and meaning—and these are the hermeneutic principles of both "the family man" and the etymologists he criticizes—must miss "Odradek" because "Odradek" means dissidence, dissense, and a defection from the order of meaning. "Odradek" thus "means" that it does not mean. His discourse says that he denies this discourse, that he runs off course, that he de-courses; his name says that he has no name. (Hamacher 320–1)

Here is the strange Oulipian poem that emerges if I just run Hamacher's paronomastic word lists along in a row, with some of Hamacher's commentary interpolated. The reader will note that Hamacher takes away with one hand what he gives with the other. He wants to have these associations and at the same time to repudiate them as all false leads. The effect of the echoing potentially interminable series of words and word fragments is that they all gradually lose meaning and become mere sound, "rad, rad, rad, rad," in a crescendo of nonsense, as does the whole word "Odradek" if you repeat it often enough, as I am doing here, with Hamacher's help:

And among the uncertain meanings of "Odradek" which "the family man"—this economist of meaning who is always concerned with certainty in matters of interpretation—would have to refuse, there are also those that recall other connections in Czech: *rada* means not only *Rat* (counsel) but also series, row, direction, rank, and line; *rád* means series, order, class, rule as well as advisable, prudent; *rádek* means small series, row, and line. Odradek would thus be the thing that carried on its mischief outside of the linguistic and literary order, outside of speech, not only severed from the order of discourse (*Rede*) but also outside of every genealogical and logical series: a *Verräter*, a "betrayer" of every party and every conceivable whole. . . . Even the remark that "Odradek" can also be read as "Od-rade-K" and "Od-Rabe-K"—or "Od-raven-K"—and thus contains a double reference to the name "Kafka" [a favored move by Hamacher; he tends to see all

Kafka's work as a hidden anagram of "Kafka" or "Franz Kafka," though he here rejects that move as illicitly explanatory]
misses this "word," a word moving outside of the order of
the word, outside of natural, national, and rational languages.
Not even the name "Kafka," its contraction into the letter K,
and its transformations into "jackdaw" and "raven" could be
a source of meaning, an origin of discourse, or a root of reference, for "Kafka" separates itself in "Odradek" precisely from
its roots, its *radix*. Odradek is the "od-radix": the one "without roots"; in Czech, *odrodek*, the one without its own kind,
the one who "steps out of the lineage" (*odroditi*—to degener-
ate, to be uprooted). "Odradek" is, in short, the one who belongs to no kind and is without counsel, the one with neither
a discourse nor a name of his own. . . . According to Kott's dictionary, *odraditi* means "to alienate," "to entice away"; *odranec*
means "rags"; *odranka* means "a piece of paper," "patchwork
of a text"; *odrati* means "tear off"; *odrbati* means "scrape off,"
"rub away"; *odrek* means "the renunciation"; *odrh* means "re-
proach," "reproof"; *odrod* and *odrodek* mean the one without
a kind." Kafka may have connected pieces from all these with
Odradek. They support the remark of Malcolm Paisley that
Kafka would always speak of his writings as "patchwork," fragments soldered together, little bits of a story running around
without a home. (Hamacher 320–1)

If I abstract just the German, Czech, and Latin words from Hamacher's series I get the following Oulipian or Cagean more or less meaningless and unreadable poem. The individual items have meaning, but put
together in this way, without grammar or syntax, they lose meaning and
become variations on a mere sound or on possible ways of arranging a
small selection of letters of the alphabet: *rada, Rat, rád, rádek, Rede, Verräter; ratio,* Od-rade-K, Od-Rabe-K, Od-raven-K, Kafka, *radix,* "od-
radix";*odrodek, odroditi, odraditi, odranec, odranka, odrati, odrbati, odrek,
odrh, odrod, odrodek, Odradek.*
This string would be akin to the many unverifiable meanings that
Jacques Derrida gives to the enigmatic phrase that starts his essay on
"How to Avoid Speaking: Denials": *"Pardon de ne pas vouloir dire"* (which

means, among other possibilities, "I beg your pardon for not wanting to speak," or "I beg your pardon for not meaning anything" (119–121; 161, 163**)), or to the variations in meaning that Thomas Pynchon, in one segment of *Gravity's Rainbow*, gives by changes in punctuation, emphasis, and context to a single word string "You never did the Kenosha Kid":

> *Dear Mr. Slothrop:*
> *You never did.*
>
> *The Kenosha Kid. (62)*
> *Old veteran hoofer: Bet you never did the "Kenosha," kid! (62)*
> *You? Never! Did the Kenosha Kid think for one instant*
>   *that you…? (62)*
> *"You never did 'the,' Kenosha Kid!" (62)*
> *But you never did the Kenosha kid. (63)*
> *You never did the Kenosha kid. Snap to, Slothrop. (63)*
>   *Voice: The Kid got busted. And you know me, Slothrop.*
>   *Remember? I'm Never.*
>   *Slothrop (peering): You, Never? (A pause.) Did the*
>   *Kenosha Kid? (72)*

Another example would be the string of words, phonemes, and putative Indo-European roots in "g" that I spin out, with help from Derrida's *Glas*, in "Line," the first chapter of *Ariadne's Thread: graph, paragraph, paraph, epigraph, graffito, graft, graphium, graphion, graphein, gluphein, gleubh-, gher-, gerebh-, gno-, guh, gn, gl, gh, gr.* (9–10). Derrida's "Telepathy" appropriates another such multilingual string from Freud's strange essays on telepathy: "Forsyth … Forsyte, foresight, *Vorsicht, Vorasussicht*, precaution, or prediction [*prevision*]." Elsewhere in "Telepathy" Derrida appropriates a dazzling sequence, generated from the name "Claude" (ambiguously both male and female) from his own *Glas*: "*glas … (cla, cl, clos, lacs, le lacs, le piége, le lacet, le lais, là, da, fort, hum … claudication* [cla, cl, closed, lakes, snare, trap, lace, the silt, there, here, yes, away, hmmm … limp])" (260–1, 234 (translation modified), 235; 269, 245, 246).[9] Other examples of such Oulipian poems can be found in the discussions of Cage, Perec, and Joyce in Louis Armand's "Constellations," referred to in footnote 8.

Given language systems or multiple interwoven language systems are non-rational assemblages in which the meaning of a given phoneme or string of phonemes may be apparently limited by context, by intonation, and by its difference from other phonemes or strings of phonemes. Nevertheless, a given string always exceeds its context and its differential limitations toward a limitless horizon of more and more remote but never entirely excludable puns, homonyms, and chance associations. The words or phrases in these lists are not ordered either by priority or temporally or as a narrative sequence. They could be given in any order. Implicitly they are simultaneous, like all the data in the Internet or like the items in a hypertext. The first item is not a beginning, nor is the last word an end. That makes Louis Armand's Mallarméan figure of the constellation appropriate, even though "constellation" implies a fixed pattern rather than the dynamically and unpredictably changing assemblage I am exemplifying here. The items in these sequences are like those bits of different colored thread knotted and twisted together that are wound on Odradek as if he were no more than a spool for saving used thread. Each list I have cited could be extended indefinitely in either direction. Ultimately, by a more and more outrageous process of substitution and permutation, such as Hamacher brilliantly deploys, as if he were a machine for making puns, any item, such as the "rad" in "Odradek," could lead to all the words in the Czeck and German languages, and to all the words in other languages too. It is no wonder sane people dislike puns and say of them what Samuel Johnson said: "He that would make a pun would pick a purse." Punning robs language of its rationality, as do the alliterations in Johnson's witty formulation. Paronomasia, like accidental alliterations, reveals that language is already an irrational machine. The will to meaning, the *"vouloir vouloir dire,"* can never capture or control this machine, anymore than the *Hausvater* can capture or control Odradek.

I have hypothesized that the thing that calls itself Odradek has an unstructuring structure that is analogous to the unworking (*désoeuvrant*) word-machine "Odradek." Let me be more specific about this. For one thing Odradek the thing is, like the word "Odradek," homeless. When the *Hausvater* asks Odradek where he lives, he says "No permanent residence (*Unbestimmter Wohnsitz*)" (73),[10] and then laughs. "But it is a kind of laughter that can only be produced without lungs. It sounds more or less like the rustling of fallen leaves (*wie das Rascheln in gefallenen Blättern*)" (73).

For me this is the most uncanny moment of *"Die Sorge des Hausvaters."* It is akin to the skin-crawling and hair-raising moment when the Hunter Gracchus, who is caught permanently on his death-barge drifting between this world and the next, says: "My barge has no tiller, it is driven by the wind that blows in the nethermost regions of death" (*Kafka's Selected Stories* 112). Laughter is, experts claim, a form of distinctively human gesture-speech. We assume that animals cannot laugh. What, however, is laughter that is produced without lungs? It is laughter without laughter, an ironic undercutting of real laughter. Odradek's laughter is directed, oddly, toward the assertion that he has no permanent residence. It is an inhuman sound, like that produced by the rustling of fallen leaves. As Hamacher has recognized, however, *"Blättern"* is also the German word for the leaves of a printed book. Odradek's laughter, one might say, is a purely literary laughter. It is a sound generated by the words on the page and by their comparison with the sound of fallen leaves. But the leaves of this text are fallen, dead, dried out. They can only rustle. They are not legible and they cannot be read, like Odradek's laughter. Why does he laugh? No reason is given for why he finds having no permanent address risible. It hardly seems a laughing matter, or even an object fit for ironic non-laughing laughter.

The *Hausvater's* description of Odradek the thing is as anomalous as the word that names him or it. Odradek is neither a human being, nor an animal, nor a thing, but rather a strange sort of talking and nimbly moving machine. Odradek is a (not very successful) robot, a technological construct that seems to have been made by someone not very good at designing robots. Or rather it is difficult to imagine that it had any designer at all. It seems to be the product of *techné* without a technician, as, it may, are the universe as a whole and human bodies within that universe, with their defective genomes, potentially self-destructive immune systems, and faulty endocrine systems. All three are prone to lethal non-working. We and our ecosystem may be the result of chance alterations over billions of years that have never yet quite got it right from the perspective of what we human beings think would be good for us.

Attractive as the argument from intelligent design is, since it gives a meaning to the creation and to all the creatures in it, the evidence strongly suggests that Darwin and recent physicists and geneticists are right: the universe and everything within it has evolved through billions of years of random variation, with the more or less random survival of the fittest determining which variations last longest. No rational designer could have put together the human genome, the endocrine system, and the immune system. Almost anyone could have done better than this *bricolage* of spare parts, with a lot of left-over parts (the nonsense sequences in the human genome) that do not seem to have any purpose or function at all. They may, however, have some hidden function that we have not yet identified, or may never be able to identify.

The same thing can be said of Odradek. The *Hausvater* says nothing at all about Odradek's genesis and genealogy. He seems to have no origin and no kin, to be *sui* generis, a one off, just as he seems to have no end in the sense of purpose or goal: "At first it looks like a flat, star-shaped spool for thread, and in fact, it does seem to be wound with thread; although these appear to be only old, torn-off pieces of thread of the most varied kinds and colors knotted together but tangled up in one another. But it is not just a spool, for a little crossbar sticks out from the middle of the star, and another little strut is joined to it at a right angle. With the help of this second little strut on the one side and one of the points of the star on the other, the whole thing can stand upright, as if on two legs" (72). If you try to imagine what this strange machine would look like, you have difficulty making sense of it. I never yet saw a spool for thread that was star-shaped, though commentators have seen a reference to the Star of David, first employed in Prague as a way of marking Jews. Nevertheless, how would you wind thread around the points of the star? In and out? They would slip off the star's points. The bits of thread are all tangled and knotted in any case, like those word and phoneme strings I discussed earlier. They have no apparent purpose beyond showing that Odradek or someone who uses him (it) is a thread-saver, though for no apparent reason. Perhaps some obscure reference may be encoded to Kafka's works as what he called a "patchwork" of narrative elements knotted together in a random sequence.

I can see how such an apparatus might stand upright, but I do not see how it can move so nimbly up and down the stairs, down the corridors, in the hallway, in the attic, as the *Hausvater* says it does. It is so extraordinarily mobile that it can never be caught: "*Odradek außerordentlich beweglich und nicht zu fangen ist.*" Though Odradek appears to be made of wood, it is self-propelled and it can speak and laugh, though it is without lungs. Like the kitten-lamb in "The Crossbreed," or the talking ape in "Report to an Academy," or like all those other talking and thinking animals in Kafka's work, Odradek belongs to no identifiable species. It is neither thing, nor plant, nor animal, nor human being, but a disturbing mixture of all these that defies reasonable classification.

The reader might be tempted to think that Odradek is incomplete, unfinished, or broken in some way, but the *Hausvater* says no proof of that exists, though he has sought evidence of it. If Odradek is incomplete and the missing parts could be found, then it might make better sense as a technological machine with some identifiable purpose: "It is tempting to think that this figure (*Gebilde*) once had some sort of functional shape {*zweckmäßige Form*] and is now merely broken. But this does not seem to be the case; at least there is no evidence for such a speculation; nowhere can you see any other beginnings or fractures that would point to anything of the kind; true, the whole thing seems meaningless yet in its own way complete (*das Ganze erscheint zwar sinnlos, aber in seiner Art abgeschlossen)*" (72). That would be a good description of Kafka's works, as well as of the paradigmatic Kafkaesque word "Odradek." All these are complete, even the works he did not finish, but meaningless.

No wonder the *Hausvater* is worried. Kafka, I imagine, must have taken great delight in imagining a thing that would defy reasonable explanation, be meaningless, and yet "in its own way" complete, *abgeschlossen*, closed in on itself. He also must have enjoyed inventing a responsible and reasonable patriarch as "narrator" whose attempts to make sense of the creature that has invaded his household lead over and over to the verdict: "meaningless (*sinnlos*)," just as the name Odradek defies all attempts to give it a verifiable meaning. Both the name and the thing are cunning technological constructions whose "purpose" seems to be to defy reasonable explanation by human beings.

The final characteristic of Odradek is the one that causes the father of the family the most worry or *Sorge*. This is his fear that Odradek may be unable to die, again like the Hunter Gracchus. Anything mortal, the *Hausvater* says, has at least an identifiable goal, that is, to die. For Heidegger, an essential feature of *Daseins* is that they can foresee their death, as, according to him, animals cannot. *Sein zum Tode,* being toward death, is therefore what *Daseins* are. "Can he die?" asks the *Hausvater* about Odradek. "Everything that dies has previously had some sort of goal (*Ziel),* some kind of activity (*Tätigkeit*), and that activity is what has worn it down (*zerrieben*); this does not apply to Odradek" (73).

The principle of reason or *Satz vom Grund* that this strange little text radically puts in question presumes that anything with a rational meaning has that meaning because its activity is goal-oriented. Its meaning can be defined in terms of its goal or purpose, its *Zweck* or *Ziel*. Odradek has no goal and therefore his (its) activity does not wear him out until he (it) dies, as even a machine, however cleverly made, ultimately wears out. Only a technological construction without goal, purpose, or meaning can be immortal, perhaps like the universe itself in its endless movement of expansion and then contraction back to a new Big Bang. The *Hausvater's* most haunting worry is that Odradek will outlive him and "that one day, with his bits of thread trailing behind him, he will come clattering down the stairs, at the feet of my children and my grandchildren[.] True, he clearly harms no one (*Er schadet ja offenbar niemandem*), but the idea that, on top of everything else, he might outlive me, that idea I find almost painful (*fast schmerzliche*)" (73).

After all this I have said about the word "Odradek" and the thing "Odradek" as a way of exemplifying the model of self-destructuring inorganic technological structures I have in mind as a replacement for thinking on the model of the organic, I can give short shrift,[11] or, to make a pun of my own, short *Schrift*, in the sense of just a few written words, to the two other forms of the inorganic machinal or technological this text exemplifies.

If "Odradek" is a word that is not a word and if Odradek it(him)self is a machine that is not a machine, *Die Sorge des Hausvaters* is an anomalous text that belongs to no recognizable genre. It is neither a story, nor a parable, nor an allegory, nor a confession, nor an autobiography, nor a scientific report, nor does it conform to the laws of any other recognized genre. It is an anomaly, an inorganic hybrid assemblage of words mixing aspects of many genres but conforming lawfully to none. It is not even much like other texts by Kafka. It is *sui generis*, a species with one exemplar, no parents and no offspring.

In a similar way, *Die Sorge des Hausvaters* does not create in the reader's mind the illusion of some recognizable character or personage. We learn little about the father of the family except that he is worried about Odradek. Kafka excels in creating a cool, slightly ironic, narrative voice that can hardly be called a "point of view," or a perspective, or either a reliable or an unreliable narrator, or the recognizable speech of a person. *"Die Sorge des Hausvaters"* is just a strange assemblage of words that seems to have fallen out of the sky, like a meteor, or like an inscribed astrolith, or like a scratched stone we might find on the beach. It just lies there like an indecipherable message in code. Though we know Kafka wrote it, nothing we can learn about Kafka the person explains or accounts for this fantastically inventive little text written in pellucid German. Its meaning is its successful resistance to interpretation, its failure to mean. It is *sinnlos*.

Whatever Works

Before turning to some present-day examples of destructuring structures, let me summarize the features of such a model as I have identified it in *"Die Sorge des Hausvaters."* Such a technological artifact seems to have no creator. It seems to be self-generated and self-generating. It is certainly not the result of human will and technological knowhow. It is best described as a machine, but as machine that is unworked, inoperative, or disarticulated, though it goes on and on doing its thing, working away, like the Energizer bunny. It is *techné* without a technologist or technician, but a mad *techné* that produces machines that do not make sense from the perspective of human needs and wants, or from any other imaginable perspective.

I want in conclusion to set in parallel five systems that I claim are understandable, if they can be understood, according to the linguistico-machinal model I have sketched out, with Kafka's help: the environment, the global financial system, the nation-community, the body, and language. These mechanical sign-systems work. They make something happen, often in the end disaster from the human perspective. Each system can be seen as a figure for the others, but no one is the literal of which the others are displacements, figures, supplements, substitutions, or symbols. All are interconnected. Together they make an all-inclusive ecotechnological non-integrated whole into which each one of "us" is plugged.

One such system is terra, the earth. The earth, scientists are more and more discovering, is a complicated machine made of almost innumerable atoms and molecules that signal to one another. This machine is out of our control. It just goes on doing what it does do, that is, create the ever-changing climate within which we live, as in our environment, our house or *oikos*. The clever scientists, technicians, and engineers who invented and perfected the internal combustion engine that uses gasoline as a fuel, and then linked it to a vehicle with wheels, like the scientists who developed chemical fertilizers and pesticides, or coal-fired electrical plants, did not intend to cause catastrophic climate change. Nor did they at first know that, once started, climate change accelerates rapidly through feedback mechanisms. Scientists these days keep saying in amazement, "This is happening much faster than we thought it would!" The rapid increase of carbon dioxide and other green house gases in the atmosphere as a result of the later stages of industrialization has intervened in the ecosystem to trigger its self-modifying gears and levers. We intended no such thing, but that did not keep it from happening, mechanically.

The earth is not a super-organism. It is not an organism at all. It is best understood as an extremely complex machine that is capable of going autodestructively berserk, at least from the limited perspective of human needs. Global warming will bring about widespread species extinction. It will flood our low-lying islands, our coastal plains, and whatever towns, cities, and houses are on them. An example is our house on the shore of Deer Isle, Maine, where I am writing this, in sight of the ocean, only fifty feet away, its surface only a few feet down, at high tide, from the ground level of our house.

Moreover, as we continue to build up carbon in the atmosphere to higher and higher levels, we never know when the next emitted carbon-dioxide molecule will tip over some ecosystem and trigger a nonlinear climate event—like melting the Siberian tundra and releasing all its methane, or drying up the Amazon, or melting all the sea ice at the North Pole. The systems I am describing are best understood by way of chaos theory and catastrophe theory, that is, in terms of instantaneous breaks. Moreover, when one ecosystem collapses, it can trigger sudden unpredictable changes in others that could abruptly alter the whole earth (Friedman).

Another such machine is the global financial system. That machine is linked now to the Internet and to a host of computer-based data-storage and data-manipulation devices. Global capitalism in 2007 imploded, causing a worldwide recession and much human suffering. The unemployment level in the United States is at almost ten per cent, not counting the millions who have stopped looking for a job. The financiers, bankers, and CEOs whose decisions brought about this catastrophe did not intend to bring the financial system to the edge of total breakdown. Each acted rationally, so they thought, to maximize profits and garner their own high salaries, bonuses, and stock options. The financial meltdown happened, apparently, because too many people believed in the magic of a simple computer program formula that was supposed (falsely) to measure risk comparatively, i.e, the joint default probability of mortgages. David X. Li, then in Canada and the United States, but now back in Beijing, wrote the formula, a Gaussian copula formula of elegant simplicity (Salmon). The formula was fatally flawed by the assumption that house values would not, could not, go down. All the bankers and investment managers believed in that assumption, however, including the ratings agencies, paid by the financial "industry," that were giving AAA ratings to bundles of eventually almost totally worthless securities.

The computer programs "quants" devised allowed linked computers and databases to do things no human brain can understand. All the bankers and heads of financial institutions like Merrill Lynch, Bear Stearns, AIG, Citigroup, Bank of America, and so on, said, as their institutions were going belly up, that they did not understand what a credit default swap is, or what a CDO (collateralized debt obligation) is, or just what are the workings of programs that make tranches and tranches of tranches to distribute subprime mortgages into more and more remote slices. This procedure was supposed to spread the risk so widely that no one would suffer appreciable loss if someone defaulted on one of the mortgages. Those in charge of banks and financial companies were not lying when they said they did not know how far in debt they were. It appears that many were totally insolvent. One hundred and four smaller banks failed in the United States by October 24, 2009, and bank failures have continued worldwide since then. CDO's added up to $4.7 trillion in 2006. By 2007 the amount of credit default swaps (CDSs) outstanding was the astounding sum of $62 trillion. The banks and financial companies were destroyed, or would have been destroyed if they had not been saved by a massive infusion of billions of dollars of taxpayers' money, by something built into the system that was not an object of cognition, though some whistle-blowers put up warning signs. This is a little like the way I do not understand just what is going on somewhere deep inside my computer when I press certain little keys on my keyboard and get this present sentence on my screen in twelve point Palatino, double-spaced, with certain pre-set margins and other automatic formatting. Our cats are adept at accidentally pressing fortuitous combinations of keys that cause my laptop to "crash," just as the stock market crashed. Like the CEOs already mentioned, in relation to their highly paid computer quants, I have no idea just what my cats have done, nor how to undo it.

It is an essential feature of the modern financial system that it depends on computer programs and elaborately interconnected computers for its workings. These workings exceed human comprehension. That does not, however, keep them from going on doing their thing, in what might be called by anthropomorphism a revenge of the robots. The unexpectedly accelerated pace of global warming and species extinction is parallel to this unknowabilty of the workings of the financial system. Experts have to keep revising the time frame for the inundation of our Deer Isle house. It keeps getting more and more imminent. "Get ready! The end of the world is at hand!" "Get ready! The financial system is in meltdown!" It will not have escaped my reader's notice that "meltdown" and "toxic," as in "toxic assets," are terms borrowed from the vocabulary of climate change. Thomas Friedman, in the New York Times Op Ed column cited above, expresses our inadvertently-caused plight as follows:

To recover from the Great Recession, we've had to go even deeper into debt. One need only look at today's record-setting price of gold, in a period of deflation, to know that a lot of people are worried that our next dollar of debt—unbalanced by spending cuts or new tax revenues—will trigger a nonlinear move out of the dollar and torpedo the U.S. currency. If people lose confidence in the dollar, we could enter a feedback loop, as with the climate, whereby the sinking dollar forces up interest rates, which raises the long-term cost of servicing our already massive debt, which adds to the deficit projections, which further undermines the dollar. If the world is unwilling to finance our deficits, except at much higher rates of interest, it would surely diminish our government's ability to make public investments and just as surely diminish our children's standard of living. As the environmentalist Rob Watson likes to say, "Mother Nature is just chemistry, biology and physics. That's all she is. You can't spin her; you can't sweet-talk her. You can't say, 'Hey, Mother Nature, we're having a bad recession, could you take a year off?'" No, she's going to do whatever chemistry, biology and physics dictate, based on the amount of carbon we put in the atmosphere, and as Watson likes to add: "Mother Nature always bats last, and she always bats a thousand." [Addendum 11/29/11: Friedman's scenario of self-destructive high interest rates has not taken place yet in the United States, but just this event has recently occurred in the "Club-Med" nations of the Euro-zone that are on the verge of bankruptcy: Greece, Ireland, Italy, Spain, Portugal. Both the Euro-zone nations and the United States, however, are making the same disastrous ideological (that is, robot-like) mistake of thinking they can return to economic well-being by slashing government spending and lowering taxes on the rich and on big corporations. This is exactly the wrong thing to do, as Ireland's present plight demonstrates. Following this strategy would be a catastrophe eventually even for the rich and for corporations because it would greatly reduce the income consumers must have to buy the goods corporations make. Meanwhile, unemployment in the United States remains at over nine percent (much higher if you count those who are underemployed or who have stopped looking for a job); hundreds of thousands of people are losing their houses through mortgage foreclosures, some illegal; the top 1% of Americans make 20% of the national income and control 40% of the nation's wealth; national health care costs are rising to 20% of GDP and will go on rising; soaring tuition costs are putting higher education out of the reach of more and more Americans, in a litany of interlocked auto-co-immune disasters.]

The third such system is a community or a nation. Such a construct is an interrelated conglomeration of human beings controlled by laws, institutions, constitutions, legislatures, and all the machinery of government, what Foucault calls "governmentality." The financial system is an important part of a given national fabric, especially in a militarist-capitalist-teletechnoscientific plutocracy like the United States. What is most conspicuous about the United States today, if we think of it not as an organism but as a technological artifact, a product of *techné*, is its penchant for mindless or at least irrational self-destruction.

Why is it that a large group of apparently well-meaning and apparently sane human beings are hell-bent on auto-destruction? The best description of this I know is Jacques Derrida's hypothesis of what he calls "auto-co-immunity," that is, a penchant within any community that turns its forces against itself. Such a community destroys itself by way of what is intended to make it safe, whole, indemnified from harm, just as autoimmunity in the human body's immune system turns the body against itself. I have discussed Derrida's "auto-co-immunity" at some length in *For Derrida* (123–9), but here are the essential passages, from Derrida's "Faith and Knowledge" and "Rogues." They speak for themselves:

But the auto-immunitary haunts the community and its system of immunitary survival like the hyperbole of its own possibility. Nothing in *common*, nothing immune, safe and sound, *heilig* and holy, nothing unscathed in the most autonomous living present without a risk of auto-immunity. . . . This excess above and beyond the living, whose life only has absolute value by being worth more than life, more than itself—this, in short, is what opens the space of death that is linked to the automaton (exemplarily "phallic"), to technics, the machine, the prosthesis, virtuality: in a word, to the dimensions of the auto-immune and self-sacrificial supplementarity, to this death drive that is silently at work in every community, every *auto-co-immunity*, constituting it in truth as such in its iterability, its heritage, its spectral tradition. Community as *com-mon auto-immunity*: no community <is possible> that would not cultivate its own auto-immunity, a principle of sacrificial self-destruction ruining the principle of self-protection (that of maintaining its self-integrity intact), and this in view of some sort of invisible and spectral sur-vival. This self-contesting attestation keeps the auto-immune community alive, which is to say, open to something other and more than itself: the other, the future, death, freedom, the coming or the love of the other, the space and time of a spectralizing messianicity beyond all messianism. It is there that the possibility of religion persists: the religious bond (scrupulous, respectful, modest, reticent, inhibited) between the value of life, its absolute "dignity," and the theological machine, the "machine for making gods. (82, 87 [translation slightly modified]); original 62, 68–9).Yet all these efforts to attenuate or neutralize the effect of the traumatism (to deny, repress, or forget it, to get over it [*pour en faire son deuil*], etc.) are, they also, but so many desperate attempts. And so many autoimmunitary movements. Which produce, invent, and feed the very monstrosity they claim to overcome.What will never let itself be forgotten is thus the perverse effect of the autoimmunitary itself. For we now know that repression in both its psychoanalytical sense and its political sense—whether it be through the police, the military, or the economy [*au sens politico-policier, politico-militaire, politico-économique*]—ends up producing, reproducing, and regenerating the very thing it seeks to disarm (99 [translation slightly modified]; original 152).The Patriot Act and the Department of Homeland Security have made United States citizens conspicuously less safe by taking away our precious civil liberties, subjecting us to universal surveillance and the danger of indefinite imprisonment, perhaps by way of "extraordinary rendition," to be tortured in a secret prison in a foreign country. I identify in iteration in variation four further regions where the United States is currently engaged in auto-immune self-destruction.

One, perhaps the worst, is the refusal to have done anything serious about global climate change until it is already too late. It is already too late, I mean, to keep the atmospheric temperature and the ocean levels from rising to levels that will make the planet in most places uninhabitable.

Another auto-immune gesture is the refusal to do anything serious to regulate the financial system. Bankers and investment officials are already returning to their old ways of excessive risk-taking along with setting outrageous salaries and bonuses for themselves. Banks and investment houses are fighting tooth and nail to keep regulation from happening. This is perhaps because they secretly know that climate change will cause devastation. They know what they are doing will cause another financial meltdown, but are squirreling away huge sums of money so they can pay to be part of the surviving remnant living in gated communities perched high above the rising waters. Or so they imagine.

A third example of auto-immune behavior is the refusal even to consider the only rational solution to our catastrophic health-care system, namely single payer government-run health care. The Republicans have sworn to repeal the modest and not very effective health care bill that was passed when Democrats still controlled both houses of Congress. They also want to eviscerate Medicare and Medicaid, which would cause tens of thousands of our citizens to die from lack of adequate healthcare, in a perhaps not entirely undeliberate process of population culling. It is difficult to believe that the Republicans, some of them at least, do not know what they are doing. Without a robust so-called "public option" the "reforms" that passed Congress and was signed by Presideny Obama will only make the health care insurance companies and the pharmaceutical companies immensely richer, costing far beyond the current sixteen to twenty per cent of the Gross Domestic Product that we spend on health care in the United States.

A fourth example, also already mentioned, is the delay in withdrawing from the war in Afghanistan and bringing our troops home. Trillions of taxpayer dollars have already been sunk into the wars of occupation in Iraq and Afghanistan, not to speak of the human toll in killed and wounded on all sides.

If you just stand back a little and look at these four problems, it is easy to see the rational solutions. Our collective auto-co-immunity, however, seems to make it extremely unlikely that any of these solutions will be chosen. Apparently we will remain blindly bent on self-destruction.

An additional realm of the technological is the "human being," thought of as soul embodied, material spirit. The body is now more and more seen as not organic in the warm fuzzy sense we have tended to mean that, but as a complex product of *techné*, with the universe as ecotechnician. The human immune system is exemplary of the body's machine-like self-functioning, as is the endocrine system. You cannot direct your antibodies to do this or that by thinking about them. They act on their own. It is *L'homme machine*, as de la Mettrie said, or *La femme machine*, but with a tendency to self-destruction built in. Hypothyroidism is, for example, apparently an autoimmune disease, as is, perhaps, pancreatic cancer, and as are many other diseases and cancers. Many forms of cancer appear to be brought about by random mishaps in the genetic code. We cannot influence by thinking the way a string of genetic code generates a certain protein or enzyme, as it is programmed to do, or the way the immune system produces antibodies against what it perceives, not always correctly, as invading alien antigens. These mechanical systems do not always work all that well. They are cumbersome, redundant, and prone to error. Recent work on the human genome and its functions, on cell biology, on the endocrine system, on the immune system with its terrifying power of self-destructive autoimmunity, and by neuroscientists on brain chemistry and the brain's "wiring" is showing that a technological paradigm is a better way than a traditional organic paradigm to understand the body and even its most human-appearing concomitants of consciousness and the accompanying senses of self-hood and volition.

An authoritative recent feature essay in *Science News*, "Enter the Virosphere," summarizes recent work on viruses in ways that indicate how the workings of genes are machine-like, but make big problems for assumptions about what constitutes "life." Viruses were thought not to be alive, but scientists are now increasingly not so sure, hence the pun in the title "Virosphere" rather than "Biosphere." On the one hand, viruses do not eat, respire, or reproduce. They have no metabolism, so they must be dead. On the other hand, viruses are made of genetic material that acts in many ways like that in "living organisms" such as bacteria, algae, rabbits, and human beings. A gene is a gene. Whether a given gene is in a virus or in the human genome, it is a pattern that constructs things like proteins. Viruses are everywhere. "A thimbleful of sea water contains millions of virus particles" (Ehrenberg 22). Viruses make up about 90 percent of the ocean's biomass, killing an estimated 20 percent of that biomass every day. "Their killing feeds the world" (22), since so many "organisms" feed on dead organisms killed by viruses. Just as a living cell's nucleus uses its surrounding cytoplasm "to replicate its own DNA using machinery outside of itself" (qtd. from Jean-Michel Claverie in Ehrenberg 25), a virus is made of genetic material that acts like a nucleus in entering a host cell and using the machinery of that cell to reproduce itself. Viruses borrow genes from other gene systems and either pass them on to "infect" other gene systems, or incorporate them in their own genomes.

It might be best to say that the new evidence does not so much lead to the conclusion that viruses are alive as suggest that all so-called living things are subject, like viruses, to the machine-like processes of gene action. It may even be that the first "living thing" was a protovirus that ultimately mutated into biological cells, though that hypothesis is highly controversial. It might aid coming to terms with *"Die Sorge des Hausvaters "* if we think of Odradek as virus-like, or at any rate of we include the virus along with thing, plant, animal, and human beings in Odradek's hybrid mixture of language-like systems. The virus's relation to language is indicated in the terminology used to describe the two different ways bacterial and animal viruses enter a host cell, replicate themselves, and then leave the cell to continue their work. This is often a work of killing. According to how virologists express this process, the viral genome enters a cell, "replicates" itself, then "transcribes" itself," then "translates" itself, finally "assembling" and "packaging" itself before the replicated viral genome exits the cell in new multiple copies, like those made by a copying machine.

Figures drawn from the workings of language are, you can see, essential to expressing the results of genetic research. The three dominant metaphors in Ehrenberg's article are "machinery," "language," and "infection." These are used unselfconsciously and unproblematically. They are the usual figurative words for the way a virus works. One paragraph, however, ostentatiously, with evident irony, uses a sustained metaphor comparing the way viruses work to the global financial system, with sinister implications for the mindless technicity of both. The paragraph also reinforces my claim that we tend to think of each of these systems by figurative analogy with the others, in the absence of any grounded literal terminology. Any description of these products of *techné* is catachrestic, that is, the borrowing from one realm of a term then used to name something whose working has no satisfactory literal name: "Viruses also may keep genes they've procured, and even bundle these assets together, as appears to be the case with several photosynthesis genes recently found in marine viruses. These findings hint at the vast viral contribution to the ocean's gross national product and viruses' significance in global energy production" (22).

Fifth: Textual systems, sign systems generally, are also machine-like in their action. This can best be seen in the interference of constative and performative forms of language. Once these systems come into being (who knows how?) they are out of our control. They do things on their own which we are powerless to stop. As Paul de Man argued, we cannot prevent ourselves from making the same errors of misreading all over again even when we have correctly identified them as errors.[12] Decisive here is de Man's idea that performative utterances work on their own, not as a result of human agency. They work mechanically, through the force of language. And they work in weird and unpredictable ways. De Man always emphasized the mechanical, non-human, and arbitrary workings of language, as does, in a somewhat different way, Louis Armand throughout *Literate Technologies*.[13] The first draft of the present essay was written by way of examples that were accessed spontaneously and somewhat randomly from the database stored somewhere in my brain's memory center. Sentences just formed themselves magically in my mind, as words were fitted into pre-existing grammatical and syntactical paradigms. This happened by a process of invention in the double sense of discovery and making up. I then typed these sentences into my laptop. I suppose most writing by anyone gets done that way. It is uneasy-making, however, to realize that writing is so little under the writer's conscious control and volition. I never know what I am going to write until I write it. *Die Sprache spricht:* Language speaks. It speaks through me by a species of ventriloquism that uses me (in the sense of my body and my computer literate, keyboard-tapping, conscious self and fingers) as medium.

For Paul de Man, a performative utterance makes something happen, but not what is intended or predicted. The last sentences of de Man's "Promises *(Social Contract)*" express this in terms of that paradigmatic performative, a promise: "The redoubtable efficacy of the text is due to the rhetorical model of which it is a version. This model is a fact of language over which Rousseau himself has no control. Just as any other reader, he is bound to misread his own text as a promise of political change. The error is not within the reader; language itself dissociates the cognition from the act. *Die Sprache verspricht (sich)*; to the extent that is necessarily misleading, language just as necessarily conveys the promise of its own truth" (de Man 277). The German phrase is an ironic allusion to

Heidegger's portentous, *Die Sprache spricht*, "Language speaks," cited earlier. *"Versprechen"* means "to promise," as a reflexive: "to promise itself," but it also means "to make a slip of the tongue." This happens because of the doubleness of the prefix *"ver-,"* which can mean both for and against. De Man's little phrase is an example of the nonsensical paronomasias, puns, and wordplay, built mechanically into language. Language speaks all right, but it says things the speaker does not intend, that are *necessarily* misleading, for example in the form of a promise that cannot be kept. De Man goes on, notoriously, to assert that such rhetorical complexities, such linguistic mixups, "generate history." As de Man expressed this unsettling feature of performative language in a graduate seminar: "you aim at a bear and an innocent bird falls out of the sky."

Put these five domains together, working like the interconnected machines that they are, linked as one big and extremely cumbersome and *désoeuvrée* machine, and you get the revolt of the robots big time. Using the technological model as a way of outlining what is happening in these five realms will not keep what is occurring from occurring. Like Odradek, my prime model in this essay of the inorganic ecotechnological, these unworked machines just keep on mindlessly doing their thing. This alternative paradigm does, however, provide a better *techné* or tool than the organic model for sketching out what is happening as the water rises around us. Unfortunately, however, as my emphasis on what is irrational or aporetic about the (non)machines of various sorts I have named, the ecotechnological model does not lead to clear cognition or understanding. At most it invites the sorts of performative action, such as passing laws about carbon emissions, that seem exceedingly unlikely to take place. The implacable law of auto-co-immunity forbids that.

This failure of both cognition and of effective action is taking place in fulfillment of a weird translation into Mayan hieroglyphs of Christ's words on the cross. The oral expressions of these hieroglyphs were then transliterated into Western letters, according to a perhaps fallacious mystery story I can no longer find among our books: "Sinking, Sinking! Black ink over nose." This essay might be thought of as the inscription in black ink, exemplifications of the technicity of the letter, written on the nose of someone drowning in black ink.

November 5, 2011, Deer Isle, Maine

Notes

1. See Heidegger's An Introduction to Metaphysics 45–50 (original 34–8).

2. See Hamacher, especially 296–300.

3. For a fuller discussion, see my *The Medium is the Maker: Browning, Freud, Derrida and the New Telepathic Ecotechnologies*.

4. This the complex word Jean-Luc Nancy uses in the title of his book about modern non-community communities: *The Inoperative Community* (*La communauté désoeuvrée*).

5. The metaphor of a "cloudy spot" in Kafka's writings, especially the parables, occurs three times in Walter Benjamin's great "Kafka" essay. Of the opening anecdote about Potemkin, Benjamin says "The enigma which beclouds this story is Kafka's enigma" (795). The famous parable "Before the Law" has a "cloudy spot at its interior" (802), and Kafka's use of gesture is said to form "the cloudy part of the parables" (808). This part is cloudy because it is the place where clear-seeing of the doctrine, teaching, or moral that the parable ought to express is impossible. The parables of Jesus have a clear meaning. The parable of the sower in Matthew is about the Kingdom of Heaven and how to get there. Jesus tells the disciples that this is the case. Kafka's parables have no such identifiable meaning. An impenetrable opacity resides where the meaning ought to be. Kafka's parables therefore mean their lack of identifiable meaning.

6. My allusion is to what Walter Benjamin says of Kafka's parables. See previous footnote.

7. "Oulipo (French pronunciation: [ulipo], short for French: *Ouvroir de littérature potentielle*; roughly translated: 'workshop of potential literature') is a loose gathering of (mainly) French-speaking writers and mathematicians which seeks to create works using constrained writing techniques. It was founded in 1960 by Raymond Queneau and François Le Lionnais. Other notable members include novelists Georges Perec and Italo Calvino, poet Oskar Pastior and poet/mathematician Jacques Roubaud. The group defines the term '*littérature potentielle*' as (rough translation): 'the seeking of new structures and patterns which may be used by writers in any way they enjoy.' Constraints are used as a means of triggering ideas and inspiration, most notably Perec's 'story-making machine' which he used in the construction of *Life: A User's Manual*. As well as established techniques, such as lipograms (Perec's novel *A Void*) and palindromes, the group devises new techniques, often based on mathematical problems such as the Knight's Tour of the chess-board and permutations" ("Oulipo"). (Underlined words are links from the Wikipedia entry, <http://en.wikipedia.org/wiki/Oulipo>. [Accessed Nov. 5, 2011.])

8. For Cage, Perec, Oulip, and Joyce as creators of texts in one way or another made by a machine-like process of permutation see the brilliantly learned and

provocative book by Louis Armand, *Literate Technologies: Language, Cognition, Technicity*, especially the final chapter, "Constellations," 165–223. Though Armand's primary focus is on the technological aspects of language, thought, and consciousness, what he calls "literate technologies," rather than on climate change, on the financial system, or on national communities, or even on the effects of new media, his book has nevertheless greatly influenced my thinking in this essay.

9.   I have discussed these sequences in *The Medium is the Maker*, 27–9.

10. For whatever it is worth, which is probably not much, Kafka himself had no permanent residence. Guides to Prague visitors, as I know from experience, point out apartment after apartment where Kafka is said to have lived, mostly with his family, if what he did can be called living, which Kafka himself doubted. Most of these apartments are around the famous Old Town Square or on adjacent side streets, but at least one is in a quite different part of the city, across the river and near Prague Castle. Like Joyce in Zurich, Kafka moved a lot. He was without permanent residence. Joyce moved from flat to flat because he could not pay his rent and was evicted. Kafka moved because his father was rising up in the world and wanted to live in always more and more pretentious apartments.

11. A "shrift" is a penalty prescribed to a Catholic parishioner by a priest after confession. Criminals sentenced to be hanged were given "short shrift" before being executed. They were shriven in a hurry. See Shakespeare, Richard III. "To give him short shrift" is in German "*kurzen Prozeß mit ihm machen*." *Prozeß* is certainly a word with Kafkesque resonances, though Joseph K's *Prozeß* is anything but short. He is told rather that his best hope is to make his trial interminable, which, unhappily, does not happen.

12. See de Man's "Allegory of Reading (Profession de foi)" in *Allegories of Reading*: "Deconstructive readings can point out the unwarranted identifications achieved by substitution, but they are powerless to prevent their recurrence even in their own discourse, and to uncross, so to speak, the aberrant exchanges that have taken place" (242).

13. See, for example, de Man's "Excuses (Confessions)" in *Allegories of Reading*: "The deconstruction of the figural dimension is a process that takes place independently of any desire; as such it is not unconscious but mechanical, systematic in its performance but arbitrary in its principle, like a grammar. This threatens the autobiographical subject not as the loss of something that once was present and that it once possessed, but as a radical estrangement between the meaning and the performance of any text" (298).

Works Cited

Armand, Louis. *Literate Technologies: Language, Cognition, Technicity.* Prague: Literaria Pragensia, 2006.

Benjamin, Walter. "Franz Kafka: On the Tenth Anniversary of His Death." *Selected Writings: Volume 2: 1927–1934.* Trans. Rodney Livingstone. Ed. Michael W. Jennings, Howard Eiland, and Gary Smith. Cambridge, MA: The Belknap Press of Harvard University Press, 1999.

de Man, Paul. *Allegories of Reading.*New Haven: Yale University Press, 1979.

Derrida, Jacques. "Literature in Secret: An Impossible Filiation." *The Gift of Death.* 2nd ed. Trans. David Wills. Chicago: University of Chicago Press, 2008. Trans. of *"La littérature au secret: Une filiation impossible." Donner la mort.* Paris: Galilée, 1999.

---. "Telepathy." Trans. Nicholas Royle. *Psyche: Inventions of the Other, Volume I.* Ed. Peggy Kamuf and Elizabeth Rottenberg. Stanford: Stanford University Press, 2007. Trans. of "Télépathie." *Psyché: Inventions de l'autre.* Paris: Galilée, 1987.

---. "Faith and Knowledge: The Two Sources of 'Religion' at the Limits of Reason Alone." Trans. Samuel Weber. *Acts of Religion.* Ed. Gil Anidjar. New York and London: Routledge, 2002. Trans. of "Foi et savoir: Les deux sources de la 'religion' aux limites de la simple raison." *La religion,* with Gianni Vattimo. Ed. Thierry Marchaisse. Paris: Seuil, 1996.

---. "Autoimmunity: Real and Symbolic Suicides." *Philosophy in a Time of Terror: Dialogues with Jürgen Habermas and Jacques Derrida,* with Jürgen Habermas and Giovanna Borradori. Chicago: University of Chicago Press, 2003. Trans. of *Le 'concept' du 11 septembre: Dialogues à New York (octobre-décembre 2001).* With Jürgen Habermas and Giovanna Borradori. Paris: Galilée, 2004.

Ehrenberg, Rachel. "Enter the Virosphere." *Science News.* 10 Oct. 2009. 22–25.

Friedman, Thomas. "Our Three Bombs." *New York Times.* 6 Oct. 2009. Web. 7 Oct. 2009. <http://www.nytimes.com/2009/10/07/opinion/07friedman.html?th&emc=th>. (Accessed Nov. 5, 2011.)

Hamacher, Werner. "The Gesture in the Name: On Benjamin and Kafka." *Premises: Essays on Philosophy and Literature from Kant to Celan.* Trans. Peter Fenves. Cambridge, MA: Harvard University Press, 1996.

Heidegger, Martin. *Being and Time.* Trans. John Macquarrie and Edward Robinson. London: SCM Press, 1962. Trans. of *Sein und Zeit.*Tübingen: Max Niemeyer, 1967.

---. *The Fundamental Concepts of Metaphysics: World, Finitude, Solitude.* Trans. William McNeill and Nicholas Walker. Bloomington: Indiana University Press, 1995. Trans. of *Die Grundbegriffe der Metaphysik.* Frankfurt am Main: Vittorio Klostermann, 1983.

---. *An Introduction to Metaphysics.* Trans. Ralph Manheim. New Haven: Yale University Press, 1959. Trans. of *Einführung in die Metaphysik.* Tübingen: Max Niemeyer, 1966.

---. "Language." *Poetry, Language, Thought.* Trans. Albert Hofstadter. New York: Harper and Row, 1971. Trans. of "Die Sprache." *Unterwegs zur Sprach.* Pfullingen: Neske, 1959.

Kafka, Franz. "The Worry of the Father of the Family." *Kafka's Selected Stories.* Ed. and trans. Stanley Corngold. New York: W.W. Norton, 2007. 72–3. Trans. of "*Die Sorge des Hausvaters.*" <http://www.kafka.org/index.php?landarzt>. (Accessed Nov. 5, 2011.)

Miller, J. Hillis. *Ariadne's Thread.* New Haven: Yale University Press, 1992.

---. *For Derrida.* New York: Fordham University Press, 2009.

---. *The Medium is the Maker: Browning, Freud, Derrida and the New Telepathic Ecotechnologies.* Brighton and Portland: Sussex Academic Press, 2009.

Nancy, Jean-Luc. *Corpus.* Paris: Métailié, 2006.

---. *The Inoperative Community.* Ed. Peter Connor. Trans. Connor, Lisa Garbus, Michael Holland, and Simona Sawney. Minneapolis: University of Minnesota Press, 1991. Trans. of *La communauté désoeuvrée.* Paris: Christian Bourgois, 2004.

"Oulipo." Wikipedia. Web. 25 Oct. 2009. <http://en.wikipedia.org/wiki/Oulipo>. (Accessed Nov. 5, 2011.)

Pynchon, Thomas. *Gravity's Rainbow.* New York: Penguin, 1973.

Ruskin, John. "Of the Pathetic Fallacy." <http://www.ourcivilisation.com/smartboard/shop/ruskinj/>. (Accessed Nov. 5, 2011.)

Salmon, Felix. "A Formula for Disaster." *Wired.* March 2008. 74+.

Williams, William Carlos. *Selected Essays.* New York: Random House, 1954.

Chapter 3

Care

Within the limits of capitalism, economizing means *taking care*

BERNARD STIEGLER

Consumers were consuming consumer items

– Raymond Queneau

The future of Europe and the world must be thought in terms of the psycho-power characteristic of control societies, the effects of which have become massive and destructive.[1] Psycho-power is the systematic organization of the capture of attention made possible by the psycho-technologies that have developed with the radio (1920), with television (1950), and with digital technologies (1990), spreading all over the planet through various forms of networks. It results in a constant industrial canalization of attention, which has provoked recently a massive phenomenon: the destruction of this attention which American nosologists call attention deficit disorder. This *destruction of attention* is a particular case, an especially serious one, of the destruction of libidinal energy whereby the capitalist libidinal economy self-destructs.

Attention is the reality of *individuation* in Gilbert Simondon's sense of the term: it is always both psychic and collective. *Attention*, which is the mental faculty of concentrating on an object, that is, of giving oneself an object, is also the social faculty of taking care of this object—as of another, or as the representative of another, as the object of the other: attention is also the name of civility as it is founded on *philia*, that is, on socialized libidinal energy. This is why the destruction of attention is both the destruction of the psychic apparatus and the destruction of the social apparatus (formed by collective individuation). This is so to the extent that the latter constitutes a system of care, given that to pay attention is also to take care. (It is also to *watch out*, which is taken up in the emphasis I will put on destruction.) Such a system of care is also a libidinal economy, wherein a psychic apparatus and a social apparatus hook up, whose destruction today is engendered by technological apparatuses. And we will see that they are in fact psychotechnological and sociotechnological apparatuses. In other words, we are confronted with a question stemming from what I call a general organology.

The major stake of attention deficit disorder and of everything stemming from the destructive effects of the exploitation of attention by psychopower is therefore the fragility inflicted upon the infantile psychic apparatus and on sociability founded on *philia*. Now, this precocious liquidation of libidinal economy is also what destroys the industrial capitalism of investment: the organ of psychopower is marketing as the arm of a financialized capitalism having become essentially speculative.

∼

The gigantic financial crisis sending tremors all over the world is the disastrous result of *the hegemony of the short term*, of which the destruction of attention is at once effect and cause. The loss of attention is a loss of capacities of long term projection (that is, of investment in objects of desire) which systemically effects the psychic apparatuses of consumers manipulated by the psychopower as well as the manipulators themselves: the speculator is typically the person who pays no attention to the objects of his speculation, and who takes no care of them either.

The act of the speculator has effects on the multitude of consciousnesses that undergo, directly or indirectly, the effects of his speculation through the psychotechnological devices of attention capture. These consciousnesses are thus always a little more enclosed in the default of attention and care, *that is, in the short term*, which *justifies a posteriori* the act of the speculator: this act is performative in the sense Jean-François Lyotard lends to it in *The Postmodern Condition*. This is how a system of the short term gets established, along with the vicious circle of the destruction of attention.

This is the context in which the colossal environmental crises rage on, now in first place in the world's concerns (*Besorgen*) and in the attention (*Sorge*) of the Nobel Academy. Here is discovered and planetarily recognized what I will later analyse as the *third limit of capitalism*, after the tendency of diminishing returns. It also follows the tendency of libidinal energy to self-destruction (resulting directly from the destruction of attention).

This is the context of an environmental crisis which suddenly considers self-evident the necessity of planning on a long term basis, that is, of re-elaborating a *politics of investment*—precisely at a time when an enormous financial crisis emerges which brings to light the calamity of speculative and short term organization induced by attention-destroying financialization. Here we can see new operations of spectacular industrial concentrations being implemented or prepared, for example the OPA by Microsoft on Yahoo, and the decision by Google to invest in a cell phone network.

The objective of these operations is to gain control over social networks, that is, the digital networks wherein new models for the capture and formation of psychic attention as well as collective attention are revealed: it is a new age of reticulation that is being implemented, and it constitutes a new stage of what I have described as a process of *grammatization*. At this stage, it is the mechanisms of transindividuation that are grammatized, that is, formalized, reproducible, and thus calculable and automatable. Now, *transindividuation* is the way psychic individuations are meta-stabilized as collective individuation: transindividuation is the operation of the fully effective socialization of the psychic.

With the social networks, the question of technologies of attention becomes manifestly and explicitly the question of technologies of transindividuation. The latter are henceforth formalized by the technologies of psychic individuation originally conceived in view of ending up with a collective individuation, with Simondon's analysis posing that psychic individuation is also and in the same stroke collective individuation receiving spectacular and organalogical confirmation. It is a matter of technologies of indexation, annotation, tags and modelized traces (M-traces), wiki technologies and collaborative technologies in general.

Here a reading of Foucault is especially necessary and promising: Foucault also showed that the techniques of the self, as techniques of psychic organisation, are always already techniques of collective organisation—which he demonstrates in his analysis of the correspondence of Seneca with Lucilius. On the other hand, Foucault did not see coming the question of psychopower, whereby marketing, from the emergence of the programme industries, transforms the psychotechniques of the self and of psychic individuation into industrial psychotechnologies of transindividuation, that is, into psychotechnologies threaded by networks, and as the organization of an industrial reticulation of transindividuation that short-circuits traditional and institutional social networks.[2] After having destroyed the traditional social networks, the psychotechnologies become socialtechnologies, and they tend to become a new milieu and a new reticular condition of transindividuation grammatizing new forms of social relations.

In order to analyze these facts, which constitute the specific context on the basis of which it is necessary and possible to think a future for Europe and the world, we must return to the question of what attention actually is. Psychic and collective individuation is essentially what forms attention insofar as the latter is necessarily both psychic and social, and attention is what results from the relation holding between retentions and protentions in the sense Husserl gives to these terms (Husserl naming intentional consciousness what I am calling attention). Now, this relation of retentions and protentions whose result is attention is always mediated by tertiary retentions—of which psychotechnologies and sociotechnologies are instances.

We must speak of tertiary retentions if we are to complete the analysis in which Husserl distinguishes between primary and secondary retentions. Primary retention is, for example, what happens when you listen to me speaking and, applying the verb I use to the subject preceding it, a subject you no longer perceive, you maintain this subject in the verb, which constitutes the maintenance/presence of my discourse which is also what maintains your attention: you conjugate the subject to the verb, with a view to projecting this action designated by the verb toward its complement, projection which is a protention, that is, an expectation.

What Husserl calls primary retention is this operation consisting of retaining a word in another (an operation that Husserl analyzes by studying the way in a melody a note maintains in itself the preceding one, and projects forward the expectation of another note—Leonard Meyer describes this as an expectation): it is the operation consisting in retaining a word which however is no longer present, the beginning of the sentence having been pronounced and in this respect already past, and yet still present in the sense that is thus elaborated as discourse.

We must distinguish the operation we are calling primary retention from secondary retention. The latter is a memory: something that belongs to a past having passed by (it is thus a former primary retention), whereas the primary retention still belongs to the present, to a passing present: it is the passage itself, per se, and in this respect the direction of the present—its sense in the sense of direction as well. Now, the secondary memory is also what permits us to select possibilities from the stock of primary retentions: primary retention is a primary selection whose criteria are furnished by the secondary retentions.

You are listening to me, but each one of you hears something different in what I say, and this is owing to the fact that your secondary retentions are singular ones: your pasts are singular ones. In the same stroke, your apprehension of what I say is each time singular: the meaning that you assign to my discourse, whereby you individualize yourself with my discourse, is each time singular—and this is the case because you select each time singularly primary retentions in the discourse I am giving for you, and through which I am trying to retain and to maintain your attention.

However, if you could, now, repeat the whole discourse that you have just heard, for example because you had recorded it on a memory stick in MP3 format, you could affect obviously new primary retentions, depending on previous primary retentions, which become in the meantime secondary retentions. You would thus call into question the meaning of this discourse already constituted by yourself: you would produce a difference in meaning on the basis of this repetition, through which this meaning would moreover reveal itself as a process much more than a state, and more precisely, the process of your own individuation hooking up with the individuation that this discourse exemplifies, which is, in this case, my own individuation. You would thus form *retentional circuits*, which I do not have time to explain why they are at the heart of what must be conceptualized as *circuits of transindividuation*.

Be that as it may, that which allows such a discourse to be repeated, for example in the form of a recording in MP3 format, is a tertiary retention with the same status as the text I am now reading for you, which allows me to repeat a discourse that I conceived elsewhere, and at another previous time: this is what Plato called a hypomnesic *pharmakon*. Such a *pharmakon* allows the production of attentional effects, that is, retentional and protentional hook-ups, whose existence entirely justifies the definition of this pharmakon as a psychotechnical device. Such a device allows, to be more precise, the control of retentional and protentional hook-ups in view of producing attentional effects.

Such effects are also those that Husserl analyzed as the condition of the origin of geometry—where writing is what allows the formation of types of rational primary and secondary retentions, through which the long circuits of transindividuation are formed, as well as those that Plato denounces in *Phaedrus* or in *Gorgias* as that which allows the short-circuiting of the anamnesic work of thought through the intermediary of ternary and hypomnesic retentions.

Tertiary retentions are therefore mnemotechnical forms of the exteriorization of psychic life constituting organized traces into retentional devices (of which the devices described in *The Order of Things*, *The Archaeology of Knowledge* or *Discipline and Punish* are cases) that characterize the systems of care, as therapeutic systems whose retentional devices are the pharmacological basis.[3]

Now, retentional devices constitute themselves in a new *distributed organization* that in fact represents a major break with the former organization of industrial society—and which is the subject of a recent book by Alexander Galloway and Eugene Thacker, *The Exploit*. I would now like to show that this break is a meeting of the ways faced with which a new industrial politics must make choices, drawing the consequences of these mutations, on the basis of which a new issue out of the hyperindustrial world could present itself. But I must first of all specify why this break, which is both an opportunity and a new danger (it is induced by a new *pharmakon*), emerges at a moment when capitalism runs up against three limits.

~

It was at the end of the 19th century and at the end of the 20th century that capitalism met with its first two limits:

The industrial revolution, as the implementation of the capitalist system of production, is the extension of the process of grammatization whereby and wherein tertiary retentions (which include psychotechniques) are formed by apparatuses of the control of gestures which allow, as machine-tools, the liquidation of workers' know-how, and, on this basis, the realization of immense gains in productivity, and the development of a new prosperity. However, besides the misery this process engenders in the form of the proletariat, it encounters the limit analysed by Marx as the tendency of diminishing returns.

To fight against this limit of capitalist development, the *American way of life* invented the figure of the consumer whose libido is systematically put to work to counter the problems of excess production, which is the social concretization of this tendency of the rate of profit to fall. This canalization of the libido operated by the capture of attention ends up by liquidating the expertise in living [savoir-vivre] of consumers, by the massive development of societies of services which let them off the hook of their own existences, that is, of their diverse responsibilities as adults having reached their legal maturity. This is what ends up provoking the liquidation of their own desire, as well as the desire of their own children, to the strict extent that the latter can no longer identify with them, both because these parents no longer know anything, and are no longer responsible for anything, having become themselves big fat children, and because the process of primary identification is short-circuited by psychopower through the psychotechnologies. This destruction of desire (that is to say also the destruction of attention and of care) is a new limit encountered by capitalism, this time not only as mode of production, but also as mode of consumption, way of life, that is, as biopower having become psychopower.

A third limit henceforth imposes itself on our attention. It consists in the fact that the development of the industrial way of life, inherited from the 19th and 20th centuries, has become not only toxic on the level of minds and of libido, but also on the geophysical and biological level. This third limit will not be able to be raised or effaced before the invention of a mode of life constitutive of a new way of taking care and of paying attention to/of the world by the invention of therapeutics: techniques, technologies and socio-pharmacological apparatuses of the formation of attention corresponding to the organological specificities of our time: to the specificities of the technologies of transindividuation forming the infrastructure of an industrial system itself functioning in an endogenous way as a system of care: making care its "chain of value" that is, its economy, and thereby renewing with the original sense of the word economy, for to economize is to take care.

Western societies, in the sway of the exportation of technologies issuing from their mode of production, have engendered industrial competitors (on whom Paul Valéry was already meditating as to their consequences to come) by a movement of financialization that could do nothing but cause a global economic war. In this new form of war, the stakes are a defense of society no longer as an enemy, exterior or interior, but against a process that ruins time, that is, the horizon of the long term, and the possibility of projecting this horizon in giving oneself objects of desire. This process spins out of control at this precise moment when the effects of the three limits of capitalism combine.

Global competition fired up by financialization has ended up in the destruction of the complex equilibrium that allowed that capitalism's development also be the social development of industrial democracies by the Keynesian organization of the redistribution of wealth under the authority of a welfare State, and it is in the context of the economic war which resulted that marketing has become, as Gilles Deleuze put it, "the instrument of social control" in the societies of control, and that the tendency of libidinal energy to self-destruct suddenly worsened.

Thus, on the side of consumption, the capitalist mode of life has become at the end of the 20th century an addictive process less and less capable of finding sustainable satisfactions—this has induced great discontent in the civilization of consumption, which has replaced culture, that is, care, if we accept that culture precedes cults of all types, that is, attachments to objects whose ensemble constitutes a system of care. It is in this context that Jenny Uechi could write in *Adbusters* that:

> According to surveys conducted recently by the sociologist Juliet Schor, 81% of Americans estimate that their country is too centered on consumption and almost 90% of them consider that it is too materialistic.

~

We all know that in no case will this new global capitalism be able to develop in reproducing the modes of production and consumption that have been characteristic of Western, Japanese, and Korean industrial democracies. For the exportation of this mode of life is also that of the growth in the rate of production of toxins of all sorts toward the greatest part of the planetary population, and which can result in nothing else but the disappearance of the human race—to say nothing of the phenomena of the destruction of psychic apparatuses that also create their effects as quickly as "growth" spreads over the world, which is indeed, by this very fact, a stunted growth [une mécroissance]. The new global capitalism will not be able to renew its energies without inventing a new logic and new objects of investment—and here the word investment must be taken literally and in all its senses: both the sense it has in industrial economy and its sense within libidinal economy.

At this stage of my exposé, it is interesting to check for heart murmurs in a text by Jeremy Rifkin which is circulating all over France and Europe. Rifkin, setting his discourse under the watchword of "the end of the age of oil," asks how we are to assure a "sustainable development" but without ever asking the question of the problem of stunted growth, that is, of a "growth" that destroys desire, and that deindividuates producers as well as consumers, stunting the dynamism of what Max Weber called the spirit of capitalism, a spirit that has to be apprehended as libidinal energy and that can be constituted only in processes of sublimation henceforth annihilated by marketing techniques.

While never taking up these questions (which were however the horizon of both his *European Dream* and *The Age of Access*), Rifkin insists, apropos the age of oil and more generally of fossil fuels, its growing "external costs" (which in economics is called negative externalities): he thus describes the third limit encountered by a capitalism become an actually globalised technological system of production and of consumption. In this context, he writes, there is a residual stock of fossil energy that we will have to learn to exploit to the hilt, that is, the most economically possible, while at the same time putting into place other processes for the production and consumption of energy:

> So as to prepare the future, each government will have to exploit new energy sources and establish new economic models.

I am myself convinced that the stakes are a change in the economic model. But I do not believe that the heart of the question is the energy of subsistence: the real question is that of an energy of existence that is libidinal energy.

Now, by only asking the question of a new production of renewable, sustainable energy of subsistence, founded on the intermediary storage by the technology of the production of hydrogen, Rifkin would have us believe that the energy crisis is a passing one and that it will be able to be surmounted, and along with it the third limit of capitalism, without having to ask the question of libidinal energy, without taking into account this second limit which is the truth of the third one: where the libido has been destroyed, and where the drives it contained, as Pandora's box enclosing every evil, henceforth are at the helm of beings devoid of attention, and incapable of taking care of their world.

Libidinal energy is essentially sustainable, except when it decomposes into drive-driven energy, which is on the contrary destructive of its objects. The drive is an energy, but an essentially destructive one, for the drive consumes its object, which is to say it consummates it. This consumption and consummation implemented by consumers is a destruction. *Consummare*, the etymology of the word to consume, and which initially meant to accomplish, to reach the goal, becomes with Christianity a synonym of to lose, *perdere*, and to destroy, *destruere*. Starting in 1580, the French word *consommer* means to *do away through use* with goods and energies. Starting in 1745 we begin to hear about consumers, and consumption designates then the usage one has of an object for the satisfaction of needs. Consumption becomes an economic term at the beginning of the 20th century. And it was only in 1972 that the word *consumerism* made its appearance in the United States.

$\sim$

If consummation is that which destroys its object, libido is to the contrary that which, as desire and not as drive, that, as the sublimation intrinsic to desire, *takes care* of its object. This is why the question of the third limit of capitalism is not that of the relinquishment of fossil fuels but rather the relinquishment of a drive-driven economy and the reconstitution of a libidinal economy, that is, a sustainable one, given that this energy increases with the frequentation of its objects. The third limit of capitalism is not only the destruction of the reserves of fossil fuel, but the limit constituted by the drive to destruction of all objects in general by consumption, in so far as they have become objects of drives, and not objects of desire and attention—the psychotechnological organization of consumption provoking the destruction of attention in all its forms, on the psychic level as well as the collective level.

Because he seems to ignore everything involved in the second limit of capitalism and its meaning once the third limit has been reached, Rifkin's discourse seems to me fraught with dangers: he would have us believe that a drive-driven growth could be sustained owing to the technology of hydrogen. And yet, this discourse is interesting and of import for at least three reasons:

1. it proposes a real alternative to the question of the energy of subsistence with this system founded on hydrogen which would allow a harmful limit to be pushed back;

2. it poses the questions about energy that are never distinct from questions on networks of communication and information, that is, hypomnesic systems and retentional devices of tertiary retentions;

3. finally, and above all, it posits that the network founded on hydrogen must be based on the model of social networks made possible by the World Wide Web and, thus, must get beyond the opposition between production and consumption.

An organization based on consumption, and constituted by its opposition to production, is dangerous not only because it produces excess quantities of carbon dioxide, but because it destroys minds. The opposition of production and consumption has as its consequence that both producers and consumers are proletarianized by the loss of their knowledge: they are reduced to an economy of subsistence, and deprived of an economy of their existence—they are deprived of libidinal economy, that is, of desire. This is why the fundamental question opened by the combination of the three limits of capitalism is the overcoming of this opposition and of the proletarinarization it engenders structurally.

Now what is extremely interesting in Rifkin's proposition consists in positing, based on the position set forth in the first lines of the study, the energy systems and information or mnemotechnical systems co-develop, that the most recent system of communication, the Internet, breaks precisely with the opposition of consumption and production and thus constitutes the possibility of implementing a new distributed and decentralized network of sustainable energies where everyone would be producer as well as consumer, by combining the technology of stockage by hydrogen and that of networking along the lines of the Internet model.

Confronted with this unprecedented challenge to planetary (planetarianized) humanity—a challenge of practically sublime dimensions, which demands an extraordinary mobilization of the forces of the spirit to meet it: a challenge convoking what Kant called the suprasensible, that is, also the infinite (infinitely renewable)—the temptation of the industrial and capitalist world is to come up with a technological and scientific response in denial of the three limits of capitalism. This temptation borne of denial cannot apprehend:

1. that these three limits, when they combine, produce a systemic evolution at a superior level, that is, a phenomenon of emergence,

2. that we must change industrial models not only to produce a new technical and scientific rationality, but to constitute a new social rationality, productive of motivation, of reasons for living together, that is, of taking care of the world and of those living there,

3. that the fundamental question is here to reorient the financial fluxes toward long-term investments by waging war against speculation, but also against modes of life founded on the short term, of which the most every-day example is the organization of society by a marketing systematically exploiting drives by destroying libido as that which evinces the capable of sustainable investment.

Consumption that becomes drive-based is profoundly dangerous for society. If there were no limit to this consumption, and if fossil fuels were inexhaustible, the catastrophe would perhaps be even greater than the one resulting from the deplenishment of fossil fuels. Perhaps this deplenishment is finally a kind of stroke of luck: the opportunity to understand that the true question of energy is not that one, that the energy of subsistence is of interest only insofar as it contributes to an energy of existence—and is such in its capacity to project what I call the plane of consistencies. Now this is the true stake of what is today called, in an ambiguous expression, ascendant innovation.

~

Over the past ten years, society as a whole (in industrialized countries and in developing countries), because of a spectacular drop in costs in the field of the electronic technologies of the fabrication of materials as well as transactions and duplications of data, acquires new practical, but also analytical and reflexive competencies, through the spread of digital apparatuses giving access to functionalities hitherto reserved to professional actors—these functionalities were hitherto organized by the industrial division of labor (and by everything coming with it, thus for example the law of intellectual property). These functionalities are those of the social networks.

This socialization of innovation calls more and more often on social forms of apprenticeship that would appear to be self-organizing and to elude the usual processes of the socialization of innovation described as "descending" (piloted by the research/development/marketing complex): it constitutes what is more and more often called "ascendant" innovation. Ascendant innovation is a structural break with the organization of social relations in the industrial world based on the oppositional couple production/consumption. It is founded on motivations oriented toward consistencies, that is, toward objects of what the Greeks and the Romans called *skholè* and *otium*, which are very specific objects of attention: the objects of knowledge (know-how, art of living, the disposition to theory, that is, to contemplation).

Digital technologies, where the technologies of information, communication, and telecommunications converge and tend to amalgamate, and on the basis of which a sector of communicating objects called "internet objects" is developing, form a new technological milieu, reticulatory and relational in nature, belonging to what Simondon called an "associated technico-geographical milieu," reconfiguring what he also called the process of psychic and collective individuation, and transforming into technologies of the spirit what hitherto has functioned essentially as technologies of control.

In this technological milieu, electronic apparatuses form a systemic ensemble with the network owing its existence to the IP protocol. Now, the resulting dynamic system, in constant evolution, grounded in a relational economy of miniaturized and personalized equipment and relational services—what is indeed called, and in particular by Jeremy Rifkin, relational technologies ("R technologies")—install new social dynamics, absolutely unheard-of with what hitherto was characteristic of industrial society, and which are propelled by a psycho-social state of the population no longer content with the classical organizational model, and which stores up, therefore, a dynamic potential in the form of expectations, and by the combination of the effects of Moore's "law" and the specificities of the IP networks.

The characteristics proper to the new technological milieu being formed with the IP protocol, which must be apprehended as a technological protocol of reticulation with structural consequences in the field of social reticulation, can be put down to its both bidirectional and intrinsically productive and collective character of a metalanguage of a new type, whereby metadata are collected and organized: it is the combination of these characteristics that founds the constitution of what are called "social networks."

This metalanguage consititues a new epoch in the *process of grammatization* that globally transforms the conditions of transindividuation. A psychic process is translated at the level of a collective individuation where the psychic individuation is marked, inscribed so to speak in the real, and is recognized by other psychic individuals: this work of collective individuation by psychic individuation, and conversely, is the process of transindividuation. Now it is precisely this *circuit* formed by the *process* of individuation that can be observed in the "social networks"—however tawdry they may appear at first sight.

This is why the dynamics induced by the technological protocol of reticulation IP must be described as the effects of a process of psychic, collective and technical individuation the likes of which have never existed before. As poor and disappointing as the social-digital networks appear to us, most of the time, they bring together, henceforth, hundreds of millions of psychic individuals in a processes of collective individuation that can sometimes be evaluated as rich and inventive—if we recall online video games, the network *Second Life*, Facebook, MSN, Skyblogs, etc. But we must also include collaborative platforms like Wikipedia, the open source communities in the field of software development with the Linux system, and so many other variegated initiatives that have taken off in the world—collaborative spaces of teaching, cooperatives of knowledge, and so on.

The Simondonian theory of psychosocial individuation is a theory of relations in which this individuation is produced via a process of transindividuation (which engenders what Simondon calls significations). The process of transindivuation consists in the formation of circuits "knitted" by these relations, whereby the process of co-individuation can be meta-stabilized. However, the conditions of formation of such circuits are quite variable. In particular, these circuits can either imply psychic individuals formed by them, this implication then being the very process of their formation, or, on the contrary they can short-circuit them and impose formations of signification in which they have not participated—the psychic individuals having been proletarianized, that is, disindividualized. The significations in which transindividuation consist then tend to loose their sense and their direction: this is what occurs in dissociated milieus.

Such milieux are created in the production/consumption dichotomy, and this causes a generalized loss of individuation, and a protean discontent and unease. The IP technology is on the contrary what allows the proliferation of new circuits of transindividuation, and that's why it is massively invested in by social practices that were neither anticipated nor programmed by any industrial or commercial strategy. It is thus that this technico-relational milieu tends to reconstitute associated and dialogical milieus (that is, where all those who participate in this milieu contribute to its individuation) by the unfolding of technologies of transindividuation.

This is not to say that these technologies cannot serve the cause of the short-circuiting of transindividuation. All attentional technologies (and these digital technologies of transindividuation belong to the group of attentional technologies) are pharmacological to the strict extent that, as technologies of the formation of attention, they can be reversed and upturned into technologies of the deformation of this attention, and short-circuit this attention, that is, exclude it from the process of transindividuation and signification: they can always produce dissociation.

This is the context that ought to spur the European Union to elaborate a new industrial model, based on what I call with my friends in the association *Ars Industrialis*, an industrial politics of the technologies of spirit—that is, of sublimation—as the only sustainable libidinal economy. It is only on this condition that Rifkin's proposition can supply a basis of subsistence (and a basis for a bio-politics conceived at the level of the biosphere) for a new politics of existence: a *noopolitics* susceptible of reversing and overcoming the deadly logic of psychopower. The actual question, for Europe as for the rest of the world, is whether it can invent with America and the other major industrialized countries a European way of life where economizing means taking care.

Notes

1. This essay was translated by Georges Collins.

2. At first sight and after a preliminary analysis, the formalization of transindividuation here appears to constitute the ultimate and perfect concretization of what I have elsewhere described as the destruction of

the associated milieux, which are the symbolic milieux, by the formation of dissociated milieux that short-circuit the transitional instances of transindividuation, which form circuits of transindividuation which are too long for the rhythms of evolution of industrial society. And yet, I also believe that the formalization of transindividuation constitutes an altogether unheard-of possibility for the reconstitution of the long circuits of transindividuation. Here is where the stakes show up in concentrated form as a crossroads for a planet having become globally hyperindustrial.

3.   Attention, call it A, is a function of tertiary retentions, that is, of mnemotechniques and mnemotechnologies, call them R3, to the extent that the latter overdetermine the relation between retentions and protentions, R and P, and given that the tertiary retentions form systems that must be called retentional devices, RD. Here is a formula: $A = fR3 = R/P$ where $RE = RD$.

Works Cited

Foucault, Michel. *The Archaelogy of Knowledge.* Trans. A. M. Sheridan Smith. New York: Pantheon Books, 1972.

---. *Discipline and Punish.* Trans. Alan Sheridan. New York: Vintage, 1977.

---. *The Order of Things.* New York: Vintage, 1970.

Galloway, Alexander R. and Eugene Thacker. *The Exploit: A Theory of Networks.* Minneapolis: University of Minnesota Press, 2007.

Lyotard, Jean-François. *The Postmodern Condition.* Trans. Geoff Bennington and Brian Massami. Minneapolis: University of Minnesota Press, 1984.

Rifkin, Jeremy. *The Age of Access.* New York: Putnam, 2000.

---. *The European Dream.* Cambridge: Polity, 2004.

Chapter 4

Unicity

JUSTIN READ

Unicity is a term produced by the 1963 poem "cidade/city/cité" by the Brazilian poet Augusto de Campos that I have derived as a concept describing world order during globalization. The "nature" of this concept is such, however, that we cannot think of "Unicity" as conceptual in a normative way. That is, "Unicity" *does* operate as an abstract concept describing the world in which we live, but its abstraction must not be assumed to be an *idealization*. The abstraction of "Unicity" as a concept is, rather, its *virtualization*—a virtual-reality through which the value of ideals, idealizations, essences, spirits, utopias, and so forth, is evacuated completely.[1] Accordingly, the Unicity is not just a concept that describes the world of globalization; the Unicity *is the world* of globalization, the world we inhabit. Framed in logico-poetic terms, the Unicity is the line at which metaphor, metonymy, analogy, symbol, identity, tautology, and contradiction cease to be *different* in concrete space.

The emergence of the Unicity is indicative of a historical, structural shift in world order, typically denoted under the name "globalization." Globalization is the process by which everything in the world approaches planetary scale: production, markets, architecture, society, *life itself*. But "planetary scale" by no means equals "massive" or "homogenous." By thinking through the Unicity, we come to understand the proportion of the planet in terms of a unified "sliding scale" that extends from sub-atomic particles out to the movement of galaxies; the Unicity is, in a word, *universal*, but only because it operates both microscopically and macroscopically, locally and globally. The planetary scale of globalization is thus a means by which to measure movement across the world, from any location to any other. There is no *difference* in the Unicity—how can anything be different if all is One? Nonetheless there are movements—flows within networks, and flows across multiple networks. Thus, there must be a way to calculate movements across mutually embedded networks. The Unicity provides the scale by which network flows may be calculated as *differential* movement within a singular space.

Stated another way, the Unicity is the line at which the world reaches absolute network integration, the mutual embedding of seemingly diverse informational networks into a complex systematic singularity. The Unicity is the "seam" or "border" between networks by which movement through one network with respect to movement across another network may be calculated and quantified. With respect to network integration, the Unicity may be thought of as the possibility of seamless measurability from one network to the next, making possible "leaps" from quanta to organic molecules to bodies to ecosystems to digital computer networks to cellphones to solar systems to economic/financial flows to warfare to linguistic translation to plumbing to garbage collection to academic publishing to whatever, *ad infinitum*, along a *singular scale of measurement*. Because movement is utterly measurable, the "leap" from one network to the next in the Unicity therefore becomes a "leap of confidence" rather than a "leap of faith." Although any particular network may appear distinct or different from another, the Unicity allows movements within one network (i.e., network traffic) and movements within another network to be measured in tandem. Thus, although there are no differences per se in the Unicity, we must always consider the Unicity to be a differential system—a differential space.

As such the Unicity is a form of virtual reality, but only in the following way: it is the seam uniting the concrete terrain of the planet and the virtual terrain of networked informational flows. The Unicity is therefore virtual reality because it is both virtual *and* reality. Perhaps we think of "virtual" in terms of "immaterial," and perhaps this connotation occurs, at least in philosophy and critical theory, because the "virtual" has been coded to mean the "possible" (though "not necessarily actualized"). In today's world order, however, we tacitly accept the virtual as both a real force and a commonplace aspect of daily life. *Everything* in the world has entered into the flow of informational networks: finance and communications, of course; but also transportation (we can go to anywhere from anywhere on the planet); energy (generated and utilized anywhere in the world); production (things can be manufactured anywhere and consumed anywhere); agriculture (food can be grown anywhere and eaten anywhere); and so forth. Ultimately, life itself has been informationalized and networked: the meaning of life is no longer a metaphysical question, but a physical process of metabolism (transmission of genetic information). The space of life (i.e., the planet) has been irrevocably altered by human production, to the point that it is no longer "natural," in the true sense of "nature." There is no nature left, only an *ecological system*, a singular network *environment*. All in all, we can think of the world in two ways: on the one hand there is the "rough" terrain of the world's geography, and on the other hand, there is the "smooth" terrain of global informational flows. We tend to think that the "smooth terrain" of globalization covers the "rough terrain" of the planet, but this is not quite correct. The Unicity is the integration of "discrete" networks (such as listed above) into a singular network, a "network of networks." But, recognizing the planet and life on the planet as networks themselves, the Unicity is also the borderline between the "rough" terrain and the "smooth" terrain: it is the line at which the informational world *saturates* the real world (rather than "covering" it). These two "hands"—the rough/real world on the one hand and the smooth/virtual world on the other—are in fact the *same* hand.

There is no reason why this shift to globalization (the emergence of Unicity) has occurred; furthermore, there is no direction—finality—towards which globalization is heading. History no longer propels us forward (it does not "overdetermine our movement") to an end, as if globalization were mandated by human *progress*. Just because things happen over time and space does not mean that things "progress" or "develop" or "perfect themselves." It is clear for a variety of reasons, however, that certain changes in world order have occurred over time. The first change is from "traditional" societies to "modern" ones. Politically, "traditional" sovereignty—primarily European feudalism, but also other social orders in the Americas, Asia, Oceania, and Africa—was based on the right to kill; the Sovereign (king, lord, cacique) maintained social order by being able to decide if someone could die, either physically (execution) or symbolically (banishment). "Modern" sovereignty, at least as theorized by Foucault and Agamben, shifted into a "biopolitical" order; sovereignty is geared to the preservation and maintenance of life (*bios*) rather than the determination of death, in large part because every human is born (symbolically) with sovereignty over him/herself, a sovereign subject. The historical shift to biopolitics has been paralleled (leaping to the terms of Henri Lefebvre) by a shift from "absolute space" (one's place in the world is determined by the divine cosmological order of the community) to "abstract space" (one's place in the world is determined by one's abstract relation to capitalist production). The Unicity would be a break with both biopolitics and abstract space in certain respects. In the space of the Unicity both the natural and the symbolic (spiritual) have been liquidated by the sheer physicality of networks; the natural gives way to the concrete, the symbolic gives way to the virtual, and all network systems are "anthropogenic." In the order of politics, whereas "biopolitics" as it has heretofore been understood operates on the level of the phenotype, life-information in the Unicity operates on the level of the genotype. If politics are possible in the Unicity, they could only take the form of an intensified *zoëpolitics*, and hence a global *ecopolitics*. The question facing any possible political order with respect to Unicity is not whether individual organisms continue to live or die; it is the process by which life itself may be synthesized within flows of information.

By describing Unicity as a "historical shift" in world order, then, one might be led to believe I am saying that a new political order has replaced an old one, just as a new spatial order displaced an old one. I am not saying this here. Although I do not discount Lefebvre's theory of "differential space" as a new progression from "abstract space," I cannot say that there has been progress from old to new, since what it "old" may very well remain contemporary to what is nominally "new" (Lefebvre, *Space* 352–400). The Unicity is not the "new world order," but merely the way in which all the various flows across informational networks may be measured quantitatively. This atlas entry is only an initial attempt to establish a cartography of flows through the Unicity *qualitatively*.

I have been reading one line of poetry for the better part of the last decade: "cidade/city/cité" (1963) by the Brazilian concrete poet Augusto de Campos (Fig. 1). This poem is both a map of the Unicity and a movement (flow) through the Unicity. At first glance the poem appears un-readable. It is a single line of letters that do not form any known lexeme, a composition of letters that convey no meaningful content. Upon closer inspection, however, we begin to notice certain amounts of order. Though not meaningful (yet), the letters are pronounceable, utterable. We begin to read, then, in fits and stops: "atrocaduca" to "ducapaca" to "pacausti" and so on. We then realize that the poem in fact consists of *partial words*—atro, cadu, capa, causti… vera, viva, uni, vora—and that these partial words have been ordered (for the most part) alphabetically. These partial words can therefore be "completed" by combining them with the poem's title, which is attached, integrated into the poem at the end of its one line. The title serves as a "key" by which we can begin to read "atro-cidade," "cadu-cidade," "capacidade," "causticidade"… "vera-cidade," "vivacidade," "unicidade," "voracidade." This string of lexemes can be instantly translated into three languages: Portuguese (just cited), English (atrocity, caducity, capacity…), and French (…veracité, vivacité, unicité, voracité). All of these terms (nominalized adjectives) may be used to describe a city, and in a sense the poem visually reproduces urban density in the way its letters mimic buildings pushed together in an urban core. But the "city" here is hardly a city at all, but just a *suffix*, an incomplete part of a word (-cidade, -city, -cité). In reality, this "city" is composed of language, of typography literally printed in the space of a poem. In reality, however, this "city" is also de-composed in language, since it generates a *virtual* list of words that may describe a city (but do not specify which city in particular they are describing). The string of lexemes generated by the poem, that is, does not exist in concrete space (the page) but only in the virtual space of reading.

In the first iteration of my reading of Augusto's poem ("Obverse Colonization"), I sought to show how the poem maps São Paulo, Brazil. Since the time of the Iberian conquests, Latin American cities have always been constructed with the idea of establishing order on the "barren" landscape of the New World. Initially the Latin American city was designed to be a harmonious space so that land could be "civilized" under the command of the Monarch and the Church. This civilizing mission was to be accomplished by a class of scribes—the "lettered city"[2]—who would maintain social, legal, and/or theological order through writing. Unlike the traditional Latin American city, however, São Paulo grew after 1870 as a *mod-*

ern city linked to international flows of goods (coffee), industrial production, and finance. Rather than the ordered, geometric grid of the colonial
city, São Paulo grew without any cohesive urban planning around the
disordered lines of factories, railroads, and *favelas*; the city emerged
around sites that both generated great wealth and concentrated unspeak-
able poverty and exploitation. Augusto's modernist poem therefore disrupts the world order initiated by the conquest of the Americas. Veering
sharply from traditional stanzaic formats, it is at once an *illiterate* poem
that cannot be read, and a *hyperliterate* poem that can be read in three
languages simultaneously. The one line of the poem marks a borderline
between illiteracy and hyperliteracy through which a city-space is generated, much in the way modern São Paulo emerged from the relation between "hyper-wealth" and "hyper-poverty." By operating in the primary
languages of the "developed First World" (English and French), the poem
would seem to be inserting "underdeveloped Third-World" Brazilian Portuguese into the league of developed nations. The poem would seem to
insist on bringing Brazil "up" to the First World. In fact, just the opposite
occurs: because information is instantly translatable between the three
languages, the poem allows the "transfection" of the hyperliterate/illiter-
ate relation (typical of "underdeveloped" nations) across the globe. The
poem is in fact about colonization—the "coloniality" of space, language,
law, and thought[3]—and yet its mode of colonization operates from the
"obverse" direction than we might expect historically.

Augusto's poem therefore marks an "internalized" border in the center of São Paulo through which the city has emerged as a global city. The
poem maps a borderline between hyperliteracy/illiteracy, development/
underdevelopment, wealth/poverty, but this map does not demarcate
the territory of one as separate from the territory of the other. The poem
does not demarcate a space-within from a space-without. Rather, the
poem works as an "internalized" border, drawn within the city of São
Paulo, to demonstrate how hyperliteracy/illiteracy, development/under-
development, wealth/poverty are all conjoined, co-dependent, united.
But once the border has been internalized, where do the city limits end?
Augusto's poem maps the point at which the city limits reach infinity. In
other words, São Paulo is "global" insofar as its city limit, being internal,

has no external bounds. The "city" mapped by the poem is no city at all, but may effectively spread across the entire planet.

The poem suggests that its form of order may be replicated and translated on a global scale. "Order" in "cidade/city/cité" is established by the alphabet of Latinate script. Yet there are instances in the poem when alphabetic order is disrupted. Indeed it may be the case that the poem is fundamentally *disordered* alphabetically. The most notable instance of disorder is the title itself: "cidade" (or "city" or "cité") does not follow alphabetically from "vora" (the last "stem" in the sequence of the poem). Of course, in the poem "-cidade" is utilized as a suffix, rather than as a lexeme meaning "city," in which case we might say that all that matters are the ordered prefixes (atro-, cadu-, etc.) comprising the majority of the verse. However, although titles usually stand distinct from their poems, in this case the title flows directly from the poem—so that "stems" ordered by the letter "v" lead directly into terms in the letter "c," suggesting a disruption in the alphabetical order of prefixes. The "cidade" also marks a physical disruption in the shape the poem, shifting the line from a horizontal axis to a vertical one.

Another instance of disorder occurs amongst the prefixes themselves: "velocity," "veracity," "vivacity," "unicity," "voracity." This particular segment of the lexical string raises questions regarding the truth (veracity) within flows at maximum speed (velocity). The truth is linked to two distinct descriptions of life: the positive energy of living, the life force (vivacity); and destructive needs, consumption of flesh, the violence of life (voracity). The truth speeds between these positive and negative nodes of life in that the poem files the four terms together under the index of the letter "v." However, this scripted (if not scriptural) index is disrupted by "unicity." The "unicity" jumps out of alphabetic order, even though the poem itself is a map of a unified urban space. Or rather, the truth of the matter is that the Unicity marks the border between the desire for life (vivacity) and the needs of life (voracity), and marks the transition from one kind of order to another, from linguistic order (lettered city) to the order of translation, information flow, the urban.

The *real* fact of the matter, however, is that there is very little alphabetic order in the poem at all. Recall that the alphabetic string of lexemes can only be created *virtually*. Translation of meaningful content can therefore only occur *virtually*. But this virtual, meaningful, and non-tactile reality can only be generated by dividing the one line of letters that actually exist on the page (or the screen or wherever) into discrete units: atro, cadu, capa, causti, dupli, elasti, and so forth. Yet nothing in the poem actually mandates that its single line of letters be divided in this way. We could just as easily divide it thus: at, roca, duc, apaca, u, stid, upliela, st, ifeli, etc. Seen this way, we must only understand that the majority of the poem has no alphabetical order in the slightest, and thus no meaningful content, and thus no possibility of being translated. The poem, which is both hyperliterate and illiterate simultaneously, is also simultaneously translatable and untranslatable. The poem establishes a syntactical chain from illiteracy to underdevelopment to poverty—just as is done by global agencies such as UNESCO, the World Bank, and myriad Non-Governmental Organizations (NGOs). But it does not create this syntax in terms of an exclusion from order and power. Rather, illiteracy and poverty are included in the order and language of power—as the *untranslatability* of order.

The Unicity is exactly what it says it is: a Uni-City or One City that covers the globe. We still assign individual names to "different" places, of course, but in fact the world is now a singular city, or more precisely a singular urban network.[4] Accordingly, world order is no longer constituted by "centers" and "peripheries," "First World vs. Third World," relations of "inside" vs. "outside," or similar binary relationalities. Globalization is a structural shift in world order, then, in the following way: at some historical threshold in the recent past, it is *as if* the relation between "interiority" and "exteriority" (which constituted the bourgeois-capitalist order of nation-states) collapsed or imploded into itself. This implosion produced an "internalized" border within the city (*any* city, *all* city), no longer demarcating a territory-within from a territory-without, but only a singular vanishing point at which the city limit reached infinity. The Unicity is therefore an "internalized border," but one that works to territorialize the entire planet as absolute *exteriority*. Although many have concluded that this exteriority of globalization represents a "smooth" or "homogenous" space of global capitalism, this is only partially correct. We live in and walk through the material, physical space of the planet, what we can call "concrete space." The "globe" of globalization, however, at first appears to us as immaterial, invisible, non-tactile; it is the movement of information across networks by which the world becomes "anthropogenic" or engineerable by human society. This "anthropogenic" globe we can call "virtual space." In fact, *there is no difference* between concrete and virtual space; if we can make a distinction between them, it is only to envision how virtual space saturates concrete space, and vice versa. The Unicity is the border where this saturation occurs, the seam at which concrete and virtual realities come into contact and merge.

The Unicity is therefore not a place in the usual way we think of "place-ment," but rather a border-zone from which spaces of translatability or untranslatability may be generated. But where does the generation of ur-ban space occur? At first glance "cidade/city/cité" resembles nothing so much as a genetic sequence as conventionally symbolized as combina-tions of "C-T-A-G" (the bases **C**ytosine, **T**hymine, **A**denine, **G**uanine):

T G C A G C C T C A A C C T C G T C A G G C T C A A G
C A A T C C T C C C A C C T C A G C C T C C A G A G T A
G C A G G G A C G A T A G G T G T G C A C C A C C A T
G C C C A G C T A A T T T T T G T A T T T T T T T T T C
T T T T T T T G A G A T G G A G T C T T G C T C T G T T
GC. (National Center for Biotechnology Information)

This is a fortuitous coincidence, but it is not meaningless. In reading Augusto's poem—the city—we have already entered into the process of *enzymatic reading.*

We can now think of cells and the molecules in them—by which I mean to say, *any living* cells including the ones in your body right now—as media for the transmission of information. In biochemistry, in fact, this is called "information metabolism," which can be defined as "the storage, retrieval, processing, and transmission of biological information" (Mat-thews, Holde, and Ahern 876). Information metabolism is the use of a nucleic acid (either DNA or RNA) as a template for the synthesis of pro-teins or other nucleic acids (another DNA or RNA molecule). As such, information metabolism has three distinct processes: DNA replication, DNA transcription, and RNA translation.

When DNA replicates, a set of enzymes (topoisomerases, helicase, and primase) "unwinds" and "stretches" the DNA molecule, which is normally coiled up in a double-helix. These enzymes effectively open a "fork" between DNA's two strands. Another set of enzymes (polymerases) then "runs through" and "reads" the genetic information sequenced on each strand; as the polymerases run through their reading they create a complementary strand for each, thus forming two "daughter" DNA molecules. DNA *replication* is thus the use of DNA as a template for the synthesis of duplicate DNA molecules. DNA *transcription*, by contrast, is the use of DNA as a template for the synthesis of RNA. In transcription, another kind of polymerase (RNA polymerase) "reads" the sequences of base pairs (C-T, A-G) coiled into the DNA molecule and "generates" a single-stranded RNA molecule. Initially this RNA has both "meaningful" bits of genetic code (called *exons*) that will ultimately be used to create proteins, but it also has "meaningless" bits of genetic code (called *introns*). These "meaningless" introns are spliced out of the RNA, so that transcription results in the production of what is called *messenger RNA* (or mRNA) that is only composed of "meaningful" exons. During RNA *translation*, finally, the mRNA serves as a template for the synthesis of proteins—the "stuff" of which all the cells in your body is composed. In RNA translation, mRNA is conjoined to a *transfer RNA* (or tRNA) by means of a rizome. In essence, the rizome uses tRNA as a kind of genetic dictionary so that information on mRNA can be transferred into a new medium—the amino acids that are chained together to form proteins.

My point in this digression on information metabolism is not to belabor the details of genetics, but only to show that biochemical metabolism has now been shown to involve processes through which information is replicated and transcribed into a useable form, and then translated into content (in the form of proteins, the "stuff" of which your body is actually made). Life as we know it has been transposed into information, and this information is replicatable, transcribable, and translatable. Through understanding and describing "natural" molecular-biological processes, molecular biology has effectively worked to "nest" genetic molecules in a virtual informational matrix. The map of this virtual matrix, in fact, is readily accessible online through the US National Institutes of Health now that the Human Genome Project has been completed. This does not mean that the life of your cells has been engineered by human hands, only that your human hands are formed by an informational process that is now *potentially engineerable by and for human society*. Just because science has infused biological systems with information, and then generates more information through experimentation, does not mean that science or scientific knowledge is always-already reductive or false. Rather, the living organism has come to be understood (and utilized) as part of an environmental system in which "natural" life and "human" knowledge recombine into one another. There is no distinction between artificial and natural here, because all "natural" systems (not just biological ones, but also environmental and climatological systems) are potentially "engineerable," thus rendering them open to social regulation.

In one sense, then, the human body is composed of cells. In another sense, each cell is a network of information, and information in one cell is networked to all others to form a body. The information in the cell, moreover, is in a constant state of decomposition and translation. In fact, when decomposition and translation reach a maximum they result in uncontrollable growth—cancer—that quickly becomes a social condition to be managed by other networks (health care systems, medical technology, pharmaceutical research, government, education, religion, family, and so forth).

It is fortuitous, therefore, that the title of "cidade/city/cité" operates *as if* it were an enzyme for the reading, replication, transcription, and translation of a sequence of letters. Fortuitous, but not mistaken. A reading of the poem allows us to "leap" from the urban network of the Latin American city to the urban network of globalization to the metabolic network of cells, as if all these networks pertained to a singular network environment. The "city" (Unicity) is nothing less than the environmental system of life generated by the saturation of the environment by information—information that flows across networks mutually embedded into each other. The border of this city is internalized: it is the border that opens between one strand of DNA and the other during replication.

The Unicity is a space of both composition and decomposition. Likewise, it is a space defined by relative (differential) flows of translatability and untranslatability. Across this space there are densities of informational flow, zones where data-streams are particularly dense. Although these densities are the same *quantitatively* (all are data, information), they may differ *qualitatively* (there are differential flows of data). Some network densities channel information that is highly translatable across the

Unicity; other network densities channel information that is highly un-translatable. Following from the DNA transcription of exons and introns, the space of the Unicity is de/composed of zones of dense "meaningful" content (translatable content) that I will call *exones*, and zones of dense "meaningless" content (untranslatable content) that I will call *introness*. Both exones and introness are necessary for the structural (emergent) sta-bility of the Unicity, although it is not yet clear why this is the case.

What is clear is that translatability in the exone tends to reach a maxi-mum when economic interests (i.e., greed) are most intense. This has be-come painfully clear in the recent financial crisis of 2008–09. From the standpoint of global economic order, it has become commonplace to see the world in terms of network "flows" (cf. Castells' "space of flows" to be discussed shortly). Capital has become informationalized—it is digital "content" that can be moved around the planet at almost the speed of light. With increasing force and dexterity since 1990, the informational-ization of capital has allowed capital to flood into any market that is "hot." Moreover, it has allowed the creation of incredibly complex derivatives designed to capitalize instantaneously on the movement of capital into "hot" markets, and to leave these markets just as instantaneously once they "cool." As Manuel Castells has written, derivatives "operate to re-combine value around the world and across time, thus generating market capitalization out of market capitalization" (104).

Unfortunately, as it has been made painfully evident recently, deriva-tives also generate market de-capitalization out of market de-capitaliza-tion. The prime example of this is the United States housing market since 2000. Because it could be moved at the push of a button (literally), capi-tal from across the planet flooded into the US real estate market faster than federal regulators of this market could manage—or rather, faster than they *cared* to manage, since the official policy of the US federal gov-ernment encouraged the flood. Capital, in other words, moved into the real estate market *virtually*. Capital then worked to transform *real* estate into *virtual* estate: mortgages were bundled into massive bonds (deriva-tives), so that real property was essentially capitalized into virtual quanti-ties (mortgages) that could then be used as collateral for further loans (bonds); in essence, banks issued loans, and then used these loans to borrow other loans, and then used these collateralized loans to take out even more loans. Banks then bought and sold these derived loans (in the form of bonds, collateralized debt obligations, etc.) from/to other banks, so that for every US$1 of *real* capital loaned out upwards of US$30 of capital was "created" virtually. Of course, when the value of *real* estate declined sharply and people defaulted on their mortgages *en masse*, the 30:1 ratio for profit turned into a 30:1 ratio for debt, and capital evaporated from the entire global market instantaneously.

Virtual gains instantly became virtual losses, and this proved to be a real problem. Since 1980 all financial activities worldwide have been networked. Thanks to the repeal of Depression-era safeguards against consolidation, financial institutions merged into one another. Behemoth financial institutions, housed in command-and-control centers (e.g. the skyscrapers of Lower Manhattan) could operate in consumer and commercial banking, securities markets, insurance, hedge funds, and any other financial activity of their creation. All of these activities were also digitized over the same time period, so that transactions could be "managed" automatically by complex algorithms over digital information networks. The informationalization of capital further allowed behemoth financial institutions to network themselves globally. In practice, all financial institutions across the globe loan each other capital to cover their daily operating expenses, facilitated by the grand instrument of digital networks. In theory, these loans should be guaranteed by other instruments like hedge funds and collateralized debt obligations. In the case of the current financial meltdown, however, financial institutions were also profiting (virtually) by issuing, buying, and selling these "guarantees." Thus, the more global capitalism "insured" itself virtually, the more capital virtually evaporated once the crisis began. And since financial institutions operated day-by-day by loaning capital to one another, the mass-scale disappearance of capital *virtually* threatened the viability of the entire market.

Global financial networks were designed in order to mitigate risk. Because capital has become informationalized, it may be withdrawn from one investment instantly and reallocated to another more profitable investment. Derivatives, moreover, were created as a hedge against risk, so that if one aspect of the market dropped profit could still be generated "on the back-end" from that drop. The current financial meltdown has demonstrated that the informationalization of capital has not yet eliminated the possibility of miscalculating risk, however. On one hand, powerful capitalists working from the exone may deliberately falsify data and then translate that falsified data throughout the system faster than can be regulated. On the other hand, and more importantly, the exone of financial networks is dependent upon introNes, and yet has no means of calculating the flow of information through introNes. In fact, "intronic" flow cannot be calculated because it is untranslatable. Thus, mortgages are issued to denizens of the introNe, even though terms of the agreement are not communicable between exone and introNe; financial and corporate exones draw upon the labor power of the introNe; "natural" resources and energy are drawn from the introNe. But the risk of dealing with introNes in this way cannot be prognosticated.

Financial flows can and must be regulated, however. That is, power in the Unicity exceeds the power of governments and international agencies, yet the Unicity still requires governments and international agencies for the regulation and maintenance of networks. For finance to flow, after all, monetary policies have to be set in place and ordered. Global corporate structures require some institution to ensure that contracts are enforced, that assets are fungible, and so forth. In this sense, the Unicity is a historical shift in world order, a step above the order of modernity, industrial modernization, and the modern nation-state. But the Unicity is *not* a progression from the old order, as if the power of the nation-state had been totally liquidated. Nothing could be further from the case; in fact, the power of the nation-state may be magnified in certain respects. History needs to be re-written in this way: The bourgeois-capitalist nation-state evidently succeeded the theological order of the Catholic church; but this never meant that the power of theological order waned, as evidenced by the incredible power exerted by religion over the world. The same will be true with the nation-state. Why? History and juridico-political paradigms are now just informational networks, to be networked into the "network of networks" that is the Unicity. The risks posed by the informationalization of history, theology, and capital cannot yet be properly calculated or prognosticated.

By linking exones and introNes, the Unicity marks the borderline between the desires of life, perceived as an immaterial life force (vivacity); and the bare necessities of life, hunger, the need to eat, the need to destroy one body so that another may live (voracity). The Unicity links desires and needs so closely that they become indistinguishable. But what are the legal and political consequences of this indistinguishability?

In thinking through an answer to this question, the worst mistake that could be made is to think of exones in terms of inclusivity, versus introns in terms of exclusivity. There are real modes of disaffection, disempowerment, and exploitation in the Unicity, but none of these has anything to do with binary relations of inclusion/exclusion. Since exones and introns are bound together as co-dependent relations of production, both are "included" in the space and flows of the Unicity.[5] By including all into a singular oneness, the Unicity functions only in terms of absolute exteriority. Everyone and everything is always already "outside."

This absolute exteriority alters how we must think of power and relations to power. Once everything is on the outside, there can be no such thing as *transcendence*, at least not as some metaphysical Being that inheres in physical matter. This should be welcome news to most practitioners of deconstruction: there is only physical matter in the Unicity. The unwelcome news for practitioners of deconstruction is this: there is only physical matter in the Unicity. Just as there is no transcendence in the Unicity, neither is there such a thing as *immanence*. Just data. The problem of course is that no institution of political power has ever been formed around streams of data. Politics have only been constituted through either transcendence (as in, heavenly order handed down through popes and kings based on the presupposition that we all have souls), or immanence (as in, all subjects are born with inherent powers that they can choose to represent rationally in the form of a republic or nation-state). Having no sense of transcendence or immanence, it is not clear how law can be enforced in the Unicity—or more precisely, by what force-of-law (*nomos*) legal powers could be deemed legitimate.

The Unicity is *anti-nomic space* in this regard, and this poses all sorts of problems for political and legal philosophy. Clearly, in terms of politics, law, and governmental organization, the Unicity represents a historical and structural shift in world order. Once the validity of both transcendent and immanent modes of subjectivity has been evacuated, it would seem that a new mode of subjective power (and/or subjugation) would be on the horizon. But this horizon will not arrive. Why? Most philosophers, theorists, and critics (operating in the exone, after all) assume a strict periodization in which the history of world order is the succession of juridico-political paradigms. Thus, Europe moves from the Roman Empire to the order of the Catholic Church; with the discovery of the Americas, the power of the Church wanes and gives way to the modern system of nation-states. The days of the nation-state are now thought to have come to an end…giving rise to what?

To my mind, Giorgio Agamben has come closest among contemporary political philosophers to providing an answer. Following from Carl Schmitt and Michel Foucault, Agamben seeks to theorize the "new" *nomos* of the planet (the force of law over the globe). Agamben knows that this *nomos* is biopolitical, directed to the incorporation of "bare life" (*zoë*) as political life (*bios*). As biopolitics—the orientation of politics towards the preservation and maintenance of life—emerges as a primary aim of the nation-state, national order paradoxically enters into crisis. In order to preserve the force of law and hence to preserve life in times of crisis, the nation-state finds it must suspend its own laws; the force of law (*nomos*) demands the force of law, the state of exception. "It is produced at the point at which the political system of the modern nation-state, which was founded on the functional nexus between a determinate localization (land) and a determinate order (the State) and mediated by automatic rules for the inscription of life (birth or the nation), enters into a lasting crisis, and the State decides to assume directly the care of the nation's biological life as one of its proper tasks" (*Homo Sacer* 175).

If I understand Agamben correctly in the totality of his work, the order of the nation-state enters into crisis because, although it is founded on the symbolic-metaphysical inscription of life into politics, the State can never properly translate the bare physicality of life into symbolic-metaphysical terms of citizenship. The state of exception is the limit between this "metaphysicality" and "physicality," the point at which the two would unite; the biopolitical imperative thus mandates entrance into the state of exception. Yet the state of exception only marks the transition of the biopolitical imperative into a "thanatopolitics," whereby sovereign power may execute bodies at will. In this respect, the Nazi concentration camp becomes the primary emblem of the crisis of national *nomos* and the supposed entrance into the new *nomos* of the planet:

The state of exception, which was essentially a temporary suspension of the juridico-political order, now becomes a new
and stable spatial arrangement inhabited by the bare life that
more and more can no longer be inscribed in that order. The
growing dissociation of birth (bare life) and the nation-state
is the new fact of politics in our day, and what we call *camp* is
this disjunction. To an order without localization (the state of
exception, in which law is suspended) there now corresponds
a localization without order (the camp as permanent space
of exception). The political system no longer orders forms of
life and juridical rules in a determinate space, but instead contains at its very center a *dislocating localization* that exceeds it
and into which every form of lie and every rule can be virtually taken. The camp as dislocating localization is the hidden
matrix of the politics in which we are still living, and it is this
structure of the camp that we must learn to recognize in all
its metamorphoses into the *zones d'attentes* of our airports and
certain outskirts of our cities. (*Homo Sacer* 175)

In order to preserve the life of its "People," the nation-state establishes
an external territory it inhabits with bodies stripped of citizenship, a zone
composed of bodies that may be voided without any possible legal rami-
fication, no protection against homicide or genocide. This new space, in
which life can no longer be inscribed into juridical order, transforms into
a space of permanent displacement that "virtually takes" the globe. Agamben concludes, "The camp, which is now securely lodged within the city's
interior, is the new biopolitical *nomos* of the planet" (*Homo Sacer* 176).

It is precisely on this point that Agamben's theories falter: in the Unicity, there is no such place as "the city's interior," only global exteriority.
Agamben certainly helps us to see how the historical shift to Unicity occurs. Nevertheless, he tends to equate historically produced spaces incor-
rectly. His temptation is to see in "Third World" zones like the *favela* or
the *maquiladora* slum a direct analogy to the Nazi concentration camp.
From the standpoint of network integration, the *favela* and *maquiladora*
slums—introne—are far more nuanced and complex than the concentration camp. This is not a comparison of relative degrees of pain and
violence, which would be utterly pointless and disgusting. Rather, I am

merely stating, first, that introries are not zones of exclusion, that they are
thoroughly inscribed into the world order of Unicity as the untranslatability of information. But the Unicity, second, is not a juridical-political
space in the way Agamben thinks of *nomos*. Agamben's main blind spot is
that in envisioning the absolute decline of one kind of sovereign *nomos*,
he assumes it to be replaced by a new *nomos*. But the Unicity is not that.

The global city has been understood as a "space of flows," in which
goods, services, and people are eminently translatable. As Manuel Castells defines the "space of flows":

> The informational, global economy is organized around com-
> mand and control centers able to coordinate, innovate, and
> manage the intertwined activities of the networks of firms.
> Advanced services, including finance, insurance, real estate,
> consulting, legal services, advertising, design, marketing,
> public relations, security, information gathering, and man-
> agement of information systems, but also R&D and scientific
> innovation, are at the core of all economic processes, be it in
> manufacturing, agriculture, energy, or services of different
> kinds. They all can be reduced to knowledge generation and
> information flows. Thus, advanced telecommunications sys-
> tems could make possible their scattered location around the
> globe. (409–10)

The networks Castells mentions can be located anywhere on the planet, facilitated not only by telecommunications networks, but also transportation (air, ground, sea) networks. Large corporations can therefore
distribute their various functions to any locale on the globe that offers
the most advantageous cost-benefit. The most notable effect of the space
of flows—notable in the sense that it has received the most critical attention—is the emergence of the global city. The global city is not only
a command-and-control node in the global network, but also a city in
which urban life (culture) resembles that of any other global city. Thus
we now have cities in far-flung locales, such as Los Angeles, New York,
Tokyo, London, São Paulo, Bangkok, which all seem to offer the same
urban existence—a translatable urban existence. This view of the global
city, however, is only partially correct, because the "global city" is in fact

partial—it is only a part of any of the places just mentioned. The evident homogeneity of urban life in global cities is of limited interest, however.

The historical transition from the "space of places" to the "space of flows" is far more significant than the emergence of global cities per se. That is, we have traditionally thought of city space as a *place* defined by a bounded center (or centers) of densely packed buildings, surrounded by houses and smaller buildings, surrounded by countryside. The space of places is one held within external city limits. We have traditionally defined "city," furthermore, according to a spatial model of centers and peripheries; this model has been extended to the world order of modern geopolitics, which was composed of "central" rich industrialized nations and "peripheral" poor dependent or agrarian nations. Yet the "center-periphery" model assumes a static kind of space, one that can be surrounded by a borderline because space is thought to be fundamentally motionless. In the space of flows all that matters is the movement "through." Data flows in, data is processed, data flows out. Capital flows in, capital is processed, capital flows out. Planes fly in, planes are processed, planes fly out. I turn on my computer (electricity flows in), I process words and send an email, I turn off my computer (electrical flow halts). Thus, it matters less that a static space can be defined as a "place" or an "area," and more how things and bodies transit through space. From this perspective it becomes clear that "city" is network of networks: not only corporate services networks, but also water, energy, food, culture, and so on, all of which transit through space, hopefully through ordered channels (but certainly not always).

The space of flows has been theorized with greatest precision by one of Augusto de Campos' contemporaries in São Paulo, the Jewish/Prussian/German/Czech/Brazilian philosopher Vilém Flusser. In "The City as Wave Trough in the Image Flood," Flusser seeks to re-image space:

> We are accustomed, for example, to see the solar system as a geographic place in which individual bodies orbit around a larger one. We see it as such because it has been shown to us in images, not because we have perceived it with our own eyes. However, today we also have other images at our disposal. Here is one that shows us the solar system as a network of wire netting, as a gravitational field, and in this netting there

are sacklike wells in which the wires are more tightly knotted together. In one of these wells we recognize our Earth once more because built into this sack there is a smaller body, namely, our moon. Both of these images of the solar system are models rather than maps. And certainly the second image is more useful for a trip to Mars than the first. In the second image one sees that one must first crawl up out of our well and then be careful not to fall into the sun's well in order to finally fall into the Mars well. The same is true of the image of the city. When we are talking about a "new urbanism," it is more useful to construct the image of the city as a field of flections. (323)

The first model of the solar system as "geographic place" corresponds to a "traditional" center-periphery model of urban space that Flusser seeks to surpass: "The typical image we construct of the city looks something like this: houses as economic private spaces that surround a marketplace, the political public sphere, and over their on a hill stands a temple, the theoretical sacred space" (323). In essence Flusser describes the idealized image of classical Athens as a public sphere of ideal relations between citizens (*polis*) engaging one another on a public marketplace (*agora*) before returning home to private space (*oikos*).

This classical urban order no longer exists. In the contemporary "space of flows" (Castells' term) of the Unicity (my term), this image of city as composed of discrete, bounded places cannot hold. The city, argues Flusser, becomes a "confusion of cables" in which public political and economic relations are literally piped into private living spaces and piped back out again. Instead of discrete spaces and places, then, there are only intersubjective flows of information. I will quote Flusser at length:

We must imagine a net of relations among human beings, an "intersubjective field of relations." The threads of this net should be seen as channels through which information like representations, feelings, intentions, or knowledge flows. The threads knot themselves together provisionally and develop into what we call human subjects. The totality of the threads constitutes the concrete lifeworld, and the knots therein are abstract extrapolations. One recognizes this when they un-knot themselves. They are hollow like onions. The Self (I) is an abstract, conceptual point around which concrete relations are wrapped. I am that to which you is said. An image of humanity of this type is obvious not only thanks to psychoanalysis and existential analysis but corresponds also to the concepts of other areas, for example, ecology (organisms are knottings together of ecosystems); molecular biology (phenotypes are knottings together of genetic information); or atomic physics (bodies are the knottings together of the four field strengths). If one holds fast to the image of an intersubjective field of relations—we is concrete, I and you are abstractions of this—then the new image of the city gains contours. It can be imagined roughly in this way: The relations among human beings are spun of differing densities on different places on the net. The denser they are, the more concrete they are. These dense places develop into wave-troughs in the field that we must imagine as oscillating back and forth. At these dense points, the knots move closer to one another; they actualize in opposition to one another. In wave-troughs of this type, the inherent possibilities of relationships among humans become more present. The wave-troughs exert an attraction on the surrounding field (including the gravitational field); ever more intersubjective relationships are drawn into them. Every wave is a flash point for the actualization of intersubjective virtualities. Such wave-troughs are called cities. (325–6)

Writing before the expansion of the Internet, it is remarkable how clearly Flusser theorizes social networking—allowing us to see what must have been wild abstract images in Flusser's day as normal parts of daily life. Now writing after the expansion of the internet, however, I must expand and modify several of his claims here. First, Flusser is correct to image the city as a density (a wave trough) of intersubjective informational flows. In such an image each subject (Self) is merely a density of information (a "knot") with respect to another knot (Other); each knot exerts a kind of force with respect to all others, such that if enough informational knots agglomerate together they form a "deep" density we call a "place." In this sense there is no such thing as subjective identity, at least in the sense of an immanent identity that inheres within an individual body. Rather, there are only relations between informational densities that may be abstracted as individual subjects. In other words, in the Unicity subjective identity is always displaced into the network(s) of informational flows, so that subjectivity per se is only experienced in the differential movement between one "density" and the next. However, the networks in the Unicity are not just human or subjective; human bodies become informational networks (information metabolism, for instance), but so do buildings, air, water, computers, plastic, book. Thus, we must view subjectivity in the Unicity in terms of *interobjective* fields of relations—how "subjective" information flows across object-networks.

Second, to this end Flusser views his "city" (the Unicity) as a kind of marketplace where "masks are lent out" (324). Since the "Self" is like a hollowed-out onion, subjects move through the city by projecting masks to one another. What Flusser calls a "mask," we could rightly now call a "username" or "avatar." In order to transit through networks, we are often called upon to prove our identities; we then produce a virtual image of our identity and guarantee this image with a unique signature or password. If the network cannot verify this virtual identity, then we are not allowed to pass through. Thus, I can check my email, voicemail, bank accounts, and use a credit card or passport anywhere in the world, so long as my avatars are verified.

This flow of masks is precisely what Marc Augé has theorized as the "non-place" (*non-lieu*). It used to be the case that one's identity was guaranteed by a sense of place: perhaps one's village assigned one's place in the community, in the world of men, and in the world of gods (absolute space); or, perhaps one's inherent sense of self united one to other selves (abstract space). In any event, one could always know one's Self just as others could recognize each other. According to Augé, however, we now routinely move through spaces (non-places) in which one's anonymity (rather than known identity) is constantly affirmed. Paradoxically, we are continually required to demonstrate our identities: we show our passports, swipe our credit cards, type in our passwords. Only by doing so, however, are we allowed to proceed on our way as *anonymous* subjects whose movement through space (a shopping mall, a road, an airport) does not have to be questioned. Augé, just like Flusser, theorizes a world in which we carry *multiple forms of identity*, each of which has been displaced into an objective network of informational flow. How else could we possibly explain identity theft? If our identities were locked inside our bodies (*placed* there), how could some other anonymous being steal our identities (now *displaced* to some network non-place) and operate as if they wore masks of our faces?

Flusser and Augé are incorrect, however, in that both find all "masks," "identities," and "non-places" to be of equal measure. *All* subjects wear masks that hide *all* identities so that *all* anonymous subjects may transit through *all* non-places. If we now turn back to Augusto de Campos's poem, we will recall that the "cidade/city/cité" is simultaneously translatable and untranslatable; the city is a singularity (a single line), but it flows through the differential movement of "hypertranslation" and "non-translation." The Unicity, then, is the unbounded informational/ urban terrain of the planet; but far from a "smooth" globe, the Unicity is pock-marked by densities, troughs, knots, black holes, across which information may flow quickly, slowly, or become suspended like fuzzy static charge (noise). Assuming the "leap" between genetics and urbanization as argued earlier to be possible, we should recall that in RNA transcription, "meaningless" content (*introns*) must be spliced out of mRNA leaving only "meaningful" content (*exons*) in order for RNA translation to proceed. Similarly, the terrain of the Unicity is marked by differential spaces of "content": exones and introns. Since the Unicity is both urban space and informational network, I would define "exones" more precisely as demographic concentrations with network densities of which information tends to be *immediately translatable* throughout the Unicity. By contrast, "introns" may perhaps be more demographically dense than exones, but they are *less dense informationally*, because information in the introne is not as readily translatable as meaningful content across the Unicity. Exones are informationally "rich" (global wealth); introns are informationally "poor" (global poverty).

One's ability to flow through an exone is maintained by protocols of subjective identification: one must have avatars (e.g., credit cards, passports, numbers) that can be verified by the network; otherwise one simply "does not make sense" to the world, and one "habits" an introne. By the same token, the introne may co-opt identities in the exone, whether deliberately or not, and thereby circulate with absolute anonymity. In any case, the borders between wealth and poverty, exones and introns, may be demarcations between *neighborhoods* within a single urban area; the lines of dependency between these zones are still in effect, of course, by which I mean that "global wealth" and "global poverty," exones and introns, are *co-dependent* relations through which global urban space is produced. The Unicity demarcates the entire world as a global border zone.

The border of this global border zone, however, does not demarcate one geographic (geopolitical) territory from a different territory. The border that is the Unicity cannot therefore *legitimate* that which belongs to one territory as opposed to that which belongs to an Other. Here there is no question of legitimacy or illegitimacy, because the Unicity is fundamentally *a-legitimate*; no legality or illegality, because the Unicity is fundamentally *extra-legal*; no civilization or barbarity, just users, denizens, avatars, and/or pirates. So what does the border that is the Unicity demarcate and territorialize? By stating that the globe is singular urban space of network traffic, we are stating that everything has become informationalized. Since "we" are only really information, *there is no difference* between a "Self" and an "Other." There are only relative densities or diffusions of network traffic (*you* are only a density of network traffic, and so am *I*).

The border therefore constitutes and distributes relative degrees of translatability—but how? This is the most difficult question raised by this present *Atlas* entry, one that I hope to have answered if only partially. As I see it, translatability must be guaranteed by certain protocols, or sets of protocols, so that a user/denizen might be able to enter and exit an exone with a particular identity (avatar) intact. These protocols are established—for no other reason than the fact that it so happens to be the case—by pre-existing social institutions. Thus, there is no force of law— no *nomos*—in the Unicity whereby such things as legality, sovereignty, citizenship, or subjectivity might be constituted as legitimate. There is no such thing as a "global citizen" because citizenship per se is precluded in the Unicity. There are no citizens, just denizens and avatars. Citizenship is a category determined by immanent subjective power, but identities are not produced immanently in the Unicity. Rather, bodies are merely phenotypes of genotypical information. As such, identities are merely verified, transcribed, and translated (or unverified, untranscribed, and untranslated) across informational networks. There can be no symbolic "People" for a State to govern—just data, streaming through bodies. And yet social institutions—States—are still required to monitor and maintain network traffic and protocols.

On the one hand, then, the Unicity is neither *nomos* nor *anomie*, but rather *anti-nomic space*. On the same hand, however, the Unicity is still a legal, political, and above all, *zoëpolitical* space, in that it requires—feeds off of—extant sphere(s) of *nomos*. The Unicity is a singular *physis* that evacuates the metaphysical foundation of *nomos*, by recombining itself into the physical residues of pre-existing *nomos*. If the *physis* of the Unicity retains a parasitical (and hence destructive) relationship with extant *nomos*, life in the Unicity nonetheless still depends upon just "so much" of laws, protocols, legitimations, contracts, enforcements, and/or subjectivities guaranteed by *nomos*. Having no *nomos* for itself, the Unicity nonetheless operates recursively, retroactively...the *retronomos of the globe*.

Buffalo, USA / Kolobrzeg, Poland

Notes

1. There is no room for some a priori or ultimate Cause or Reason in the Unicity, not even as a negative recess.

2. This is the general argument advanced by the Uruguayan critic Angel Rama, in one of the most important works of Latin American cultural theory, *La ciudad letrada*.

3. Cf. Aníbal Quijano. Quijano and his interlocutors see "coloniality" (not just colonialism) as the dominant epistemological paradigm of global power (capitalism) since the European conquest of the Americas. Any attempt to critique epistemology and power without recognizing a connection to coloniality is doomed only to reiterate the dominance of coloniality. Thus, interlocutors such as Walter Mignolo seek to operate from the "exteriority" of coloniality—the borderline, the margin—since speaking from a position of "interiority" would only be self-destructive and ineffectual. My theory of Unicity concurs with this world-view in certain respects, but diverges robustly in others. The reason it is ineffectual to speak from "interiority" is that there is no such thing as an interior. The Unicity only exists in absolute

exteriority—primarily because the historical roots of the Unicity are to be found in the lines of political-economic and techonological dependency between global wealth and global poverty. Global wealth and global poverty, in other words, are not different but rather produced simultaneously as co-dependent differential relations. In spatial terms, wealth and poverty occupy, respectively, the exones and introries that compose the Unicity (terms which will be defined later in this essay). Thus, Mignolo and Quijano do speak from the exteriority of the coloniality of power, but only to the extent that the Unicity represents the "obverse" re-colonization of the planet as absolute exteriority. They speak from the exteriority because exteriority is all there is. Their critical work will only prove moderately successful at best, because both operate from an exone, even though they purport to speak for the introne.

4. As a clarification, we may follow Lefebvre and think of the Unicity as "the urban" rather as "a city." Writing in 1970 Lefebvre states: "I'll begin with the following hypothesis: Society has become completely urbanized. This hypothesis implies a definition: An urban society is a society that results from a process of complete urbanization. This urbanization is virtual today, but will becomre real in the future" (Lefebvre, Urban Revolution 1). And later in the same work: "From this point on I will no longer refer to the city but to the urban" (45).

5. For this reason it is not possible to "include" those who habit the introne by giving them computers or credit cards or microcredit, since they were never "excluded" in the first place.

Works Cited

Agamben, Giorgio. *Homo Sacer: Sovereign Power and Bare Life*. Trans. Daniel Heller-Roazen. Stanford, CA: Stanford University Press, 1998.

---. *State of Exception*. Trans. Kevin Attell. Chicago: The University of Chicago Press, 2005.

Augé, Marc. *Non-Places: Introduction to an Anthropology of Supermodernity*. Trans. John Howe. London: Verso, 1995.

de Campos, Augusto. "cidade/city/cité." *Viva Vaia, Poesia 1949–1979*. São Paulo: Editora Brasiliense, 1963. 115.

Castells, Manuel. *The Rise of the Network Society*. Malden, MA: Blackwell Publishing, 2000.

Flusser, Vilém. "The City as Wave-Trough in the Image-Flood." Trans. Phil Gochenour. *Critical Inquiry* 31 (Winter 2005): 320–8.

Foucault, Michel. *Society Must Be Defended: Lectures at the Collège de France, 1975–1976.* Trans. David Macey. New York: Picador, 2003.

Hardt, Michael and Antonio Negri. *Empire.* Cambridge, MA: Harvard University Press, 2000.

Lefebvre, Henri. *The Production of Space.* Trans. Donald Nicholson-Smith. Malden, MA: Blackwell Publishing, 1991.

---. *The Urban Revolution.* Trans. Robert Bononno. Minneapolis: University of Minnesota Press, 2003.

Matthews, Christopher K., K. E. van Holde, and Kevin G. Ahern. *Biochemistry.* 3rd edition. San Francisco: Addison Wesley Longman, Inc., 2000.

Mignolo, Walter D. "The Geopolitics of Knowledge and the Colonial Difference." *The South Atlantic Quarterly* 101.1 (Winter 2002): 57–96.

National Center for Biotechnology Information (NCBI). "NCBI Reference Sequence: NG_005905.1 (Homo sapiens breast cancer 1, early onset (BRCA1) on chromosome 17)." Web. 1 July 2009. http://www.ncbi.nlm.nih.gov/nuccore/1 26015854?from=10479&to=91667&report=fasta

Quijano, Aníbal Quijano. "The Coloniality of Power, Eurocentrism, and Latin America." Trans. Michael Ennis. *Nepantla: Views from the South* 1.3 (2000): 533–80.

Rama, Angel. *The Lettered City.* Trans. John Charles Chasteen. Durham, NC: Duke University Press, 1996.

Read, Justin. "Obverse Colonization: São Paulo, Global Urbanization, and the Poetics of the Latin American City." *Journal of Latin American Cultural Studies.* 15.3 (December 2006): 281–300.

---. "Speculations on Unicity: Rearticulations of Urban Space and Theory during Global Crisis." *CR: The New Centennial Review* 9.2. In press.

Chapter 5

Scale

Derangements of Scale

TIMOTHY CLARK

> *When we observe the environment, we necessarily*
> *do so only on a limited range of scales; therefore our*
> *perception of events provides us with only a low-*
> *dimensional slice through a high-dimensional cake*
>
> – Simon A. Levin

Introduction: Scale Effects

You are lost in a small town, late for a vital appointment somewhere in its streets. You stop a friendly-looking stranger and ask the way. Generously, he offers to give you a small map which he happens to have in his briefcase. The whole town is there, he says. You thank him and walk on, opening the map to pinpoint a route. It turns out to be a map of the whole earth.

The wrong scale.

A scale (from the Latin *scala* for ladder, step or stairs) usually enables a calibrated and useful extrapolation between dimensions of space or time. Thus a "cartographic scale" describes the ratio of distance on a map to real distances on the earth's surface. To move from a large to small scale or vice versa implies a calculable shift of resolution on the same area or features, a smooth zooming out or in. With climate change, however, we have a map, its scale includes the whole earth but when it comes to relating the threat to daily questions of politics, ethics or specific interpretations of history, culture, literature, etc., the map is often almost mockingly useless. Policies and concepts relating to climate change invariably seem undermined or even derided by considerations of scale: a campaign for environmental reform in one country may be already effectively negated by the lack of such measures on the other side of the world. A long fought-for nature reserve, designed to protect a rare ecosystem, becomes, zooming out, a different place. Even the climatology works on a less than helpful scale: "Paradoxically, it is simpler to predict what will happen to the planet, a closed system, than to make forecasts for specific regions" (Litfin 137).

Cartographic scale is itself an inadequate concept here. Non-cartographic concepts of scale are not a smooth zooming in and out but involve jumps and discontinuities with sometimes incalculable "*scale effects.*" For instance:

> In the engineering sciences, scale effects are those that result from size differences between a model and the real system. Even though a miniature model of a building made of wood is structurally sound, it is not necessarily appropriate to infer that the same process maintaining structural stability could hold for a full-size building made of wood. (Jenerette and Wu 104)

To give another instance, a map of the whole earth, at a "small" scale in cartographic terms, is at an enormous scale ecologically, one at which other non-linear scale effects become decisive and sometimes incalculable. Garrett Hardin writes:

> Many stupid actions taken by society could be avoided if more people were acutely aware of scale effects. Whenever the scale is shifted upward, one should always be alert for possible contradictions of the conventional wisdom that served so well when the unit was smaller.... Failure of the electorate to appreciate scale effects can put the survival of a democratic nation in jeopardy. (52)

Some thinkers less controversial than Hardin draw on complexity theory to suggest the necessary emergence of scale effects with merely the increasing complexity of globalizing civilization: "once a society develops beyond a certain level of complexity it becomes increasingly fragile.

Eventually it reaches a point at which even a relatively minor disturbance can bring everything crashing down" (MacKenzie 33). For others, the environmental crisis is in part caused by the effects of conflicting scales in the government of human affairs. Jim Dator writes:

> Environmental, economic, technological and health factors are global, but our governance systems are still based on the nation state, while our economic system ('free market' capitalism) and many national political systems (interest group 'democracy') remain profoundly individualistic in input, albeit tragically collective in output (215–6).

Scale effects in relation to climate change are confusing because they take the easy, daily equations of moral and political accounting and drop into them both a zero and an infinity: the greater the number of people engaged in modern forms of consumption then the less the relative influence or responsibility of each but the worse the cumulative impact of their insignificance. As a result of scale effects what is self-evident or rational at one scale may well be destructive or unjust at another. Hence, progressive social and economic policies designed to disseminate Western levels of prosperity may even resemble, on another scale, an insane plan to destroy the biosphere. Yet, for any individual household, motorist, etc., a scale effect in their actions is invisible. It is not present in any phenomenon in itself (no eidetic reduction will flush it out), but only in the contingency of how many other such phenomena there are, have been and will be, at even vast distances in space or time. Human agency becomes, as it were, displaced from within by its own act, a kind of demonic iterability.

The argument of this paper is that dominant modes of literary and cultural criticism are blind to scale effects in ways that now need to be addressed.

Derangements of Scale

One symptom of a now widespread crisis of scale is a derangement of linguistic and intellectual proportion in the way people often talk about the environment, a breakdown of "decorum" in the strict sense. Thus a sen-

tence about the possible collapse of civilization can end, no less solemn-
ly, with the injunction never to fill the kettle more than necessary when
making tea. A poster in many workplaces depicts the whole earth as giant
thermostat dial, with the absurd but intelligible caption "You control climate change." A motorist buying a slightly less destructive make of car is
now "saving the planet."

These deranged jumps in scale and fantasies of agency may recall rhetoric associated with the atomic bomb in the 1950s and after. Maurice
Blanchot argued then that talk of humanity having power over the whole
earth, or being able to "destroy itself," was deeply misleading. "Humanity" is not some grand mega-subject or unitary agent in the sense this
trope implies. In practice such destruction would certainly not be some
sort of consciously performed act of self-harm, "humanity destroying itself." It would be as arbitrary as was "the turtle that fell from the sky" and
crushed the head of Aeschylus (Blanchot 106).

The almost nonsensical rhetoric of environmental slogans makes
Blanchot's point even more forcefully. Received concepts of agency, rationality and responsibility are being strained or even begin to fall apart
in a bewildering generalizing of the political that can make even filling a
kettle as public an act as voting. The very notion of a "carbon footprint"
alters the distinctions of public and private built into the foundations of
the modern liberal state. Normally, demands in a political context to face
the future take the form of some rousing call to regained authenticity,
whether personal, cultural or national, and they reinforce given norms of
morality or responsibility, with an enhanced sense of determination and
purpose. With climate change this is not the case. Here a barely calculable nonhuman agency brings about a general but unfocused sense of
delegitimation and uncertainty, a confusion of previously clear arenas of
action or concepts of equity; boundaries between the scientific and the
political become newly uncertain, the distinction between the state and
civil society less clear, and once normal procedures and modes of understanding begin to resemble dubious modes of political, ethical and intellectual containment. Even a great deal of environmental criticism, modeling itself on kinds of progressive oppositional politics and trying (like
Murray Bookchin's "social ecology") to explain environmental degradation by reference solely to human-to-human hierarchies and oppressions

can look like an evasion of the need to accord to the nonhuman a disconcerting agency of its own.

The environmental crisis also questions given boundaries between intellectual disciplines. The daily news confirms repeatedly the impossibility of reducing many environmental issues to any *one* coherent problem, dysfunction, or injustice. Overpopulation and atmospheric pollution, for instance, form social, moral, political, medical, technical, ethical and "animal rights" issues, all at once. If that tired term "the environment" has often seemed too vague—for it means, ultimately, "everything"—yet the difficulty of conceptualizing a politics of climate change may be precisely that of having to think "everything at once". The overall force is of an implosion of scales, implicating seemingly trivial or small actions with enormous stakes while intellectual boundaries and lines of demarcation fold in upon each other. The inundation of received intellectual boundaries and the horror of many probable future scenarios has the deranging effect, for instance, of making deeply unsure which of the following two statements is finally the more responsible—(1) "climate change is now acknowledged as a legitimate and serious concern and the government will continue to support measures to improve the fuel efficiency of motor vehicles" or (2) "the only defensible relationship to have with a car is with a well aimed brick"?[1]

Contra "Liberal Criticism"

How then can a literary or cultural critic engage with the sudden sense that most given thought about literature and culture has been taking place on the wrong scale?

The most controversial political effect of climate change may be its challenge to basic dominant assumptions about the nature and seeming self-evident value of "democracy" as the most enlightened way to conduct human affairs. David Shearman and Joseph Wayne Smith write: "colossal environmental problems, both existing and impending, have been accelerated by the freedoms and corruption of democracy and are unlikely to be solved by this system of governance" (15). The decisive target here is "liberal democracy" and the now dominant liberal tradition in political thought, i.e. the tradition that combines institutions of private property, market-based economics, individualistic-rights-based notions of personhood and the conception of the state as "existing to secure the freedom of individuals on a formally egalitarian basis" (Brown, *Edgework* 39). The liberal political tradition looking back to Thomas Hobbes and John Locke sees politics as essentially a matter of compacts between individuals for the unmolested use of individual property and exploitation of natural resources. Such concepts of right seem at first merely neutral: the rights that apply to a hundred people, or to a hundred million, could surely also apply to billions? Some questions about scale, however, emerge when it is remembered that the founding conceptions of the liberal tradition emerged in the seventeenth and eighteenth centuries "in low-population-density and low-technology societies, with seemingly unlimited access to land and other resources," in a world, that is, that has now been consumed (Jamieson 148). On top of this, "[Locke] takes for granted that there will be enough, that the goodness of things provides enough so that taking by one or a group does not deprive others" (Ross 57). Structurally committed to a process of continuous economic growth, modern Western society effectively projected as its material condition an ever-expandable frontier of new land or resources. This impossible demand or assumption, long disguised by the free gift of fossil fuels, has now become visible and problematic. What Hans Jonas writes of "all traditional ethics" applies here: it "reckoned only with noncumulative behaviour" (7).

Liberal notions of extending the status of the rights-bearing individual to more and more people are caught up in a complex and bewildering economy of violence. Climate change disrupts the scale at which one must think, skews categories of internal and external and resists inherited closed economies of accounting or explanation in a way even Jacques Derrida seems not to have suspected. Referring to Derrida's well-known account in *Specters of Marx* (1993) of the "10 plagues" (81–3) held to be threatening the world, Tom Cohen notes the puzzling absence of any reference to environmental crisis, arguably the most deadly of all:

> [Derrida's] manoeuvre looks weak today, all ten being fairly standard and all human-to-human political miseries—from worklessness to weak international law. Today, as we "know," the entire gameboard has been invisibly haunted by its own

drive to auto-erase, or auto-eviscerate its non-anthropic premises. (qtd. in Wood 287)

True, Derrida writes of incalculable responsibility and the conceptual and physical destabilization of borders, of national frontiers and the "at home." His *On Hospitality* (2000) argues how the supposedly inviolable interiority of the home is already de-constituted, turned inside-out, by its multiple embeddings in public space, the state, the telephone line, monitored emails, etc., yet there is residual idealism in Derrida's exclusive attention to systems of law and communication (61). The focus on the moment of decision in individual consciousness and its pathos (its ordeal of undecidablity, etc.) seems narrow and inadequate in a context in which things have now become overwhelmingly more political than people. Nothing in his work seems to allow for a situation in which it is not irrational to connect a patio heater in London immediately with the slow inundation of Tuvalu in the Pacific. Thus *On Hospitality* mentions TV, email and internet but not the central heating system, cooking appliances, washing machine or car (or, for that matter, the institution of private property itself, despite its crucial connection to Derrida's topic of personal sovereignty). In effect, "All reality is politics, but not all politics is human" (Harman 89).

Wendy Brown argues that Derrida's "treatment of freedom reveals the hold of liberalism on his formulations of democracy," ("Sovereign Hesitations" 127) that his arguments still work within an essentially liberal conception of politics as devising systems to enable the space of individuals' seeming freedom to live as they choose, the challenge being to extend such politics beyond current borders and even beyond an exclusively human reference.[2] Reconfiguring a notion of the subject as openness to the other etc. instead of an autonomous self-presence, and attention to aporias of freedom/equality and conditional and unconditional hospitality, do not alter the basic terms of Derrida's commitment to a liberal progressivist tradition whose assumptions of scale are here at issue. In support of Brown's point one can argue that a seeming blindness to nonhuman agency and to scale effects tends to preserve the political in *On Hospitality* as a factitiously separate sphere. Yet environmental issues enact a bewildering generalization of the political that makes Derrida's focus on human norms, institutions, and decisions look like a kind of containment.

His conception of the moment of decision as a negotiation with the undecidable is simultaneously both trivialized and magnified by scale effects in relation to such minutiae as turning a light on or deciding to buy a freezer. The later Derrida's frontier questions of conditional or unconditional hospitality can seem foreclosed in scale, two-dimensional, for they ignore that ubiquitous border already contiguous with all other countries at the same time, a shared atmosphere. To live the hourly trivia of an affluent lifestyle in France is *already* to lurk as a destructive interloper in the living space of a farmer on the massive floodplains of Bangladesh.

A nonhuman politics also raises questions about the dominant, liberal/progressive cultural politics of much mainstream professional literary criticism. The frequent method now is to read all issues as forms of cultural politics within an understanding of the text analogous to way the liberal tradition sees civic society generally, viz. as an arena for the contestation of individual or collective interests, rights or identity claims. For example, Group A is seen to achieve its self-celebratory image through its (implicit) denigration of Group B, while Group C is seen as itself "marginalized" by the way Group B always seems to identify it with Group A, instead of being a distinct set with its own claims...and so on.[3] Yet each, at the same time, is staking its own rights to air, water, space and material resources and to focus solely on the rights of the individual person or group elides the issue of the violence continually and problematically being waged against the earth itself, whose own agency is both taken for granted and disregarded. It is as if critics were still writing on a flat and passive earth of indefinite extension, not a round, active one whose furthest distance comes from behind to tap you uncomfortably on the shoulder. Modes of thinking and practice that may once have seemed justified, internally coherent, self-evident or progressive now need to be reassessed in terms of hidden exclusions, disguised costs, or as offering a merely imaginary or temporary closure. How this will work out in practice, however, is harder to predict—at least beyond the trivially obvious ("Well, I always thought Kerouac's *On the Road* was an irresponsible book, but now this!").

Perhaps then the most trenchant environmental and postcolonial criticism in relation to climate change would be one which took up the more meta-critical role of examining assumptions of scale in the individualist rhetoric of liberalism that still pervades a large body of given cultural and literary criticism. An ethic attending such work would also breach current notions of decorum, redrawing the seeming boundaries of privacy whereby, say, a critic's professed views on history, religion, colonialism or ethics are all seen to belong in the realm of "public" controversy, seminars, papers and conferences while the resources sequestered to that person's sole use remain a supposedly "private" matter, with a high salary and its attendant life-style still regarded, if at all, as a matter of prestige.

Reading Raymond Carver's "Elephant" on a scale of six centuries

In what ways are inherited and currently dominant modes of reading in literary and cultural criticism blind to questions of scale? The issue can be tested through a practical reading experiment. How would it be to read and reread the same text through a series of increasingly broad spatial and temporal scales, one after the other, paying particular attention to the strain this puts on given critical assumptions and currently dominant modes of reading?

Let us turn here to a specific literary example, Raymond Carver's late short story, "Elephant" (1988). This text is a comic monologue consisting of the complaints and then gradual acceptance of a male blue-collar worker who is continually being pestered for money by hard-pressed relatives in other parts of the country. Most of "Elephant" happens between domestic interiors linked by telephone. The narrator's recently unemployed brother, a thousand miles away in California, requiring immediate help to pay the mortgage on his house, seems later to be able to forgo more borrowing because his wife might sell some land in her family but finally comes asking for money once more. He has already had to sell their second car and pawn the TV. The narrator's daughter has two children and is married to:

> A swine who won't even *look* for work, a guy who couldn't hold a job if they handed him one. The time or two he did find something, he overslept, or his car broke down on the way to work, or he'd just be let go, no explanation and that was that. (77)

The narrator's aged mother, "poor and greedy," (74) relies on the support of both her sons to maintain her independent lifestyle amid signs of failing health. The narrator's son demands money to enable him to emigrate and a divorced wife has to be paid alimony. Struggling with his resentment as he writes all the cheques, the narrator reaches a turning point with two dreams, one of them being about how his father used to carry him on his shoulder when he was a child, and he would feel safe, stretch out his arms and fantasize that he was riding an elephant. The next morning, giving a kind of private blessing to all his relatives despite their demands, he decides to walk rather than drive to work, leaving his house unlocked. Walking along the road, he is stretching out his arms as in his dream of childhood when a workmate called George stops to pick him up. George has a cigar and has just borrowed money to improve his car. Together they test it for speed:

> "Go," I said. "What are you waiting for, George." And that's when we really flew. Wind howled outside the windows. He had it floored, and we were going flat out. We streaked down that road in his big unpaid-for car. (90)

With the new questions posed by climate change in mind, what kinds of readings emerge of such a text?

Firstly, perhaps, that if "Capitalism must be regarded as an economy of unpaid costs," (K. William Kapp, qtd. in Foster 37) then "Elephant" could easily read as a kind of environmental allegory, as a narrative of a chain of unpaid debt and unearned support extending itself into the final image of the large unpaid for car. This relatively obvious first reading, however, can be deepened by considerations of scale.

Any broadly mimetic interpretation of a text, mapping it onto different if hopefully illuminating terms, always assumes a physical and temporal scale of some sort. It is a precondition of any such mapping, though almost never explicit in the interpretation. The scale in which one reads a text drastically alters the kinds of significance attached to elements of it, but, as we will see, it cannot itself give criteria for judgment.

Three scales can be used. Firstly, we could read the text on a (critically naïve) personal scale that takes into account only the narrator's immediate circle of family and acquaintances over a time scale of several years.

At this scale there is a certain humanist coziness about the text, as if the Carver story were already a commercial screenplay. Family loyalty wins out against misfortune; love and forgiveness prevail in a tale of minor but genuine domestic heroism. The reading could refer to Carver's defense of the short story as throwing "some light on what it is that makes and keeps us, often against great odds, recognizably human" (Nesset 104). In this respect "Elephant" would even come close to being a kind of Carver schmaltz.

A second scale is that almost always assumed in literary criticism. Spatially, it is that of a national culture and its inhabitants, with a time frame of perhaps a few decades, a "historical period" of some kind. Almost all criticism of Carver is situated at this scale, placing his work in the cultural context of the late twentieth century United States (or sometimes, on a broader scale, that of the modern short story after Edgar Allan Poe). Kirk Nesset, writing in 1995, is representative: "Carver's figures dramatize and indirectly comment upon the problems besetting American culture, particularly lower middle-class culture, today" (7). Other topics prominent in discussions of Carver are broadly located at this scale, such as unemployment and consumer culture as they affect personal relationships, the ideals and realities of American domesticity, that society's materialism, and its concepts of gender, especially masculinity. This scale enables an interpretation of the final scene of "Elephant" as an affirmative but temporary moment of escape from the denigrations and frustrations of American consumer capitalism, focused on the private car as an image of individual freedom and mobility.

The third, hypothetical scale is, of course, the difficult one. It could be, spatially, that of the whole earth and its inhabitants, and placing "Elephant" in the middle of a, let us say, six hundred year time frame i.e. from three hundred years before 1988 to 2288, three hundred after, and bearing in mind authoritative plausible scenarios for the habitability of the planet at that time.

What does this do? An initial impulse is that trying to read "Elephant" at this scale simply does not "make sense." It seems deliberately to repeat the kind of derangement of scale familiar in environmental slogans ("eat less meat and save the planet"). At the same time, the feeling of paralysis or arbitrariness in the experiment cannot override the conviction that to read at scales that used, familiarly, to "make sense" may now also be a form of intellectual and ethical containment.

What, then, is being held off? Viewed on very long time scales, human history and culture can take on unfamiliar shapes, as work in environmental history repeatedly demonstrates, altering conceptions of what makes something "important" and what does not.[4] Nonhuman entities take on a decisive agency. Thus some would argue that, globally, the two major events of the past three centuries have been the industrial exploitation of fossil fuels and a worldwide supplanting of local biota in favor of an imported portmanteau of profitable species: cattle, wheat, sheep, maize, sugar, coffee, eucalyptus, palm oil, etc. Thus it is that most of the world's wheat, a crop originally from the middle east, now comes from other areas—Canada, the United States, Argentina, Australia—just as people of originally European descent now dominate a large proportion of the earth's surface. This huge shift in human populations, including slaves as well as domesticated animals and plants, has largely determined the modern world, with its close connections between destructive monocultures in food production, exploitative systems of international trade and exchange and the institution of the modern state. At its bleakest, an ecological overview of the current state of the planet shows a huge bubble of population and consumption in one species intensifying exponentially and expanding at a rate that cannot be supported by the planet's resources for long. It is the transitory world of this bizarre, destructive and temporary energy imbalance that Western populations currently inhabit and take for a stable and familiar reality.

One element of containment in lower scale readings of "Elephant," blind to this bigger reality, is the "methodological nationalism" of readings located at the middle scale. "Methodological nationalism" is a term taken from A.D. Smith and used by Ulrich Beck: "While reality is becoming [or always was?] thoroughly cosmopolitan, our habits of thought and consciousness, like the well-worn paths of academic teaching and research, disguise the growing unreality of the world of nation-states" (21). That is, we often still think, interpret and judge as if the territorial bounds of the nation state acted as a self-evident principle of overall coherence and intelligibility within which a history and culture can be understood—ignoring anything that does not fit such a narrative. After all, literary criticism itself evolved primarily as an institution of cultural self-definition at this scale. Almost all literary criticism of Carver could be instanced here. Even so seemingly innocent a phrase as Carver's "the dark side of Reagan's America" (qtd. in Nesset 4) may instantiate methodological nationalism in proportion to the degree in which the national sphere and its cultural agenda serve exclusively to enframe, contain, and shape an analysis or the familiar—but contained—judgments of social "inclusion" and "exclusion."

The expanded scale makes familiar critical assumptions about the adequacy of a national context look parochial, self-interested and damaging. What happens if one deploys at the third global scale the methodology of mainstream cultural criticism, with its broadly liberal, progressive agenda and questions of equity, those topoi of "inclusion" and "exclusion"? The rhetoric of marginalization and impoverishment common in readings of Carver becomes at the very least complicated by the fact, on a global scale, that while their distress is undeniable none of the characters in "Elephant" is actually poor in a material sense. The narrator has a house to himself and also a car. The supposedly impoverished brother had two cars and was forced to sell one of them to help keep his house. The supposedly poverty stricken daughter, with her husband and children, lives in a trailer but has at least one car. The brother's wife is a landowner and the son requires money to do something most living people will never do, travel in an airplane to another country. The mother does not live with any of her children but is maintained in a household of her own. It is not the number of people but the number of separate households demanding support that is the real economic issue in "Elephant," keeping the property each represents. The culture of independence affirmed in the narrator's indignant work-ethic also effectively serves economic and infrastructure systems that set up a continuous dependency on high levels of consumption and, as a result, produces a pervasive and intensifying sense of entrapment. "If nothing succeeds like success, nothing also entraps like success" (Jonas 9).

Derrida argued how the supposedly self-contained "inner" realm of the at home, the house, the personal household, is constitutively breached by its embeddedness in public space, yet his very set up repeated liberal conceptions of politics, even if it complicated them. At the third scale, however, everything and everyone is always "outside": a person registers there less in terms of familiar social coordinates (race, class, gender and so on) than as a physical entity, representing so much consumption of resources and expenditure of waste (not the personality, but the "footprint"). Like a great deal of twentieth century literature (including, say, *On the Road*), the effect of embedding "Elephant" within the third scale is to turn the text into a peculiar kind of gothic, a doppelganger narrative. Characters as "persons" and responsible agents are now doubled by themselves as mere physical entities. The larger the scale the more thing-like becomes the significance of the person registered on it (even as scale effects have given human beings the status of a geological force). Plots, characters, setting and trivia that seemed normal and harmless on the personal or national scale reappear as destructive doubles of themselves on the third scale, part of a disturbing and encroaching parallel universe, whose malign reality it is becoming impossible to deny. It becomes impossible to sustain the fiction that significant historical agency is the preserve of human beings alone. The material infrastructure that surrounds and largely dictates the lives of the people, the houses, the cars, the roads, may partially displace more familiar issues of identity and cultural representation as a focus of significance. Technology and infrastructures emerge not only as inherently political but as unpredictably doubly politicized in scale effects that deride the intentions of their users or builders. "Elephant" could be described in terms of what William Ophuls calls "energy slavery,"[5] the oppressive, all-pervading, and destructive effects of being born into a fossil fuel based infrastructure as aggressive as an occupying army. A futural reading of "Elephant" would thus be more object-centered, aware of the capricious nature of nonhuman agency and suspicious of the way contemporary criticism, even ecocriticism, tends to interiorize all environmental issues as ultimately questions of subjective attitudes or belief, of humanity acting reflexively upon itself (even "humanity destroying itself"). For instance, there is nothing really "private" about a car, just as, ironically, the average person's decisions to fill or not fill a kettle will almost certainly be of more real consequence, however minuscule, than their political opinions ever will.[6] Along with the households demanding to be sustained, the politics of energy slavery reappear even in such seeming daily trivia as how the daughter's partner allegedly loses the chance of a job because his car broke down, or the way the narrator's brother prom-ises," I've got this job lined up. It's definite. I'll have to drive fifty miles round trip every day, but that's no problem—hell, no. I'd drive a hundred and fifty if I had too" (83). Cars also proliferate themselves through the parasitism of ideologies of individual "freedom"—"Elephant" ends with the narrator in the passenger seat, on a high of speed urging on George, complete with cigar, to drive as fast as he possibly can.

To highlight nonhuman agency adds a missing dimension to such fa-miliar critical topoi, in reading Carver, as the erosion of communal val-ues, or to the social/cultural force of Carver's so-called minimalism in short story technique, its projection of a late-capitalist society of disjunc-tive surfaces and personal isolation in which the lack of a completely reli-able sense of relation between cause and effect, intention and result, ef-fort and reward, is accompanied by a pervading sense of insecurity. The futural reading further decenters human agency, underlining the fragility and contingency of effective boundaries between public and private, ob-jects and persons, the "innocent" and "guilty," human history and natural history, the traumatic and the banal, and (with technology) the conve-nient and the disenfranchising. In sum, at the third scale, a kind of non-anthropic irony deranges the short story as any easily assimilable object of any given kind of moral/political reading.

Simon Levin writes "That there is no single correct scale or level at which to describe a system does not mean that all scales serve equally well or that there are not scaling laws" (1953). However, there are cru-cial differences between reading a literary text at multiple scales and the function of scales in scientific modeling and explanation. In such model-ing, suppression of detail is seen as strength of work at large scales, where broad patterns can emerge overriding individual variations. A literary reading clearly works in no such way. Assumptions of scale are always at work in any reading, but these may enable different judgments of value, not decide them. The three scales produce readings of "Elephant" that conflict with each other, yet can the third scale act as some final frame of reference or court of last appeal deciding for us how to read the text? An ecological overview is in danger of feeding a reductive but increasingly familiar green moralism, keen to turn ecological facts into moral impera-tives on how to live, blind to the sense of helplessness dominant in "Elephant" at the first scale. While it highlights the hidden costs of lower scale thinking, the third scale's tendency to register a person primarily as a physical thing is evidently problematic, almost too brutally removed from the daily interpersonal ethics, hopes and struggles that it ironizes. For instance, although this essay chose the less controversial example of cars, the most environmentally significant aspect of the situation projected by the text would be the reproduction of people themselves. The fact that the narrator has fathered two children would be more crucial—in the brutal terms of physical emissions—than either his lifestyle or property. This highlights an issue, overpopulation, which reduces even Donna Haraway to contradiction—or, more strictly, to thinking on conflicting scales at the same time—when she says in an interview "as a biologist," "in the face of a planet that's got well over 6 billion people now":

> the carrying capacity of the planet probably isn't that. And I don't care how many times you talk about the regressive nature of anti-natalist ideologies and population control ideologies. All true, but without serious population reduction we aren't going to make it as a species, and neither are thousands or millions of other species….So you can hate the Chinese for the one-child policy and also think they are right (*laughs*). (qtd. in Schneider 153)

In sum, reading at several scales at once cannot be just the abolition of one scale in the greater claim of another but a way of enriching, singularizing and yet also creatively deranging the text through embedding it in multiple and even contradictory frames at the same time (so that even the most enlightened seeming progressive social argument may have one in agreement on one scale and reaching for a conceptual brick on another). The overall interpretation of "Elephant" offered here can only be a multiple, self-conflictual one. The acts of the narrator remain ones of great personal generosity even if, at the same time, scale effects ironically implicate them in incalculable evil. The text emerges, simultaneously, depending on the scale at issue, as (1) a wry anecdote of personal heroism, (2) a protest against social exclusion, and (3) a confrontation with the entrapment of human actions and decisions within a disastrous impersonal dynamic they do not comprehend, as well as the various containments of inherited modes of thinking.

A further conclusion seems clear. Thinking of climate change in relation to literary or cultural criticism will not be a matter of inventing some new method of reading per se, for its most prominent effect is of a derangement of scales that is also an implosion of intellectual competences. It is far easier for critics to stay inside the professionally familiar circle of cultural representations, ideas, ideals and prejudices, than to engage with long-term relations of physical cause and effect, or the environmental costs of an infrastructure, questions that involve nonhuman agency and which engage modes of expertise that may lie outside the humanities as currently constituted. This would also suggest that the humanities as currently constituted make up forms of ideological containment that now need to change.

Notes

1. This does not exclude that deceptive fix, the electric car. Most of the polluting emissions associated with any car come from the process of its manufacture. The electricity that powers a supposedly eco-friendly car would need to have been generated somewhere.

2. Brown contrasts the alternative notion of democracy as the difficult challenge of genuinely sharing power to the liberal conception of delegated power as supposedly forming the outward-facing barrier behind which individual "freedom" is lived out. Vincent B. Leitch, querying the absence of any communitarian element in Derrida's political thinking, finds "a long rightward-leaning libertarian shadow [cast] over Derrida's left-wing democratic politics" (242).

3. I go into more detail on this in the chapter "Freedoms and the Institutional Americanism of Literary Study," in my *The Poetics of Singularity: The Counter-Culturalist Turn in Heidegger, Derrida, Blanchot and the Later Gadamer* 11–31.

4. See, for instance, Ponting, Crosby, Chew, and Diamond.

5. See Ophuls 169–74.

6. Michael Northcott writes: "The ascription 'private' is increasingly problematic when applied to automobiles. Their use requires the public maintenance of an extensive concrete, steel and tarmac infrastructure, representing one half of the built space of European and American cities" (215–6).

Works Cited

Beck, Ulrich. *The Cosmopolitan Vision.* Cambridge: Polity Press, 2006.

Blanchot, Maurice. "The Apocalypse is Disappointing." *Friendship.* Trans. Elizabeth Rottenberg. Stanford: Stanford University Press, 1997. 101–8.

Brown, Wendy. *Edgework: Critical Essays on Knowledge and Politics.* Princeton: Princeton University Press, 2005.

---. "Sovereign Hesitations." *Derrida and the Time of the Political.* Ed. Pheng Cheah and Suzanne Guerlac. Durham, NC: Duke University Press, 2009. 114–32.

Carver, Raymond. "Elephant." *Elephant.* London: The Harvill Press, 1998. 73–90.

Chew, Sing C. *World Ecological Degradation: Accumulation, Urbanization, and Deforestation 3000 BC–AD 2000.* Walnut Creek, CA: Altamira Press, 2001.

Clark, Timothy. *The Poetics of Singularity: The Counter-Culturalist Turn in Heidegger, Derrida, Blanchot and the Later Gadamer.* Edinburgh: Edinburgh University Press, 2005.

Crosby, Alfred W. *Ecological Imperialism: The Biological Expansion of Europe, 900–1900.* Cambridge: Cambridge University Press, 1986.

Dator, Jim. "Assuming 'responsibility for our rose.'" *Environmental Values in a Globalizing World: Nature, Justice and Governance.* Ed. Jouni Paavola and Ian Lowe. London: Routledge, 2005. 215–35.

Derrida, Jacques. *On Hospitality: Anne Dufourmantelle Invites Jacques Derrida to Respond.* Trans. Rachel Bowlby. Stanford: Stanford University Press, 2000.

---. *Specters of Marx: The State of Debt, the Work of Mourning & the New International.* Trans. Peggy Kamuf. New York: Routledge, 1994.

Diamond, Jared. *Collapse: How Societies Choose to Fail or Survive.* London: Penguin, 2005.

---. *Guns, Germs, and Steel: The Fates of Human Societies.* New York: Norton, 1997.

Foster, John Bellamy. *Ecology Against Capitalism.* New York: Monthly Review Press, 2002.

Hardin, Garrett. *Living Within Limits: Ecology, Economics, and Population Taboos.* New York: Oxford University Press, 1993.

Harman, Graham. *Prince of Networks: Bruno Latour and Metaphysics.* Melbourne: re.press, 2009.

Jamieson, Dale. "Ethics, Public Policy, and Global Warning." *Science Technology, & Human Values.* 17 (1992): 139–53.

Jenerette, G. Darrel, and Jiango Wu. "On the Definitions of Scale." *Bulletin of the Ecological Society of America.* 81.1 (2000): 104–5.

Jonas, Hans. *The Imperative of Responsibility: In Search of an Ethics for the Technological Age.* Trans. Hans Jonas and David Herr. Chicago: University of Chicago Press, 1984.

Leitch, Vincent B. "Late Derrida: The Politics of Sovereignty." *Critical Inquiry* 33 (Winter 2007): 229–47.

Levin, Simon A. "The Problem of Pattern and Scale in Ecology." The Robert H. MacArthur Award Lecture 1989. *Ecology* 73 (1992): 1943–1967.

Litfin, Karen T. "Environment, Wealth, and Authority: Global Climate Change and Emerging Modes of Legitimation." *International Studies Review.* 2.2 (Summer 2000): 119–48.

MacKenzie, Debora. "Are We Doomed?" *New Scientist.* 5 April 2008. 33–5.

McNeill, John R. *Something New Under the Sun.* New York: Norton, 2000.

Nesset, Kirk. *The Stories of Raymond Carver: A Critical Study.* Athens: Ohio University Press, 1995.

Northcott, Michael S. *A Moral Climate: The Ethics of Global Warming.* Maryknoll, NY: Orbis Books, 2007.

Ophuls, William. *Requiem for Modern Politics: The Tragedy of the Enlightenment and the Challenge of the New Millennium.* Boulder, CO: Westview Press, 1997.

Ponting, Clive. *A Green History of the World.* New York: St. Martin's Press, 1991.

Ross, Stephen David. *The Gift of Property: Having the Good.* Albany: SUNY Press, 2001.

Schneider, Joseph. *Donna Haraway: Live Theory.* New York: Continuum, 2005.

Shearman, David, and Joseph Wayne Smith. *The Climate Change Challenge and the Failure of Democracy.* Westport, CT: Praeger, 2007.

Wood, David. "On Being Haunted by the Future." *Research in Phenomenology* 36 (2006): 274–98.

Chapter 6

Sexual Indifference

CLAIRE COLEBROOK

There has been much talk recently regarding the extinction of sexual difference, both in a highly specific sense and in a broader sense. In humans the y chromosome has recently been interrogated with regard to its evolutionary value, with some scientists suggesting its days are numbered. In addition to that quite localized prospect of annihilation, it is also possible that life, if it survives on this planet, will have to alter so radically that it will no longer take the forms of organic sexual reproduction that seem to have so dominated the imaginary, especially in these present times when thoughts of the inhuman and posthuman often stretch no further than imagining animal organic life, itself of the rather comforting sexually dual mode.[1] Sexual *indifference*—or the thought of production and 'life' that does not take the form of the bounded organism reproducing itself through relation to its complementing other might not just be a thought worth entertaining for the curiosity it presents to the life sciences. Such a thought might provoke us to think beyond the lures and laziness that the sexual dyad as a figure has offered for thinking. There were, in the early days of what has come to be known as 'theory' (at least) two diagnoses of this image of redemptive unity-in-otherness: Lacan's insistence that ethics might begin if one could imagine the non-existence of woman, precluding the dependence of the subject on some fulfillment to come; and Paul de Man's reading of the logic of growth, fruition and genesis as relapses into the myopic quiescence of meaning. Today, however, despite a few exceptions the dyad of sexual difference as fulfillment has taken on a new life in theory and has, I would argue, precluded the thought of the logic of extinction that at once resides within sexual reproduction but that also demands a thought of reproduction beyond that of sexuality. The two senses of the extinction of sexual difference—both sexuality's necessary relation to extinction and the possibility of sexual difference itself becoming extinct—despite coming to the fore in a series of recent scientific studies has not only failed to dent theory's commitment to a binary organicism, but has seemed to provoke a return or retreat to the figure of the sexual couple.

It is possible that the earth's previous significant mass extinction event was directly related to annihilation via sexual difference: if dinosaur genders were, like present day turtles and lizards, determined via temperature, then the severe cold caused by a comet would have precluded the birth of females, this in turn leading to a surfeit of males and species extinction. Recent research has opened the possibility of generating sperm from stem cells; further into the future—100 to 200 thousand years (which is a mere blink in evolutionary time)—the y chromosome has been predicted to face extinction. Many species already reproduce without dual sexual reproduction, or via sexual reproduction that does not generate distinct sexes. Non-sexual reproduction has recently been reported beyond the plant kingdom in a species of Amazonian ant that replicates itself from the queen without coming into contact with other gene lines. Far, then, from relation to sexual alterity being the *sine qua non* of life, the human sexual dyad is both an event within evolutionary life and possibly within human organic life—if the species lives long enough to realize its dreams of reproduction via stems cells, sperm generated from stem cells, cloning, inorganic artificial replication, and the mastery of a virtual reality that negates organic finitude. At a broader level, and in a temporal trajectory that conflicts with scenarios of liberation through stem cell technologies and anticipated evolutionary timelines of multiple millennia, sexual difference is not only a factor in species evolution but also faces annihilation via the extinction of organic life. Any number of (mutually exclusive but over-determined) threats promise to wipe out the existence of organisms: global warming, resource depletion, viral pandemic, bio-terrorism, the resurgence of nuclear warfare from 'rogue' states, economic collapse leading to social chaos, and the lawlessness that would preclude the managerial measures required to deal with the other threats. Indeed, the number of factors and their unpredictability intensify the possibility of panic and chaos precisely because procedures for adaptation and mitigation in one domain preclude the attention and resources being devoted to another. One might recall here, just to cite one example, the ways in which calls for population control by certain environmentalists have been criticized by left-wing feminists for (once again) focusing on the control of women and reproduction as the first port of call in a crisis regarding the viability of life. If extinction is certain as part of the natural logic of evolving life, it is also possible that extinction might—by virtue of the panic that accompanies the attempts to maintain human life at all costs—annihilate organic life as such, sweeping away sexual difference in any of its currently known or imagined forms. How then, we might ask—facing these crises and their ramifications—has theory and gender studies addressed the question of climate change in its broadest sense? The change of the literal climate cannot be delimited from the accompanying change in intellectual, social, political and systemic climates. At the very least, this is because a certain sexual feedback, whereby the imaginary of human reproduction that has allowed human life to figure itself as organically self-sustaining, has come to destroy the very system that would allow human life to sustain itself into a future imaginable as human.

Work on the relation between climate change and gender has generally focused on the ways in which disasters caused by global warming and resource depletion have tended to affect women more adversely than men, and this because women are the first to suffer in a shortage of labor opportunities and also because crises in general do not allow the status quo of inequality to be addressed. But this use of the concept of gender difference to nuance the effects of climate change needs to be extended to consider the ways in which all that comes under the rubric of climate change—all the ways in which organic human life has rendered itself unsustainable precisely by sustaining itself—has a figure of sexual difference and justice pervading its imagination of itself. Climate change, after all, is not change of the climate, as though it were nothing more than the human being observing an alteration of its surround; climate change 'includes' a confrontation with what goes beyond any topology of 'environ' or oikos, no longer being conceivable of the place in which the human resides so much as an infiltration of the human by forces beyond its organic modes of comprehension. What such an over-determined and chaotic domain of possibilities alerts us to is that questions of sexual difference can no longer be located *within life*, within questions of living organisms and their relations to each other. It is no longer a question of addressing the ways in which sexual difference does or does not play itself out in the relation among humans. For it is sexual difference, both in its genetic reality and in its imaginary figuration, that is one of the crucial factors in organic life's possible survival and possible disappearance; and this is because sexual difference is a strange and seemingly perverse logic of life, both enhancing organic variability (and survival) and yet also diverting perception, attention, and affectivity into the organism's own bounds. What I would like to insist upon here is that the extinction of sexual difference does not arrive from without as some type of accident that befalls an otherwise benevolent living system. On the contrary: the possibility of sexual difference is essentially intertwined with the possibility of extinction. An organism and a species that combines reproduction with sexual difference abandons the efficient replication of simple cloning, but nevertheless allows for greater gene survival through the multiplication of variability in recombinant DNA. (Only through the coupling of chromosomes can mutations of single gene lines be added to create new distinctions in such an effective evolutionary speed.) Sexual difference, or the living being's complex relation to the otherness it requires for genetic continuity alongside the identity that marks it as a living being as such, has always been considered (normatively and morally) in terms of the gendered couple. It is the failure to confront the potentiality of sexual indifference—or difference beyond bounded organisms—that has precipitated the accelerated trajectory towards the annihilation of sexually differentiated and organic life.

So how is sexual difference intrinsically bound up with the potentiality of extinction? Sexual difference requires something like the bounded forms of distinct kinds, requires genres or relatively stable forms whose coupling then allows for greater chances of a gene line's continuity. One of the basic principles of evolutionary theory—rendered annoyingly familiar through popular evolutionary psychology—is that the gene's survival can often occur at the expense of the organism, allowing for seemingly perverse or disinterested behavior to have some rationale at the level of populations or at the level of surviving genetic archaisms. Sexual difference allows for a maximal chance of a gene line's survival but can only do so at the expense of the organism's self-interest. Whereas simple cloning or replication would allow the maintenance of the being's identity, reproduction through sexual difference enables only a fragment of the being's genetic makeup to survive. Reproduction through sexual coupling admits a large degree of variation, allowing for a greater chance of survival, but this survival is never that of an identity, organism or natural kind. If a being or organism were to remain simply as it is, without exposure to the risks of sexual reproduction, its gene line would not couple with this diversity, maximizing survival. Sexual difference therefore requires something like the boundedness and ongoing stability (achieved through difference) of organic life; at the same time, sexual difference operates beyond the bounds of organic closure and identity, proceeding beyond the organism and the lived.

It is just this time and dynamic relationality of sexual difference—allowing the organism both to be of a certain kind or genre, while also open to living on through what is not itself—that has underpinned the highly normative images of life that have precluded the thought of the forces of life that threaten to annihilate sexual difference in its organic mode. An unthinking privileging of this logic of sexual difference has been extrapolated to much of the celebration of life *tout court*. Ecocriticism and many modes of environmentalism begin from the affirmation of humanity's necessary coupling with nature, insisting that we are not detached and isolated Cartesian units. But these grounding concepts of climate environment and ecology betray the very anthropocentrism they insist is not primary: for if we were to consider life *not* as that of the bounded being empathetically attached to its complementing other but as a play of annihilating and dominating forces then we would have to jettison the figure of the climate, tied as it is (from *klima*) to the surface of the earth (or to region—as in the notion of 'climes'), to the bounded and delimitable. Sexual *indifference*—or the forces of life, mutation, generation and exchange *without* any sense of ongoing identity or temporal synthesis—have always been warded off as evil and unthinkable, usually associated with a monstrous inhumanity. The shrill insistence on proper sexual difference—that creation must occur with a sense of continuity, intentionality, identity and dynamic self-becoming—precludes the organism from paying heed to those other rhythms that are now (for want of being perceived) exacerbating the annihilation of organic life. Had man recognized the inhuman—the monstrous mutations he has always warded off as evil, indifferent, and chaotically unbounded—he may have been more perturbed by those forces that are not of the life-world or intentional horizon, might have been able to face the encroaching sexual indifference that to date has been deemed to be unthinkable.

We might note, then, that it is just at the point that bounded sexual difference unravels and opens to a milieu of rampant self-destruction that theory and culture has returned to, and reaffirmed, a bounded gendered enclosure. And similarly, it is just at the point that capitalism appears to be in a state of collapse—precisely because it was too self-enclosed and too sheltered from radical exchange and difference—that theory retreats to archaisms of community, identity, sociality, the polity, and humanity. To make this clearer, we might say that the event that will ultimately precipitate human extinction is not its radical openness to dissolution but its suicidal self-enclosure, its self-bounded integrity that will allow it only to imagine its own world from its own imaginative horizon. As has become all too evident recently, what may trigger utter economic collapse is not radical capitalism—an absolutely free and open market—but self-enclosing narcissisms, privileges, feudal lineages, knots of self-interest, archaic nepotisms, and good old-fashioned individualist self-interest. So, when figures of the nightmares of an indifferent, inhuman, purely technical capitalist world of mere exchange and replication are imagined through depictions of an equally mechanistic, inhuman, and contingent replication, it is always something like the well-bounded whole of intentionality and meaning that is seen as a corrective. And this is so despite the fact that the wholeness of bounded, meaningful and intentional life constitutes just the self-enclosed blindness that has eliminated any possibility of witnessing the lines of life beyond our own myopia.

Before considering the ways in which the properly bounded, creative, and organic figure of sexual difference has operated as a moralism in theories of life, it might be worth pausing to ask how, today, 'theory' has responded to the milieu of extinction, to the increasing likelihood that what is now been imagined as the delimited anthropocene era may come to an end and take with it organic life in general. Far from confronting the surfeit of scientific information—or confronting the affective lag between influx of information and paralysis of response—theory has retreated from a position of theory (or inhuman disengagement) to a traditional figure of the sexual binary. In all cases what is rehearsed is a theological-anthropomorphic insistence on the fruitful, productive, relatively closed sexually dynamic couple, set over and against a (supposedly a-political) circulation of difference, exchange and possibly unproductive and senseless proliferation.

Consider some quite specific examples. After an earlier career that insisted that there was no doer behind the deed, and that 'sex' was a retroactive effect of a performance without intentional agent, Judith Butler has considered structures of recognition and familial alliance as at least the starting point of political theorization. Symptomatically, Butler has retrieved the face to face encounter that is both formative of human recognition, and that remains the ultimate horizon of a political theory that will be focused on the normativity of humanity (even if who or what counts as the norm is the site of a battle). It is the face that marks, for Butler, the rupture of representation and the limits of cognition:

For representation to convey the human, then, representation must not only fail, but it must *show* its failure. There is something unrepresentable that we nevertheless seek to represent, and the paradox must be maintained in the representation we give.In this sense, the human is not identified with the unrepresentable; it is, rather, that which limits the success of any available practice. The face is not 'effaced' in this failure of representation, but is constituted in that very possibility. Something altogether different happens, however, when the face operates in the service of personification. (*Precarious Life* 144)Butler opens with the promising and urgent question of the disruption of narcissistic self-enclosure, a disturbance that is not willed, and yet she thinks this intrusion in terms of *the Other* (via a Levinas whose entire project was founded on the primacy of the ethical, reinforcing the homeliness of *ethos* against the inhumanity of mere force). Butler's model of the self and life remains primarily traumatic; she may see infraction as necessary and constitutive, but it remains the case that the self/other, or border/trauma limit is foundational for her theory:

> Perhaps we might have to think, along with Levinas, that
> self-preservation is not the highest goal, and the defense of a
> narcissistic point of view not the most urgent psychic need.
> That we are impinged upon primarily and against our will is
> the sign of a vulnerability and a beholdenness that we cannot
> will away. We can defend against it only by prizing the asocial-
> ity of the subject over and against a difficult and intractable,
> even sometimes unbearable relationality. What might it mean
> to make an ethic from the region of the unwilled? It might
> mean that one does not foreclose upon that primary exposure
> to the Other, that one does not try to transform the unwilled
> into the willed, but rather, to take the very unbearability of ex-
> posure as the sign, the reminder, of a common vulnerability
> (even as 'common' does not mean 'symmetrical' for Levinas).
> (*Giving an Account of Oneself* 100)

This primarily self-other mode of trauma precludes any consideration
of the thousand tiny micro-events that take place beyond the lived. The
attention to trauma maintains the self as a bordered whole, even if that
surface can be punctured; the focus on the other as the agent of this disturbance both allows the self to *await* intrusion, and localizes that intrusion in the human-human relation. Drawing on Laplanche, as well as
Levinas, Butler leaves behind the diagnosis of this sexual imaginary articulated by Lacan. The Other does not exist; its fantasmatic presence—the
lure that if only one could decipher the other's desire one might attain a
plentiude beyond the self's fragmentation. Lacan's account of love would
look forward to a relation of non-dependence, but is this the best we can
do with his critique? Is a reconfiguring of the human sexual relation as far
as we can go? Both in Laplanche and Lacan there is another path indicated for thinking beyond the seduction of the human-human lure. And
yet the interest that has been attained in their work has tended to devolve
on the question of the sexual relation, the other and love.

Alain Badiou places the encounter of love as one of the four generic
conditions of events. The properly evental mode of love that may not always be that of a couple is explicated most fully in Badiou's work on St
Paul. The privileging of love operates as a valorization of love as truth, in

which human love would strive to achieve through the other, something of the universality of Pauline Christian love.

Thus, the new faith consists in deploying the power of self-love in the direction of others, addressing it to everyone, in a way made possible by subjectivation (conviction). *Love is precisely what faith is capable of.*

I call this universal power of subjectivation an eventual fidelity, and it is correct to say that fidelity is the law of a truth. In Paul's thought, love is precisely fidelity to the Christ event, in accordance with a power that addresses the love of self universally. Love is what makes of thought a power, which is why love alone, and not faith, bears the *force* of salvation (90).Love is set alongside other generic conditions such as mathematics, politics, and poetry: all of which are other than what Badiou deems to be the evil of the present. Evil is the merely senseless ever-sameness of communication, the circulation of unthought content, the capitalist and bourgeois indifference of a world without *proper thinking.* Thinking is neither the reception of information nor a consideration of how bodily life or worldly life might survive. (As an aside one might observe that all those *indifferent* conditions that Badiou associates with the unthinking world of bourgeois normality are also figurally tied to a certain notion of woman: passive consumption, mere chatter, moral ambivalence, and a society of hedonistic spectacle.)

Indifference—the loss of individuation, the subsumption of the thinking subject by opinion, and a mode of aesthetics of easy consumption and enjoyment rather than the creation of social relations—all these, too, are evils for Giorgio Agamben. Despite his theological heritage Agamben does not use the concept of evil to target the modern world's loss of the political, but he does see the terrors of contemporary bio-politics as located primarily in the lack of distinction between *bios* and *zoe.* If the ancient origin of the *polis* was possible because of a continual working of the anthropological machine, whereby man set himself in distinction from the mere life that was at once internal and yet externalized, then modernity has increasingly lost the polis in its falling back upon a managed biological existence that is no longer formed collectively, practically and politically. The human becomes merely managed substance, not that which springs forth from itself to open its own world. Agamben, lamenting the loss of the political, concludes *The Open* by finding a way beyond the opposition between bare (or simply surviving) life and properly human (or lawfully ordered and recognized) life in the figure of two lovers as presented in a Titian canvas. Here, facing one's sexual other, one is neither a mere body—for one's natural existence is witnessed by another—nor is one fully humanized and politicized, precisely because sexual desire is the desire of the other's bodily being. The lovers figure a threshold—for Agamben *the* political human threshold—of a fragile coming into existence as human from the natural:

> In their fulfillment the lovers learn something of each other
> that they should not have known—they have lost their mystery—and yet have not become any less impenetrable. But in
> this mutual disenchantment from their secret…they enter a
> new and more blessed life, one that is neither animal nor human. It is not nature that is reached in their fulfillment, but
> rather…a higher stage beyond both nature and knowledge,
> beyond concealment and disconcealment. (87)

Even though Michael Hardt and Antonio Negri argue for a new creative mode of humanity (or *homohomo*) beyond the normalized sex of the family, it is human embodied love that opens the way to a new politics. Rather than move away from the bourgeois couple to impersonal forces beyond the human, Hardt and Negri return to a pre-bourgeois theological love—the godly love that had served to render heterosexual marriage spiritually proper to the life of man: "There is really nothing necessarily metaphysical about the Christian and Judaic love of God: both God's love of humanity and humanity's love of God are expressed and incarnated in the common material political project of the multitude" (*Multitude* 351–52). This love is artifice precisely because it is fully grounded in art and knowledge, not the mere life of *zoe*, and certainly not the simple experiences of mixture:

> This creative evolution does not merely occupy any existing
> place, but rather invents a new place; it is a desire that creates a new body. … In addition to being radically unprepared
> for normalization, however, the new body must also be able
> to create a new life. We must go further to define the new
> place of the non-place, well beyond the simple experiences

of mixture and hybridization, and the experiments that are conducted around them. We have to arrive at constituting a coherent political artifice, an *artificial becoming* in the sense that the humanists spoke of a *homohomo* produced by art and knowledge, and that Spinoza spoke of a powerful body produced by the highest consciousness that is infused with love. (*Empire* 216–217)

What all these appeals to redemptive love share, apart from their repetition of normative figures of life depicted through bounded and gendered distinction, is an alignment with a moralizing anti-capitalism. What must be expelled as evil is a proliferation of differences without limit, an exchange without sense, a chaotic productivity that is divorced from the vital normativity of organic being. Sexual indifference has always been warded off precisely because it opens the human organism to mutation, production, lines of descent and annihilation beyond that of its own intentionality. And this is so even if the evolutionary logic of sexual difference entails a necessary loss of distinction and opening to annihilation. A gene line survives not if it remains sufficient unto itself, remaining as it is and fully actualized. Not only is every individual life a negotiation between maintaining a border of identity and exposing the body to the contingency of an outside, gene line survival occurs through an encounter with other gene lines, the creation of maximum mutation without any sense of certainty of living on. And yet it is just this logic of necessary and positive extinction—this necessary production of differences that will not survive—that is repressed in the shrill affirmation of the vitality of sexual binary difference. Indeed, one might ask whether the human species is now facing its end precisely because it has only been able to respond to what it recognizes as its own political—that is, human to human—milieu?

Apart from the standard anxieties regarding the engineering of life—which is, after all, an anxiety directed against the loss of chance, mystery or exposure to something other than the will making itself from itself, or an anxiety about a pure techne that would be a system maintaining itself with no sense or end other than its own efficiency—fears of the loss of sexual difference occlude a recognition of positive extinction that is the aporia of life as such. Sexual difference—if set against replication by splitting or parthenogenesis, or contemporary potentials for cloning—relies upon continuing a gene line through coupling with a diversifying other. This coupling of difference harbors three general structures of identity and difference: first, continuity of a living being occurs through a specific mode of becoming, whereby a being must neither remain simply the same through time (the inertia of a corpse) nor be radically different from moment to moment without relation; becoming is the becoming *of* this or that specified being. But what the substratum for becoming *is* can only be known after the event of becoming, and not as its logic. That is, it is never certain at what point a differentiation increases the complexity of a natural kind, or opens the first branching out of another natural kind. It cannot be clear, in other words, whether an event of sexual difference is the maximization of a being's continuity *or* the opening to its eventual annihilation or supplementation. The continuity of life requires some degree of ongoing destruction, both of the individual closed forms that make up any species, and of species themselves. At what point an event of death represents the means by which a species continues itself or passes over into extinction for the sake of other forms is undecidable.

Further, sexual difference as the motor for evolution and survival evidences an even more complex passage through a thousand tiny annihilations: if organisms were governed solely by the economic efficiency of survival it is hard to imagine how complexity would develop; complexity can—one imagines—only occur with the production of redundancy or not immediately useful differences that may or may not have some fit with the creation of an ongoing stability. This relation between immediate efficiency and risky redundancy is highly pertinent for sexual difference: a simply cloning species can double itself at twice the speed of a species that requires coupling, but its capacity to produce complex mutations is diminished. The same applies as sexual difference becomes increasingly complex. The *lure* of sexual difference, seen in its human mode, can appear as a manifest excess above and beyond any calculable benefit for continuity. Sexual display may impede a body's organic functioning—including everything from peacock feathers to silicon breasts and high heels—rendering the living being's boundedness less secure, opening its becoming to the eyes, ears, and olfactory sense of other beings. The inflections of becoming grounded in the lures of sexual difference at once evidence a logic of life as continuity *and* a disregard for the individual being. If this were not so, if organisms could only act in such a way that all actions and reactions were grounded in their own survival, then life in general would grind to a halt. Sexual difference appears to be the mark that explains the organism's surpassing of itself for the sake of life, its passage beyond its bounded form to the becoming of life in general. At the same time, this indicates that the life of sexual difference is more than organic and bounded life, even though all the figures, logics and moralisms of sexual difference are haunted precisely by a fear of sexual indifference that is intertwined with a loss of individuation.

Finally, sexual difference has, at its heart, a positive tendency of annihilation: not only do the lures of sexual difference act less for the organism's own survival and more for the becoming and differentiating life of which it is an expression; the coupling with other gene lines enables survival—not of the same—but of that which lives on only by taking on a line of life other than its own. One might note that it is precisely because of a certain clinging to bounded sexual difference and a fear of individual extinction, that the human species is now forced to confront a species extinction that may well lead to the extinction of sexual difference in general, in the annihilation of organic and organized life. What would follow—a difference beyond the bounded organism—may be neither difference or indifference, having no longer that strange relationship to self-maintenance that is figured in all the moralisms of gender difference that have marked normative figures of life.

As already noted, there has always been an anxiety regarding sexual indifference as the mere proliferation of life and production without the sense, identity and individuation of bounded forms. If life were simply to remain as it is, without alteration, becoming or creation then one would be left with nothing other than the inertia of matter, the ever-same of the inorganic. But that becoming must be a becoming of bounded and marked kinds, remaining both the same and other through the ongoing recognizable stability of gene lines issuing in kinds. Even so, alongside the anxiety regarding sexual *in*difference there is also—within the very insistence on creation through relation among individuated kinds—a refusal of sexual difference beyond kinds. It is precisely this moralism of sexual difference, an organicism that would contain difference in the bounded forms of self-recognising life, that reaches its limit today as the human species confronts an intensification both of extinction threats and sexual indifference scenarios. To broach a conclusion I would suggest that it is sexual difference and its figural imaginary that has underpinned the suicidal logic of human organicism.

According to this persistent figural imaginary life in its proper, bounded, and organic form must at once become and realize itself through a creative coupling with an other kind. Not to do so would be a refusal of the creativity of which the bounded form is the distinct expression. And yet this becoming through what is not oneself must not be so open as to risk utter annihilation. Good sexual difference is relation to otherness that at once reinforces the bounded stability of the closed form, while nevertheless remaining open to a creative potentiality of that form that can be achieved by encounter with a complementary other. What cannot be admitted is what is figured as sexual *in*difference—the mere replication, simulation, or proliferation of chaotic and unbounded life that has neither sense of itself nor of its individuating relation to the whole. Good sexual coupling is a binary in which each term is more than itself by recognizing in the other not a merely present body that would be some object for consumption, but another open relation, enabling in turn an ongoing life and becoming of the future. Such a good coupling is situated between the extremity of an utterly bounded and fixed form—something that simply is, as fully actualized and without change or life—and the other pole of proliferating difference without identity or limit.

Has not this normative figure of sexual difference, a difference that would seemingly ward off the chaos of indifference, randomness, mindless proliferation and closed completion, operated as the imaginary that has precluded us from thinking the positive indifference and extinction that would enable the human species to confront its current milieu? Why, we might ask, as extinction and indifference become possible, imagined, and even predicted scenarios, has there been a reaction formation asserting the bounds and sense of the organism? Today there is no shortage of scenarios for the annihilation of sexual difference, ranging from stem cell research that could produce sperm—a possible boon for lesbian couples—to predictions that evolution will close down the sexually distinct male human, and even further to the annihilation of organic life in general which would entail the extinction of the sexually differentiated in all its forms, allowing other modes of microbial life (possibly) to start some other line of becoming.

One might suggest that this actual threat of annihilation and extinction followed directly from a logic of organic and sexually differentiated survival and self-maintenance. It is because the human organism fears sexual indifference, fears the loss of its bounded being and its differentiated world of fixed kinds, that it has been unable to perceive, consider or allow differences and rhythms beyond those of its own sensory-motor apparatus. That is, the normative dyad of creative human coupling that has warded off difference and production beyond its own bounded life, has been the figure that has precluded a sense of life beyond *oikos*, polity, organism, sense and man. One might say that it is the insistence on proper sexual difference—a sexual difference that would not extinguish itself in chaos and would allow for the ongoing maintenance of distinct lines— that will ultimately lead to the annihilation or extinction of sexual difference in general, in the extinction of life as such. Indeed, faced with the potentiality of a sexual difference beyond that of the organic couple, both popular culture and theory have responded by reaffirming the normative image of life that has always enclosed the human within its own suicidal logic of survival. The fear of sexual indifference—a circulation, exchange and proliferation beyond bounded forms—is precisely that which has imprisoned human species within its logic of self-enclosing sameness.

The present continuation of the shrill affirmation of the life and fruition of sexual difference, along with the constant references to love and coupling, preclude recognizing all those forces beyond the organism whose play has been essential to our milieu. By only admitting the lived differences of bounded kinds we have been unable to consider the difference of lifelines and force lines beyond our purview.

Notes

1. Why, we might ask, does one of the Ur-text's for the turn to animality in theory—Derrida's—take the form of the classically existential self-other "look"? Why is the relation that might challenge anthropo-morpho-centrism one of the eye-to-eye confrontation of duality? In the other two core texts of

animal human bordering, Agamben's *The Open* and Deleuze and Guattari's plateau on becoming in *A Thousand Plateaus,* it is the border of the human that takes primacy. While all these texts challenge human specificity and supremacy they share two features: first, it is the *human relation* to the animal that opens the question of life and becoming; second, the problem of the future and the break with human boundedness nevertheless takes place in relation to organic and productive life. Deleuze and Guattari insist that the human relation to the animal will not be one of imitation, nor of sympathy and empathy but will, rather, extract 'traits' that will liberate thought from the "lived," the organic and—most importantly—the being of woman. Despite that departing gesture, their phrase of "becoming-woman" has either been criticized for appropriating the force of "woman" from women themselves or has, more recently, seemed to justify maintaining a logic of woman as point of redemption. This essay will argue that this gesture of Deleuze and Guattari's to move from becoming-animal and becoming-woman to becoming-imperceptible—thinking the non-existence of the human organism—has been occluded in the recent turn to life and praxis in contemporary theory.

Works Cited

Agamben, Giorgio. *The Open: Man and Animal.* Trans. Kevin Attell. Stanford, CA: Stanford University Press, 2004.

Badiou, Alain. *Saint Paul: The Foundation of Universalism.* Trans. Ray Brassier. Stanford, CA: Stanford University Press, 2003.

Butler, Judith. *Giving an Account of Oneself.* New York: Fordham University Press, 2005.

---. *Precarious Life: The Powers of Mourning and Violence.* London: Verso, 2004.

Deleuze, Gilles and Felix Guattari. *A Thousand Plateaus: Capitalism and Schizophrenia.* Trans. Brian Massumi. Minneapolis: University of Minnesota Press, 1987.

Derrida, Jacques. *The Animal That Therefore I Am.* Ed. Marie-Louise Mallet. Trans. David Wills. New York: Fordham University Press, 2008.

Hardt, Michael and Antonio Negri. *Empire.* Cambridge, MA: Harvard University Press, 2000.

---. *Multitude: War and Democracy in the Age of Empire.* New York: Penguin, 2004.

Chapter 7

Nonspecies Invasion

The Eco-logic of Late Capitalism

JASON GROVES

How do you deal with an enemy that has no government, no money trail, and no qualms about killing women and children? screamed protectingamerica. org, a consortium of insurance companies clamoring for public funding, in an advertisement published in the *New York Times* on the one-year anniversary of Katrina. Out of this enemy without a face materializes the face of the earth in the next sentence. *The enemy is Mother Nature.* And then: *On August 29, 2005, in the form of hurricane Katrina, she killed 1,836 people, devastated a land area larger than Great Britain and caused over 100 million dollars worth of destruction.* Never mind that Katrina remains by most accounts an unnatural disaster, an atmospheric disturbance mobilized by a strategic negligence to become what Tom Cohen and Mike Hill have called the "preemptive first strike in an undeclared US civil war" (12). For the moment this is beside the point. The miscalculation made by protectingamerica.org, its disavowal of a political ecology, is that coming disasters will arrive from a subterranean or atmospheric beyond in the form of a hurricane, earthquake, storm, or any other discrete meteorological or seismic event.

The Enemy is Mother Nature

Especially in the migrations, explosions, expansions, and contractions of species assembled under the term *biological invasion*, the very proliferation of the biophysical world is increasingly perceived and conceived in ecological and economic arenas as the unmitigated disaster of the 21st

century. From microorganisms to megafauna, from killer algae to plagues of rats and rubber vines, species are participating in an outbreak of migration greater than any in the history of the planet. Whether in ballast tanks of container ships or on the landing gear of military cargo planes, the biophysical world is on the move, and Robert Kaplan's call in "The Coming Anarchy" for a dynamic cartography, one that can serve as an "ever-mutating representation of chaos," is as both appropriate and as unavailable for ecology today as it was for political science in 1994 (75). "Make no mistake," Charles Elton writes in the seminal *Ecology of Invasions*, "we are living in a period of the world's history when the mingling of thousands of kinds of organisms from different parts of the world is setting up terrific dislocations in nature" (8). Yet these novel configurations of nonhuman life have proliferated so extensively as to have infiltrated the locus itself and in the process naturalized dislocation. The explosion of translocated life spells the end of endemism, even as the conceptualization of those species as invasives (other common designations include *non-indigenous, exotic,* and *alien* species) promises to preserve the integrity of the border and the bounded community, but only in the very susceptibility and receptivity of those communities to transgression and dissolution. That is to say, the *acceptation* of invasion, the "favorable reception" by practically every ecosystem to species previously exotic, undermines the acceptation—the "meaning given to a word"—of "invasion" as deployed by invasion biology. What is called bioinvasion or species invasion could be read as an invasion of monstrous *nonspecies* into the biological, glossed by Derrida as "the as yet unnamable which is proclaiming itself and which can do so [...] only under the species of the nonspecies, in the formless, mute, infant, and terrifying form of monstrosity" ("Structure" 292–3).

Like *Kulturkritik,* "bioinvasion" has an offensive ring to it, not in the least because of the collision between the Greek *bios* and the Latin *vadere.* Polytopic, then, the word itself is the scene of an invasion, a trespassing of territories and temporalities, a disregarding of linguistic proprieties, antiquity gone feral. This unlikely constellation has found a foothold both in biological discourse and the popular imagination. What the latter predominantly responds to is the couched appeal to a smoldering nativism, whereas the former insists it is a mere description of life forms wandering in space. But if ideology can be defined loosely as a command disguised

as description, then bioinvasion, with its close ties to conservation practices and its soft exhortations to eradicate non-native species, might be
inseparable from a conservative ideology. Yet persisting terminological
debates within the blooming field of invasion biology, no matter how "deconstructed" or otherwise meticulous in tracing (or disavowing) an ideological subtext, tend to fail to remark on the extent to which mutations in
the terrestrial itself, rather than the suggestiveness of certain key words
like "invasion," frustrate the articulation of key ecological concepts.[1] Calls
to "demilitarize" invasion biology will go only so far, since the movement
of invasive species oftentimes can be overlain over military expansion,
the case of the introduction of the Brown tree snake to Guam by U.S.
military cargo planes being the most prolific.[2] With increasing insistence
the impinging by shifting configurations of nonhuman life upon agricultural and economic systems requires models capable of comprehending
(containing) these emerging and emergent biogeographies, yet the radical and relatively recent changes in the spatial distribution of both human and nonhuman life have delegitimized the retrograde nativisms and
oversimplified dichotomies (native vs. exotic; invasive vs. non-invasive;
indigenous vs. non-indigenous) with which biology has accounted for
these shifts. Instead of polysemy it is the dissemination of polytopic species that insists on retiring the image of an inimical mother—nature—
and her unsolicited hospitality. Containment—whether cartographic,
conceptual, conservationist, or indemnificatory—increasingly is frus-
trated. The possibility that the conceptual framework rigidly imposed on
the land by these dichotomies is responsible for the perceived material
effects on the ground (environmental degradation, decreasing biodiversity, dwindling resources) remains more than plausible; the least required
is some critical recognition of the entanglement between linguistic performance and historical event in the arena of bioinvasion, if not a diagnosis of a full blown *mal d'archive*. While key operators in invasion biology,
whose ideological valences can be gauged by their association with conservationist imperatives, would seem to have warranted a more substantial critical investment, the generous lavishing of theoretical attention on
domesticated companion species has taken precedent over invasive species, which, after all, cannot be handled so easily. But undomesticated, or
should one say *underdomesticated* species are our companions too: Rus-

sian wheat aphids ate an estimated 600 million dollars worth of U.S. cereal crops in the years 1987–1989 (followed, remarkably, by a dramatic drop in reported damages) (US Congress 58). Invasive species are also highly critical of dominant geographic paradigms: not only human geographers but also those migrating species identified as invasives are busy dismantling what Lewis and Wigan call "the myth of continents." The liquidation of the continental scheme, registered by the geographers as a crisis in conceptualization, continues to occur robustly without academic institutions. What is more, and what remains drastically underconsidered, the turbulent outbreak of undomesticated species from established frontiers demonstrates the astonishing capacity of nonhuman life to opportunistically appropriate the space-time compression called globalization for their own proliferation.

The Reconstitution of Pangaea, or the Generosity of Infrastructure

Of all the sea-changes emerging out of the establishment of a global transportation infrastructure the most unsettling might be what Alfred Crosby in *Ecological Imperialism* calls "the reconstitution of Pangaea": the uneasy reunion, ecologically speaking, of the planet's disparate landmasses into a single if splintered supercontinent, facilitated by various transport systems (12). Although Crosby generally considers the space between continents more of a seam than a divide, for most genera the blossoming of species diversity depended upon the break-up of the supercontinent approximately 180 million years ago. The subsequent development of insurmountable geological and climatological obstacles to migration led to the abatement of transoceanic flows of biomatter. As the interchange of genetic material across these seams was extremely limited, evolutionary divergence could take place and biodiversity could flourish. This scheme—usually attributed to Alfred Russel Wallace's division of the planet's surface into six highly distinct biogeographic realms, roughly falling along the "seams of Pangaea," later identified with the tectonic plates—explained the rise of biodiversity over the last 180 million years (Crosby 9–13). Yet the very industrial, economic, and military technological apparatus that prepared the way for Wallace's extensive field work was at the same time working to render these evolutionary systems and geographic schemes biogeographically obsolete.

The outbreaks of bioinvasion mark an ecological watershed and a massive blind spot in Crosby's argument: the drifting networks of adventitious disseminules, which first caught a ride on the imperialist envoys and which tremendously facilitated the expansion of empire (as *colonization by other means*), mark the limit of any hegemonic biological scheme. Today the "neo-Europes" that Crosby describes are more like neo-Pangeas; contemporary ecologies are no longer imperial but multinational, overwhelmingly cosmopolitan, and in some instances utopically inclusive. Consider the anecdote of a biologist who in 1976 described a hypothetical south Floridian watching "a walking Siamese catfish crawl out of a canal choked with the Asian weed hydrilla while Columbian iguanas scampered through Australian pines beneath a squadron of Amazonian parakeets" (Coates 2). The interspecies soiree undermines its own language, though, because the emphasis on nationality flagrantly disregards the inappropriateness, outside of taxonomical considerations, of a single point or continent of origin. Such scenes also require significant revision of the opening lines of *Ecological Imperialism*: "European immigrants are all over the place, which requires explanation" (Crosby 2). If the reconstitution of Pangaea by trade once led to the biological hegemony of Europe, increasing ecological awareness shows quite the opposite movement taking place today.

Whereas biological expansion for Crosby is a one-way street, contemporary invasives unravel Crosby's narrative of biological imperialism. While the pre-18th century proliferation of political and biological Neo-Europes is undeniably robust—"While some American plants," Manuel de Landa writes, "including maize and potatoes, tomatoes and chili peppers, did 'invade' Europe, they did so exclusively in the hands of humans and not on their own" (154)—the lines opened up by conquest had more than one direction, the dissemination more a product of a pedestrian dispersal than a manual distribution.[3] In the physiology of industrial empire, as Benton MacKaye once pointed out, a source is also a mouth. Consequently the related thesis of the biological unassailability of Europe requires revision on two points: most instances of translocated life today take place outside of humans hands and without so much as a

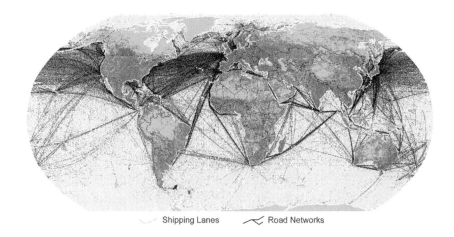

Shipping Lanes   Road Networks

steady grasp, a *Begriff*, of what is happening, since it is much more a matter of a footloose invader. Secondly, species native to North America have come to invade Europe with the frequency that the European ones invaded North America. As is becoming apparent, for every ship that went to a Neo-Europe, bearing not only articles of trade but also the weeds that would flourish in this new environment, another ship returned, bearing more blind passengers than paying.

A map published in a 2007 *Science* article vividly if obliviously illustrates the emergence of said reconstitution.[4] Here the vast oceanic space between Asia, North America and Europe has been virtually filled in by probes marking transoceanic travel, creating a new supercontinent of the Northern hemisphere, a neo-Laurasia. The myth of continents is cartographically, if not yet conceptually, exploded.

Because of the exceedingly large scale, the individual dots bleed into one another, forming solid lines that suggest land bridges connecting every continent and substantial island. (If air travel were depicted as well surely the same would be true of skybridges; the scintillating flight webs visualized by Aaron Koblin of UCLA's celestial mechanics lab, foreshadows the pathway of some as yet unknown zoonotic disease). This inference belongs only to a necessary distortion, yet this accident of scale makes an otherwise counter-intuitive claim visually compelling: the continental system is entering a phase of biogeographic obsolescence. So what exactly is mapped in this cartography of maritime and terrestrial commerce? This question must pass through the still-timely "fundamental representational problem" highlighted by Jameson in *The Geopolitical Aesthetic*:

> Bergson's warning about the temptations of spatializing thought remain current in the age of the intercontinental ballistic missile and the new infra-red and laser systems of which we are so proud; it is even more timely in an era of urban-dissolution and re-ghettoization, in which we might be tempted to think that the social can be mapped that way, by following across a map insurance red lines and the electrified borders of private police and surveillance forces. Both images are, however, only caricatures of the mode of production itself (most often called late capitalism) whose mechanisms and dynamics are not visible in that sense, cannot be detected on the surfaces scanned by satellites, and therefore stand as a fundamental representational problem—indeed a problem of a historically new and original type. (2)

A performative reading of the map, however, has the capacity to reprogram reference: what emerges out of the lines is not only a caricature of global commerce but also of a different traffic entirely, namely, some of the otherwise invisible direct dispersal routes currently facilitating a floral and faunal interchange unprecedented in its magnitude and frequency. Major contemporary ecological developments can be read out of this map: that the spatial distribution of nonhuman life today is increasingly the result of this reemergence of a global supercontinent stitched together by transcontinental and transoceanic transportation systems servicing commercial, military, and tourism sectors; that emergent biogeographies are decreasingly the result of natural-historical processes of species dispersion; in other words, that plate tectonics, sea-floor spreading, glaciation, continental drift and the other primary geomorphological factors have had their relevance eclipsed by military expansion, industrial development, integration of financial markets, foreign-direct investment, trans-national trade agreements, and international tourism—movements of capital to which the distribution and frequency of these expendable shipping probes attest. The great physical migration barriers, erected by the massive geological processes, which once gave rise to species differentiation, are being rendered irrelevant by the global transportation infrastructure. The reconstitution of Pangea thus does not signal a return to a state of primeval unity, but rather a further iteration of a tectonic agglomeration that occurs without so much as an earthquake.

Elsewhere the urge to map human influence takes a more problematic turn for a mapping of the social, as in the case of the phantasmagoric dissemination of the footprint in the ecological imagination. Consumption footprints, carbon footprints, water footprints: the human footprint today bears the mark of a planetary Oedipus, in that the average ecological footprint in the U.S.—which measures how much land and water area a human population requires to produce the resource it consumes and to absorb its wastes—has swollen to an estimated 9.4 global hectares, or roughly a million square feet (WWF). *Per pair of feet*. At first glance none need ask today, in the manner of that infamous Theban biped, *Where shall now be found the footprint, hard to trace, of ancient guilt?* Yet the ecological debt of the global North, for all its unmistakability in an industrial and agricultural setting, leaves a harder to trace, but no less destructive *legacy* (itself bearing the traces of Derrida's leg work in *legs de Freud*) in those terrestrial systems otherwise undisturbed by human activity. These hard to trace tracks of bioinvasion—the absence of a familiar birdsong, a persistent cough, a mottled leaf, the soft touch of algae on an otherwise sandy ocean floor—point to a fundamental shift in the organization of the biophysical, one that often goes unregistered topographically, is soundless as opposed to merely "silent", and seemingly unspectacular, but potentially more destructive and deconstructive of the environment than any other form of climate change. Paradoxically a bioregional attunement to local changes leads to the dissolution of the locus into a polytopic confluence of "socioecological processes occurring at quite different scales" that David Harvey and others have analyzed (542). Following Harvey and Jameson outside of the *polis*, or less adventurously to the (hardly) vacant lots within the city, I want to argue that the social, its dissolution, and its potential recuperation achieve a certain visibility, and sets off an archive fever, in the promised disaggregation of vibrant ecosystems into "ecoslums" of "weedy species, relics, and ghosts" (Meyer 7).

Biotic Globalization and the End(s) of Oikopolitics

These largely untheorized and scarcely administrated spaces contain the traces to which I propose (re)introducing to critical attention. In ecosystems least subjected to administrative control, technological mediation, and economic exploitation we can nonetheless make out the imprint of globalization. This claim can be made without falling into the trap, identified by Bergson and Jameson, that the proliferation of "multinational species" throughout ecosystems, for example, would be so many caricatures of corporate conglomerates. These nonhuman, post-cosmos cosmopolitans are not caricatures but products, however unmarketable, signifying how late capitalism is ghostwriting and multinational corporations underwriting ecosystems across the planet. But there is another side to this story. What is startling is not the eclipse of nature—divested of aura and defined as "a bundle of ecosystem services" (Kareiva 1869)—by history but rather the glimmering awareness that *globalization is capable of jumping species.* There remains the promise, not unconsidered by growing ranks of biosecurity specialists, that these ghastly and ghostly ecologies of invasion will sabotage the mode of production that unintentionally produced them. As species continue to opportunistically appropriate the global transportation infrastructure for their own dissemination, an unintended modality of globalization appears on the horizon: *biotic globalization.*[6] Understanding this shift necessitates something of a critical climate change: a turn away from the urban(e) common-places of multinational capital—those spaces well articulated by architect Keller Easterling as "organization space"—and toward the peripheral underinstrumentalized spaces currently in the process of being non-deliberately formatted by globalization: the increasingly cosmopolitan and multinational life systems inhabiting streams, valleys, lakes, meadows, forests and tropical islands.[7]

Such a call for a change of critical venue might appear embarrassingly belated following the acknowledged penetration of the market into both the most intimate and peripheral spaces and the attendant unavailability of a tenable concept of distance in political and critical theory. This redundancy can be exaggerated by recalling the image of the shipping lanes and the reading that the infrastructures of a global economy underwrite contemporary restructurings of biogeography. But even when the natural-historical production of local ecological communities is facilitated (in both productive and destructive senses of a *Bahnung*) by a global economic system, and even when the "integrity" and health of the remaining "intact" ecosystems is increasingly dependent on the management of conservationists, the translocation of life referred to as biological invasion signals that these mutating ecosystems cannot be simply absorbed into the dominant economic system. This is where things get interesting. While Timothy Morton offers a compelling account of an "ecology without nature" the unmanageable ecologies of invasion present the apparent aporia of an *ecology without the oikos*—an ecological thought shorn of the aesthetic ideology of the household, immune to domestication, and requiring a critical vocabulary of the terrestrial that does not prep, already at the level of perception, the landscape for an inevitable anthropogeomorphological modification.

In the sheer desperation of the sentence, *The enemy is Mother Nature,* the limit of the economics of nature-as-oikos announces itself. More than an accountable mother, making "nature" an enemy, a *hostis*, must be understood as a form of primitive accumulation, an *underwriting*, a first step or first strike toward making nature a *host*, and thereby subject to the law of hospitality (with statistically calculable lapses into inhospitability), ultimately subject and subjected to the law of the anthropomorphic household, an *oikonomia*. Derrida's thinking around the sentence, *nous ne savons pas ce que c'est, l'hospitalité*, could be a pivot point of a critical reorientation in an era of invasion meltdowns. Hospitality, or *Wirtbarkeit* as Kant defines and delimits *Hospitalität* in the third definitive article of perpetual peace, is glossed by Derrida on the basis of the *Wirt* that "governs the whole lexicon of *Wirtschaft*, which is to say, economy and, thus, *oikonomia*, law of the household" ("Hospitality" 6). But what is the subject of hospitality when ecosystems, overrun by exotics, increasingly stand *before* the law of the household?[8] Species invasion does not pose a novel challenge to hospitality—the shock comes from the generosity of the ecosystem to the foreigner—but rather illuminates the self-contradiction that hospitality, as latent *hostipitality*, harbors in its own body. The limit of the project of conflating the feral ecosystem with the "natural" (as "bundle of ecosystem services") is evident in the fact that most ecosystems not currently expropriated for human or corporate welfare are operating at a loss; the managerial and budgetary framework furnished by oikonomia registers everywhere only "ecological debt" and a sharp downturn in the availability of "ecological services."

Out of a politically, administratively, and more or less commercially disciplined movement of the majority of the biophysical world—witness not only these statistics but the budgetary consciousness that registers ecosystems in economic terms: a global North that appropriates nearly half of the planet's net primary productivity, consumes over one-third of the productivity of the oceanic shelf, uses a majority of freshwater run-off, and operates over 36,000 dams—out of this "administered world" (Adorno) an unregulated, unadministratable and undisciplined circulation of life is emerging under the banner of the invasive, commencing to undermine cemented conceptual frameworks and tropologies—including that of the topos itself, revealed as the polytopic—and even to undermine the economy that bases itself on the anticipated stability of the ecosystems (agricultural and otherwise), whose hospitality to exotics and invasives has been severely underestimated.[9] As the return of the repressed on a planetary scale, species invasion exacerbates, in the frustration of the global attempt to fold ecology into the economy, coming agricultural crises. It portends the invasion of multiple species into every arena of human life, including the political, and in this sense the discourse, or the trope taking the place of a discourse, of "invasion" in ecology could be read as the paroxysm of what Angela Mitropoulos, following Hannah Arendt, terms an *oikopolitics*—articulated doubly in the blurring of the public (commons) and the private (enterprise) as well as in the attempt of politics to secure "an intimately normative disposition" on grounds "both familial and national" (72).

Less abruptly dismissive of an oikopolitics we could instead pose the question: if habitat loss and species invasion, as two of the leading forces shaping ecosystems, could stand to alter the make-up of the *oikos* (as paleonymy designating squat or slum rather than affluent single-family household), then what might an actual oikopolitics, readjusted for this eviction of past associations and occupation by new ones, promise? For the scope of this essay such a question is too speculative to answer, but in the foreclosure of oikopolitics emerges, no matter how rudimentary, a political ecology. In the rise of feral ecologies the eco- will not come out unscathed, but neither will the political where as it is based on, and projects, a certain normative disposition of the domestic. The insolvency of oikopolitics in an era of ecological invasion might be softened, then, to the foreclosure of the purchase of the oikos.

> There's a loss of features that allow you to describe where you live. When you characterize where you're from, you look out the window at the plants and animals even if you don't notice them immediately. I think there's something wrong with the loss of a distinct sense of being. It comes down to: where's my home? (Burdick 11)

Hardly just a question of the house. Already some time ago Adorno identified the contiguity between the seemingly apolitical "protective hand" of the gardener—like the biologist quoted above from *Out of Eden: An Odyssey of Ecological Invasion*—and an extreme hostility to immigration.

> The caring hand that even now tends the little garden as if it had not long since become a 'lot', but fearfully wards off the unknown intruder, is already that which denies the political refugee asylum. (34)

And it should be no surprise that same presidency that in 1999 produced Executive Order 13112, which authorized U.S. federal agencies to prevent the introduction and/or control the spread of alien invasive species had in 1994 militarized the U.S. / Mexico border with the establishment of Operation Gatekeeper; both are, in the words of Mike Davis, not originary events but only so much "gas on the flames of nativism" (11). But before the increasing absurdity of nativism, and the increasingly frequent irruption of nonspecies, the magnitude of the dissolution of the ecological "home" into the "lot" should have the capacity to inform political practice (encompassing even immigration policy) and not the other way around.

Dissemination

For all that a technologically assisted passage may be an aspect of adventure, biological life's willingness to take advantage of new openings suggests a capacity for mobilism, dispersal and self-transformation that is not reducible to any anthropic principle, let alone any single moment in the development of the technological apparatus. (Clark 104)

The task of this critical climate change is no longer to consider the extent to which globalization intervenes in, structures, disarms, imprints, or otherwise acts upon life systems; rather the explosion of translocated life invites consideration of how the biophysical world itself capitalizes on the generosity of infrastructure and the transportation industry for its own dissemination and proliferation. This shift in agency has been posed by Michael Pollan in *The Botany of Desire*: what if it is the plant that exploits us for its own proliferation and not the other way around? But what if this perspectival shift goes feral, leaving the *hortus conclusus* in which Pollan, the human bumblebee, is content to dwell? Such a perspective might find in biotic globalization an extreme and perhaps contentious case of what has been called "globalization from below" and in doing so would follow Nigel Clark, who argues that "there is no final cut-off point to this 'below,' no guard rail to keep us to the realm of the already humanized" (105).

By its very deterritorializing capabilities, plurality of affiliations, openness to mutation and hybridization, dissemination operates in a deconstructive modality far outside those textfields to which it has been discursively delimited. The exploitation of the accidental filiations between seme and semen, seeds and semes, is what dissemination is all about: finding new corridors, new communication networks, novel contacts and vectors of contagion, and new generative possibilities. Biotic modalities of dissemination capitalize on these entirely fortuitous resemblances too: the similarity, for a disseminule, between a drifting timber mass and the deck of a steamer, between a prolonged gale and the sail of a ship, between a land bridge and the landing gear of a 747. Floating as well as *flying* signifiers: "the force and form of [dissemination's] disruption explode the semantic horizon" (Derrida, *Points* 41). The extensification of dissemination takes form today in the ecological explosion, not only in the upheavals in the distribution of life, but first in the "enormous increase in numbers of some kind of living organism" (Elton 1). This novel usage of "explosion," popularized by Elton, itself signals an explosion by the word "explosion" out of a fixed semantic horizon. "I use the word 'explosion' deliberately," Elton confirms on the opening page of *The Ecology of Invasions*, "because it means the bursting out from control of forces that were previously held in restraint by other forces. Indeed, the word was originally used to describe the barracking of actors by an audience whom they were no longer able to restrain by the quality of their performance" (1). The OED corroborates Elton's etymology: "to explode: to clap and hoot a player off the stage; to drive away with expressions of disapprobation; to cry down; to banish ignominiously." The metaphoric "ecological explosion" is at the same time an explosion of the metaphor: an outbreak of the allegorical and a breakdown of the monosemantic within an ecological treatise, and moreover an outbreak that "explodes" out of the semantic horizon of the theater and into the wild: *the explosion goes feral*. And what does species invasion portend if not an explosion of dissemination in the transgression of one boundary after another? The inverse also deserves consideration: that species invasion signals the implosion of the oikos, and thus a mutation of the eco- into a horizon not constrained by any anthropology.

A Willingness to Take Advantage of New Openings

Yet, to return to an earlier point, Nigel Clark's compelling suggestion—that the explosive dissemination of invasive species could be attributed to a polymorphous perverse "willingness to take advantage of new openings"—still offends the dominant scientific sensibility. A survey of ecological literature evidences a refusal to consider the Pollanian possibility of dissemination outside of an anthropogenesis. "Humans," one reads, "have surpassed natural forces as the principal global disperser of vascular plants" (Mack and Lonsdale 95). More recently and more encompassing: "Species transfer though human agency is much more frequent, efficient and effective than through natural mechanisms and has no parallel in evolutionary history" (Kowarik and von der Lippe). While the initial articulation as such of "Man as a Dispersal Agent" may stem from a talk given in 1958 by botanist F.R. Fosberg, this talk is limited to domesticated species in agricultural space, whose proliferation and maintenance is dependent at every stage of life on a horticultural agency. Yet today species transfer increasingly deals with "escaped" and non-target *nonspecies* in peripheral spaces not actively managed. And the extent to which "human agency" is an adequate designation for such non-deliberate proliferation, often occurring outside of agricultural space, remains highly dubious. While the most noxious weeds in Australia, for example, consist mostly of exotics deliberately imported for ornamental gardens, their proliferation outside of horticultural space could not be achieved without their willingness to take advantage of new openings. The very problem of bioinvasion, if one may put it this way, is based on an extreme ecological irresponsibility on the part of human specie(s), coupled with an equally radical response-ability by biological life to technological development.

To wind down—both this paper and the anthropological machine—I propose turning to a critical passage of American literature, the close of Cormac McCarthy's *Blood Meridian*. Set in a crucial moment in American history, the years directly following the colonization and genocide of the Southwest, the closing scene of the novel takes place in a crude theater, which doubles as a bordello, situated amidst a theater of war populated only by "enormous ricks" and "colossal dikes" of buffalo skeletons, the blood of the massacres having evaporated. Amidst this landscape a bear in a crinoline dress, dancing to the sound of a barrel organ, is shot during a drunken altercation, and, though bleeding profusely, continues dancing in the eerie stillness, until it collapses and dies. The Judge, the monstrous Judge Holden, nonspecies *par excellence*, falls to speaking to the Kid, the novel's protagonist, of this stage. "There is room on this stage," says the Judge, "for one beast and one beast alone. All others are destined for a night that is eternal and without name. One by one they will step down into the darkness beyond the footlamps. Bears that dance, bears that don't" (331). What Judge Holden describes is the subscript of a species whose emblem consists in the image of an unruly audience that will not cease exploding until it has driven every other actor off the stage. As definitive as his totalitarian proclamation sounds in a country currently defined by a military doctrine of full-spectrum domination, the mutually assured destruction of the environmental and financial crises, both greatly amplified by wars abroad, supplants such outdated asymmetries. And while conservationists now propose programs of "managed relocation" and "assisted deportation" for species unable to track climate change fast enough, at the same time new (and far better funded) bureaucracies and biosecurity agencies have been established to stop the flow of invasives into and throughout the country.[10] These seemingly opposing movements, however, work in tandem with the wealth of commercial activities tied to the destruction of habitat—namely, to ensure the subjection of the biosphere to political, administrative, and commercial control. Of all the hats he wears—scalp-hunter, natural-historian, scientist, and politician—Judge Holden's legendary ledger book, in which he inscribes his anthropological discoveries before consigning them to the fire, places him foremost in the position of a administrator, a manager of budgets.

> Whatever in creation exists without my knowledge exists without my consent. He looked out at the dark forest in which they were bivouacked. He nodded toward the specimens he'd collected. These anonymous creatures, he said, may seem little or nothing in the world. Yet the smallest crumb can devour us. Any smallest thing beneath yon rock out of men's knowing. Only nature can enslave man and only when the existence of each last entity is routed out and made to stand naked before him will he be properly suzerain of the earth. [...] The Judge placed his hands on the ground. He looked at his inquisitor. This is my claim, he said. And yet everywhere upon it are pockets of autonomous life. Autonomous. In order for it to be mine nothing must be permitted to occur upon it save by my dispensation. (199)

But suzerains as well as stewards of the earth, subjected to dialectical *Umschlag*, both belong to ruined mythologies. In our ecologies of war only a limited and highly discrete control is capable of being exercised. The novel pathways of biotic migration are too engrained in a modern technicity to be eradicated without a total collapse of the global economy, and yet metropolitan space is too sprawling to permit the unassisted passage of most species. Until further notice these government agencies, as well as Judge Holden's apocalyptic pronouncements, will remain, as one aptly calls them, a security theater.

Notes

1. See Keulartz and Van der Weele.

2. See Larson.

3. "On the return to England of the Durham University Exploration Society's Eire Expedition in 1954," writes H.T. Clifford, "the members were asked to scrape off the mud from any footwear worn on the expedition, but not since their return" (129–30). The results of this ingenious experiment, when the mud samples were placed in sterilized pots in an unheated greenhouse, were robust: from 22.1 grams of dry mud sixty-five plants were raised. In a later experiment involving the writer's own footwear, a sample from a single boot yielded 176 seedlings of Poa annua (annual bluegrass) alone.

4. See Kareiva et al.

5. From Peter Kareiva, Sean Watts, Robert McDonald and Tim Boucher, "Domesticated Nature: Shaping Landscapes and Ecosystems for Human Welfare", *Science* (29 June 2007): 1866-1869. Reprinted with permission from AAAS. Readers may view, browse, and/or download material for temporary copying purposes only, provided these uses are for noncommercial personal purposes. Except as provided by law, this material may not be further reproduced, distributed, transmitted, modified, adapted, performed, displayed, published, or sold in whole or in part, without prior written permission from the publisher.

6. See Mark Davis.

7. See Easterling.

8. As the *Wall Street Journal* recently reported, the global foreclosure crisis has spawned an unlikely ecosystem: the backyard swimming pool. Thousands of swimming pools of foreclosed properties are rapidly transforming from chemical baths to vernal pools. As pioneered in the aftermath of Hurricane Katrina, city officials are introducing *Gambusia affinis*, commonly known as the "mosquito fish," into these pools. Now known as the "foreclosure fish," these organisms point to the capacity of the abandoned house to transform into an ecosystem in its own right. "The mosquito fish is well suited for a prolonged housing slump. Hardy creatures with big appetites, they can survive in oxygen-depleted swimming pools for many months, eating up to 500 larvae a day and giving birth to 60 fry a month" (Corkey).

9. See Sanderson et. al.

10. See McLachan, Hellman, and Schwartz's "A Framework for Debate of
    Assisted Migration in an Era of Climate Change."

Works Cited

Adorno, Theodor. *Minima Moralia: Reflections on Damaged Life*. Trans. E. F. N.
    Jephcott. London: Verso, 1984.

Burdick, Alan. *Out of Eden: An Odyssey of Ecological Invasion*. New York: Farrar,
    Strauss & Giroux, 2005.

Clark, Nigel. "The Demon-Seed: Bioinvasion as the Unsettling of Environmental
    Cosmopolitanism." *Theory, Culture & Society* 19 (2002): 101–125.

Clifford, H.T. "Seed Dispersal on Footwear." *Proceedings of the Botanical Society of the
    British Isles* 2 (1956): 129–130.

Coates, Peter. *American Perceptions of Immigrant and Invasive Species: Strangers on the
    Land*. Berkeley: University of California Press, 2006.

Cohen, Tom and Mike Hill. "Introduction: Black Swans and Pop-up Militias: War
    and the 'Re-rolling' of Imagination." *The Global South* 3.1 (2009): 1–17.

Corkey, Michael. "For Mortgages Underwater, Help Swims In." *Wall Street Journal*. 9
    May 2008, eastern ed.: A1+.

Crosby, Alfred W. Ecological Imperialism: The Biological Expansion of Europe,
    900–1900. New York: Cambridge University Press, 1986.

Davis, Mark. "Biotic Globalization: Does Competition from Introduced Species
    Threaten Biodiversity." *Bioscience* 53 (2003): 481–489.

Davis, Mike. Introduction. *Operation Gatekeeper*. By Josesph Nevins. New York:
    Routledge, 2001. 1–11.

De Landa, Manuel. *A Thousand Years of Nonlinear History*. New York: Swerve, 2002.

Derrida, Jacques. "Hostipitality." *Angelaki* 5.3 (2000): 5–18.

---. *Points… : Interviews, 1974–1994*. Trans. Peggy Kampf. Stanford: Stanford
    University Press, 1995.

---. "Structure, Sign, and Play in the Discourse of the Human Sciences." *Writing and
    Difference*. Trans. Alan Bass. Chicago: University of Chicago Press, 1978. 278–93.

Easterling, Keller. *Organization Space*. Cambridge: MIT Press, 1999.

Elton, Charles S. *The Ecology of Invasions by Animals and Plants*. London: Methuen, 1958.

Fosberg, F.R. "Man as a Dispersal Agent." *The Southwestern Naturalist* 3 (1958): 1–6.

Harvey, David. "Cosmopolitanism and the Banality of Geographical Evils." *Public Culture* 12:2 (2000): 529–64.

Jameson, Fredric. *The Geopolitical Aesthetic: Cinema and Space in the World System*. Bloomington: Indiana University Press, 1992.

Kaplan, Robert D. "The Coming Anarchy." *The Atlantic Monthly* 273.2 (1994): 44–76.

Kareiva, Peter, et al. "Domesticated nature: shaping landscapes and ecosystems for human welfare." *Science* 316 (2007): 1866–1869.

Keulartz, Jozef and Cor Van der Weele. "Framing and Reframing in Invasion Biology." *Configurations* 16 (2008): 93–115.

Kowarik, I. and M. von der Lippe. "Pathways in Plant Invasions." *Biological Invasions. Ecological Studies* 193 (2007): 29–47.

Larson, Brendon. "The war of the roses: demilitarizing invasion biology." *Frontiers in Ecology and Environment* 3.9 (2005): 495–500.

Lewis, Martin W. and Karen Wigen. *The Myth of Continents: A Critique of Metageography*. Berkeley: University of California Press, 1997.

Mack, R.N. and W.M. Lonsdale. "Humans as Global Plant Dispersers: Getting More than We Bargained For." *Bioscience* 51.2 (2001): 95–102.

McCarthy, Cormac. *Blood Meridian*. New York: Vintage, 1992.

McLachan, J. S., J.J. Hellman, and M.W. Schwartz. "A Framework for Debate of Assisted Migration in an Era of Climate Change." *Conservation Biology* 21 (2007): 297–302.

Meyer, Stephen M. *The End of the Wild*. Somerville, MA: Boston Review, 2006.

Mitropoulos, Angela. "Oikopolitics, and Storms." *The Global South* 3:1 (2009): 66–82.

Morton, Timothy. *Ecology Without Nature: Rethinking Environmental Aesthetics*. Cambridge, MA: Harvard University Press, 2007.

Pollan, Michael. *The Botany of Desire: A Plant's Eye View of the World*. New York: Random House, 2001.

Sanderson, et al. "The Human Footprint and the Last of the Wild." *Bioscience* 52 (2002): 891–904.

US Congress. Office of Technology Assessment, Harmful Non-Indigenous Species in the United States, OTA-F-565. Washington, DC: US Government Printing Office, 1993.

WWF. "*Living Planet Report* 2008." Web. 22 Apr. 2010. <http://assets.panda.org/downloads/living_planet_report_2008.pdf>.

Chapter 8

Bioethics

Bioethics Otherwise, or, How to Live with Machines, Humans, and Other Animals

JOANNA ZYLINSKA

For thinking concerning the animal, if there is such a thing,
derives from poetry. There you have a thesis: it is what
philosophy has, essentially, had to deprive itself of.

– Jacques Derrida, *The Animal That Therefore I Am*

It seems that an animal is in the world as water in the water.

– Bojan Šarčević, video project, Galerie BQ, Cologne

I never wanted to be posthuman, or posthumanist,
any more than I wanted to be postfeminist.

– Donna Haraway, *When Species Meet*

Broken Wings

How can the human speak in the shadow of the post-humanist critique? This essay arises out of a prolonged moment of doubt, a cognitive and affective confusion over the ontology and status of what goes under the name of "man." Now, that confusion is of course nothing new. It has been inherent to the disciplinary inquiry within the *human*ities conducted under the aegis of philosophical positions broadly associated with post-structuralism over the last few decades. The early twenty-first century attempts on the part of humanities scholars to turn to a more serious engagement with those hard sciences that deal with different human parts and particles—anatomy, neurology, genetics—have contributed even further to this uncertainty, as has the discovery that the typical signal points of the human such as language, tool use, culture (or "leaving traces"), and emotions are to be found across the species barrier.[1] Rather than aim at ascertaining the identity of the human/non-human animal, in all its biodigital configurations, what I am predominantly concerned with in this essay is discussing how this transformed understanding of the human can help us not only *think better* about ourselves and others who may or may not be like us, but also *live better* with others—machines, humans, and other animals. The emphasis in this investigation falls on the pragmatics of the "how" as much as on the nature of that "we." My focus here is therefore primarily ethical rather than ontological. And yet the very inquiry into ways of living a good life must be accompanied by the assessment not only of who will do the living but also of who will be involved in the process of judging its goodness, and in structuring a theoretical discourse around our biological and political forms of existence.

In a certain sense this essay is an attempt to return to the human "after the cyborg."[2] This attempt is underpinned by an intellectual and, dare I say it, personal imperative to find a way out of what I see as the posthumanist impasse of some strands of contemporary cultural theory, whereby the widespread acceptance of the notions of transhuman relationality, interspecies kinship, and machinic becoming by many humanities scholars seems to have diminished the need for a more rigorous interrogation of the singularity of trans-species and intra-species difference. It is thus armed with doubt and singularity as my analytical tools, coupled with the intransigent use of the "I" pronoun, which simultaneously undermines and reasserts the humanist pretence of this piece of writing, that I set out to explore these issues. Obviously, there is also a possibility that this posthuman, all-too-human interrogation is just another exercise in narcissism, a desperate attempt to return to the self and hang on to a fantasy of human exceptionalism. In this context, Jacques Derrida's query "Is there animal narcissism?" (51–52) becomes something of an accusation, aimed perhaps at those of us who are still obsessed by Descartes' question: "But as for me, who am I?"

Still, post Freud, this fantasy of human exceptionalism is not an easy one to retain, as Donna Haraway explains poignantly in her book, *When Species Meet*. The three great wounds to the primary narcissism of the human—the Copernican revolution, the Darwinian theory of evolution, and the Freudian excavation of the unconscious—have seriously destabilized humanity's geographical, historical, and psychic self-centeredness.[3] To these Haraway adds a fourth, "informatic or cyborgian" wound, "which infolds organic and technological flesh" (*Species* 12). As a result, the human has to think of her- or himself as always already technological, as co-constituted and co-evolving with the world which is made up of animate and inanimate entities. To explain this performative process, Haraway takes recourse to the metaphor of dance and argues that this process of co-constitution is never fully stabilized or accomplished, and that each intervention, each movement, generates a new state of becoming. "All the dancers are redone through the patterns they enact," she writes (25).

Applying a critical lens to the theoretical offerings on interspecies relations by Haraway and two other theorists of becoming-with-animals, Matthew Calarco and Paul Patton, I want to raise some broader questions about the emergent (inter)discipline of animal studies which has gone some way towards thinking human-nonhuman relations precisely *as relations*. This is why "animal studies" is sometimes referred to as "human-animal studies" (Calarco 3). "While there is no widely agreed upon definition of what precisely constitutes animal studies," as Calarco acknowledges in the introduction to his *Zoographies*, "it is clear that most authors and activists working in the field share the conviction that 'the question of the animal' should be seen as one of the central issues in contemporary critical discourse" (1). The key debates within animal studies thus focus, on the one hand, on the being or (for the lack of a better word) "nature" of animals, and, on the other, on the possibility of making the human-animal distinction (2). Within this, the question of *living-with* but also of *living-as* animals becomes central to this field of inquiry.

It is the promises and limitations of the very notion of interspecies or companion ethics as outlined by animal studies theorists that are of particular interest to me in this piece. To let the cat out of the bag, so to speak, I am not going to be too optimistic about the viability of any such ethical framework or model. This conceptual hesitation will be outlined against the wider canvas of what I called in my earlier work "alternative bioethics." "Departing from the more accepted definition of bioethics as the interrogation of 'ethical issues arising from the biological and medical sciences,' ... [b]ioethics for me stands for an 'ethics of life,' whereby life names both the physical, material existence of singular organisms (what the Greeks called *zoē*) and their political organization into populations (*bios*)" (Zylinska, *Bioethics* xii–xiii). Traditionally, the bioethical debate about issues of health and life management has been primarily procedural, with questions of moral agency, political influence, and economic interest already pre-decided in many of the dominant ethical paradigms which are applied to resolving the so-called moral dilemmas concerning genomic interventions, cosmetic surgery, and cloning. Rooted in the philosophy of alterity, the "alternative" non-systemic bioethics I propose instead takes as its focal point relationality and kinship between humans and non-humans—such as animals and machines. Yet, for all my consideration of interspecies relationality and the recognition of its significance as both a set of material circumstances and an ethical injunction, I stop short of embracing companion or interspecies ethics as a viable proposition for what we can tentatively (but not unproblematically) call the posthuman age. In the argument that follows I will attempt to provide a justification for this ethical stoppage on my part and work through the three fundamental blind spots that the intermeshed trajectories of thought in animal studies have frequently run into. These are, to shoot from the hip:

The humanist blind spot, which is centered around issues of language, culture, affect, and the violence of imposition. Arguably, the majority of what we can call distributed positions on interspecies ethics return (to) the human through the back door, even if the theorist has temporarily descended into the kennel, looked her cat seriously in the eye or his horse in the mouth. That return in itself is not so much of a problem, I will argue, provided it is recognized as such, rather than slid or galloped over.

The technicist blind spot, where much work goes into recognizing the animal's anima, i.e. its "subjecitivity," with the animal becoming an extension of the human. Entities designated as "human" and "animal" then get carved out of a complex field of co-constitutive technical forces and situated on the side of "nature."

The violentist blind spot, where violence is posited as the enemy of ethics, something that should be overcome both in "us" and in "the world," rather than being seen as a structuring and inevitable condition of all relationality.[4]

The reason I have decided to reroute my discussion of (the difficulties of) interspecies ethics here via the thought of Haraway, Calarco, and Patton is not because I am positioning these thinkers as the representatives or figureheads of "animal studies"—although of course they cannot by themselves fully resist such an interpellation. I am turning to them primarily because in their respective works they have actually taken some significant steps towards addressing, more or less explicitly, the three blind spots outlined above. To what extent these efforts have been successful and whether they can help us envisage some better ways of living with non-human others is something I will discuss in the course of what follows. The essay will end with a tentative outline of a bioethics for the twenty-first century, a kind of "in-the-clouds" proposal that piggybacks on the ideas of the animal studies scholars such as Haraway, even if it ultimately takes many of their notions in a somewhat different direction.

Haraway's *When Species Meet* is an exceptional book precisely because of its consistently playful yet rigorous effort to undermine human exceptionalism through a series of philosophical exegeses, scientific reports, auto-ethnographic accounts, and personal anecdotes. It is also an attempt to enact what we may describe as lived philosophy, whereby the theorist lays on the table, for all to see, both her well-processed intellectual trajectories and her much more convoluted desires and passions. Such an act of dual revelation is not entirely new: feminist and queer scholars have been attempting to incorporate, literally and figuratively, their passions, desires, and everyday foibles into their theoretical and activist projects for a few decades now. Importantly, Haraway is prepared to turn her own critical lens not only on her ideas, but also on her own everyday lived practices—her agility training with her dog Cayenne, her family history—while also exposing, for all to see, the weaknesses and contradictions of any such "live/d theory." It is precisely while stumbling and becoming entangled in the texts and textures of human-nonhuman environments made up of academics, dogs, bureaucrats, Californian sunshine, wine, training competitions, research papers, French philosophers, and technologies big and small that Haraway's argument becomes most powerful.

Puppy Love

Haraway has frequently been accused of either hedging around ethical questions in her earlier books, or of resorting all too early to the American legal discourse, with its clearly identified, individualized moral and political subjects. However, in her latest offerings—primarily her 2003 text, *The Companion Species Manifesto*—she makes a more explicit effort to outline an alternative (bio)ethics of living-with, and emerging-with, other beings. The origins of her ethics of companion species are experiential and spring from "taking dog-human relationships seriously" (3). Significantly, the natural habitats for these cross-species acts of encounter and emergence are always already technological. In her attempt at thinking how to live well together, Haraway insists that the orientation of this ethical project has to transcend the wishes and desires of man as the sole arbitrator of "goodness." This is when she makes one of those well-known gestures of hers which tend to leave many of her critics, myself included, somewhat baffled: namely, she proposes "love" as the source of an ethical bind between companion species. Although she is careful to distinguish it from technophiliac or canonophiliac narcissism (i.e. the belief that dogs are either "tools" for human activity or sources of unconditional affection and spiritual fulfillment for humans), this notion of love as ethical co-emergence and cohabitation entails a number of problems. Not least among these is the way in which the values that underpin her ethics of companion species—love, respect, happiness, and achievement—have a distinctly human "feel" to them precisely because it is the human who defines the meaning of these values and their appropriateness for all companion species. There is no escape from the philosophical quandary that even the most committed of efforts to give dogs what they want, and not what humans merely want for them, inevitably depend on the human ideas of "want," "satisfaction," and "gift." This is not to say that dogs should tell "us" what "they" want; only that a value-driven theory of good is not the most appropriate basis for this kind of ethics.[5]

To a certain extent, *When Species Meet* is a continuation of Haraway's attempt to think an interspecies ethics, but one of the most significant developments in this book concerns the suspension of any programmatic, value-driven intimations of Haraway's prior ethical outlook. Instead, she is much more self-reflexive and hesitant. Picking up a thread from her earlier work, Haraway proposes that "to be a situated human being is to be shaped by and with animal familiars" (47). While this is an ontological given for her, an ethical way of being-with needs to involve curiosity about our ontology and our becoming—i.e., about those who are not us, but who constantly challenge us through their gaze, their touch or through the lick of their tongue.

Sealed with a Kiss

Haraway lays out her ethical injunction for animal curiosity—arguably the softest and yet, paradoxically, also the strongest building block of any ethics of interspecies cohabitation—through an encounter with that oft-cited text within the posthumanist circles, Jacques Derrida's essay, "The Animal That Therefore I Am (More to Follow)." In this text Derrida provides an account of finding himself naked, gazed at, and thus put to shame, by his own cat—"a real cat, truly, believe me," he insists (6). Now, Haraway is very upfront about her affections: she loves her dog— "We have had forbidden conversations; we have had oral intercourse," she confesses (16)—and rather likes Derrida. She is just slightly worried about the latter's actual feelings for his cat. More precisely, she is disappointed with Derrida for ultimately using his cat as a stepping stone for a nice philosophical parable about human unknowingness, and for not being intimate enough with his cat or curious enough about her. Begrudgingly, Haraway writes: "he did not seriously consider an alternative form of engagement...one that risked knowing something more about cats and *how to look back*, perhaps even scientifically, biologically, and *therefore* also philosophically and intimately" (20). Derrida himself admits as much: "my having confessed to feeling disarmed before a small mute living being, and my avowed desire to escape the alternative of a projection that appropriates and an interruption that excludes, all that might lead one to guess that I am not ready to interpret or experience the gaze that a cat fixes, without a word, on my nakedness..." (18). In this very event Derrida came "right to the edge of respect" but then got sidetracked by himself, by his own nakedness and his pee-pee, and hence his own philosophico-anthropocentric narcissism. He thus "failed a simple obligation of companion species; he did not become curious about what the cat might actually be doing, feeling, thinking, or perhaps making available to him in looking back at him that morning." In Haraway's reading, that day Derrida "missed a possible invitation, a possible introduction to otherworlding" (20).

This is a serious admonition; one as a failed animal lover—i.e. someone who has never owned a dog, does not coo over kittens, and has no desire to go horse riding—I take personally, which is also perhaps the sign of the aforementioned narcissism (as well as unreconstructed humanism). Yet what if Derrida did indeed "get curious," but then refused to rechannel this curiosity through his own imagined ideas of desire, love, respect, and companionship?

Love is Not Enough

The uneasiness of these admonitions raised by Haraway—not just against Derrida, but also against other "metropolitan" theorists of critical persuasion (like myself) who are somehow prevented by their own disciplinary corset and urban upbringing from caring sufficiently and adequately about animals—raises for me the important issue of what it actually means to become undone by another species, and to redo oneself after the encounter. Is this "becoming-undone" the best post-humanism can hope for, where the "post-" refers to the transformative interspecies encounter rather than any straightforward overcoming of the human (Haraway, *Species* 21)? In which case what happens if this animal is not just a dog, a cat, or a horse from the family of befriended or domestic animals, but rather a parasite, bacteria, or fungus? (Incidentally, all these are also included in Haraway's notion of companion species, even if they are not really properly "encountered" as such in her writings.) In a review of *When Species Meet*, Boria Sax similarly criticizes Haraway for showing "hardly any interest in wild creatures, except when these offer opportunities to display human ingenuity." Love for Ms Cayenne Pepper, as Haraway's Australian shepherd is often referred to affectionately, seems to win over an obligation to tell a multispecies story, with what Derrida calls "unsubstitutable singularity" (9) giving way to mere particularism—or, to put it in less generous terms, to being undone by pet love. Rather than worry about overcoming the human-animal difference via the shared experience of "other-worlding," perhaps we should spend more time tracing the already embedded, "worlded" differences between animals, breeds, and kinds, and analyze what they *mean*, not just how they unfold? Horses, for example, are said to induce either reticence or careless familiarity in those who do not know them, according to Australian sociologist Ann Game. "But to live relationally with horses," writes Game, "is to know and respect their otherness and difference, which, in turn, implies recognition of the otherness in us" (10).

What shall we do then with Calarco's postulate that "*the human-animal distinction can no longer and ought no longer to be maintained*" (3)? If by distinction we mean the listing of structural differences that safely place different beings in entirely discrete categories—Homo sapiens, Canis lupus familiaris, Erinaceus europaeus—then perhaps there are good reasons for suspending, at least temporarily, such a typology, especially given how it can be used to justify interspecies dependency and exploitation (even if we are to conclude eventually that power relations inevitably define human-animal coexistence). Yet the acknowledgement of a gap between human and animal as conceptual categories at our disposal is necessary if we are not to fall all too easily into uncritical species continuism, a theory that claims that "we" are basically "animals" professed by neo-Darwinists such as Richard Dawkins. The latter of course exerts all his human cognitive privileges in carrying out the theoretical maneuver of subsuming one conceptual category—i.e., "the human," under another—"the animal." In the same way, Calarco's statement about the need to obviate "*the human-animal distinction*" can only ever be made *from the point of species difference*.

When Calarco asserts that "philosophy still has a unique and significant role to play" in transforming "our thinking about what we call animals," he seemingly remains unaware of the fact that his proposition reaffirms the very distinction he is trying to overcome (4). In describing Derrida's reluctance to "abandon the human-animal distinction" altogether as "dogmatic" (145), Calarco reveals and simultaneously conceals his own gesture of attempting to continue philosophizing about the animal, even if the latter is seen as part of a broader system of co-emerging materialities. Now, I do not want to enter into a discussion as to whether the animal can or cannot do philosophy, since I am not sure such a discussion would get us very far. I only aim to foreground this differential, cutting gesture of *philosophizing about the other*—which is singularly different from, say, *eating the other*. It is not therefore surprising that Derrida would not abandon this evidently troublesome and politically sensitive human-animal distinction. After all, any such act of "abandonment" could only ever be conducted from within the most anthropocentric position of not just "I am," but also "I decide" and "I profess," with all the hegemonic authority this carries. What Calarco therefore sees as Derrida's "refusal" is perhaps only a hesitation, one that actually adds strength to the latter's attempt at practicing "animal studies." Incorporating such a moment of hesitation as a condition of responsible interspecies ethics, however, is not something either Calarco or Haraway particularly want to consider. Significantly, in turning to the latter's "Cyborg Manifesto" on the penultimate page of his own book, Calarco takes as a statement of fact what is evidently a normative proposition—i.e., that "the boundary between human and animal is thoroughly breached" (148)—a proposition that, incidentally, remains disconnected from any particular material context and that carries all the rhetorical force of an "I" that writes, signs, and breaches. Ironically, Calarco proposes that a better solution than Derrida's "refusal" is to be found in Haraway's closing statement that "many *people* no longer feel the need for such a separation" (140) (I hope I do not need to explain the unwitting joke once I've italicized it for you, dear reader?).

Don't Let the Stars Get in Your Eyes

Where do we go from here? How far can this hesitation about the animal take us—epistemologically and ethically? Derrida provides us with the following, much more jagged but perhaps also much more responsible and thought out (in that old-fashioned anthropocentric way) suggestion:

There is no interest to be found in debating something like a discontinuity, rupture, or even abyss between those who call themselves men and what so-called men, those who name themselves men, call the animal. Everybody agrees on this; discussion is closed in advance; one would have to be more asinine than any beast...to think otherwise....The discussion is worth undertaking once it is a matter of determining the number, form, sense, or structure, the foliated consistency, of this abyssal limit, these edges, this plural and repeatedly folded frontier. The discussion becomes interesting once, instead of asking whether or not there is a limit that produces a discontinuity, one attempts to think what a limit becomes once it is abyssal, once the frontier no longer forms a single indivisible line but more than one internally divided line; once, as a result, it can no longer be traced, objectified, or counted as single and indivisible. What are the edges of a limit that grows and multiplies by feeding on an abyss? (30–31)

From there, Derrida develops a threefold thesis, which asserts that: (1) this abyssal rupture does not mark a straight and clear-cut distinction between two entities: Man and Animal; (2) the border of this abyssal rupture has a history which we cannot ignore or dismiss all too quickly; (3) beyond the border of the human there exists a heterogeneous multiplicity of the living, or "a multiplicity of organizations of relations among realms that are more and more difficult to dissociate by means of the figures of the organic and inorganic, of life and/or death" (31).

There is perhaps a similarity between what Derrida calls "a multiplicity of organizations" between indissociable realms and what Haraway understands as the co-evolution and co-emergence of the organic and the inorganic. This line of argument also points to the technical dimension of these multiple ontologies, whereby beings come to life precisely via the technical process of bringing-forth or creation, in which no fixed elements precede their mutual becoming. However, even if we are to take co-evolution and co-emergence as a starting point for considering ethical relations between species and kinds, I suggest we need to get there via the Derridean detour of caring not only about other beings and other species but also about the history and meaning of these processes of "saming" and "othering." This, in turn, requires us to recognize "our" kinship not just with animals but also with machines(s), with technics. Ethical responsibility stands for the ability and need to respond—"responders are themselves co-constituted in the responding" (Haraway, "Becoming" 116)—which applies to people as well as lab and domestic animals. It also entails acknowledging the inevitability of relations of dependency between and among humans, animals, and machines, some of which may include causing pain and killing—even though, as Haraway insists, such practices "should never leave their practitioners in moral comfort, sure of their righteousness" (*Species* 75).[6]

What emerges from the above is that violence and dependency are positioned as inevitable conditions of "worlding." This conclusion should not be seen as a get-out clause from ethical responsibility. The recognition of the inevitability of violence in any relation with alterity does not take away the injunction to both minimize the violence and reflect on it. An ethical theory that embeds violence into its framework—rather than just pushing it aside in a fantasy gesture of moral purification—promises to address the question of dependency in all its complexity. This does not imply imposing moral equivalence between all forms of violence and all forms of dependency, even if we accept that "[*a*]*ny* act of identification, naming, or relation is a betrayal of and a violence toward the Other" (Calarco 136).[7] Yet in spite of recognizing that there is no "pure" ethical position, "no way of living that is not also a way of someone, not just something, else dying differentially" (Haraway, *Species* 80), Haraway's proposal for "ruthlessly mundane," non-utilitarian interspecies ethics ultimately sounds rather fuzzy when she writes that "The needed morality, in my view, is culturing a radical ability to remember and feel what is going on and performing the epistemological, emotional, and technical work to respond practically in the face of the permanent complexity not resolved by taxonomic hierarchies and with no humanist philosophical or religious guarantees" (75). By saying this she seems to fall prey to what Simon Glendinning calls the "cognitivist presumption" of humanism, in the sense that the human acts and processes of "remembering," "feeling what is going on," and "performing practically" are not adequately assessed for their anthropocentrism (184). Again, this is not to say that humans need to invite "others"—animals, sentient machines—into their thinking, feeling, and acting circle: such a gesture would only confirm the taxonomic hierarchy. It is only to suggest that a certain doubt or hesitation should perhaps be introduced at the very foundation of any such ethical endeavor. Yes, there is a danger that this *ego dubito* will only be an extension of the Cartesian thinking and reasoning. Yet for it to be about the ethics of the other, rather than primarily about the ontology of the self, the outcome of this doubting process needs to be pointed elsewhere. *Ethical* doubt has the potential to turn the focus and attention of the study of interspecies relationality precisely to the alterity that is not in me. It does not therefore serve the ultimate reaffirmation of the human "I."

Anything else—no matter if I was to defend the special positioning of the human as a being with its own teleology and truth, or the species continuism of modern naturalism which only affirms differences of degree, not of kind—would require the reinstatement of the position of *knowing* the nature of interspecies difference and being able to arbitrate over it once and for all. There is ethical value in the injunction for curiosity about "animals," yet this curiosity has to be combined with the recognition of not knowing all that much about "them." Otherwise we face the danger that this curiosity will lead to the projection of our most unreformed beliefs, ideas, and desires onto "the animal other," with the alleged knowledge being a mere extension of what we thought we knew in the first place, a filtration of some observed behavior through the cognitive and conceptual apparatus at our disposal which also makes us believe that we have been co-constituted together—while in fact we have only constituted this "animal" in our own image (of "us" or "them"). The *ethical* recognition of this difference between human and animal does not therefore amount to knowing its nature once and for all. Indeed, any attempt to cognitively master it will only be a narrative, a story, one that inevitably has a mythical character. It will also be another technical prosthesis—alongside flint tools, hammers and computers—that shapes our systemic co-emergence in and with the world.[8]

Side Saddle

If stories and myths shape the human as much as technical tools and apparatuses do, one particular story that is of interest to me in the context of this enquiry into interspecies ethics concerns animal training as narrated by both Haraway and Paul Patton. Reflecting on training to a high standard of performance for competitions with her dog Cayenne, Haraway remains aware of the economies of class, leisure, and geography that shape this particular sport. She also acknowledges that it is the human who decides that training will take place, even though "[t]he human must [then] respond to the authority of the dog's actual performance" (221), and hence take account of what Game calls animal (or, to be more precise, horse) "sociality" (4). But even if we recognize, with Game, that in any training situation animals need to "*allow* people to teach them to be led" (4), we also need to acknowledge the problem of multiple temporalities—i.e., a difference between the animal present and the human future, which is also a difference between (strategic) necessity and expediency. Haraway admits to having had the same reservations regarding the perfecting of the breed to "produce dogs who could herd with matchless skill, win in conformation, excel in obedience and agility sports, and serve as pets with dignity" that many cultural theorists display, but she apparently changed her mind after she "fell in love" (129). Now, we should take this confession less as an acknowledgement that what she calls "the love of the breed" has clouded her critico-ethical judgment and more as an admittance to being with, amongst and close to animals; and thus also an admonition against critical theorists (such as myself perhaps) who only ever look at animals from far away, treating them as objects of interpretation while also reducing them to two-dimensional figures of speech. Haraway seems to be saying to us: some of you know *how to think* with animals but not really *how to live* with them—and actually *what to do* with them.

Analogous concerns underpin Paul Patton's attempt to think animal philosophy from the bottom, or rather saddle, up. His essay, "Language, Power, and the Training of Horses" in Cary Wolfe's edited collection, *Zoontologies*, opens with a generic declaration of animal love: "People love horses for all kinds of reason" (83). Patton himself fell in love with horses through the experience of learning to train them. In a similar vein to Haraway, he is attempting to combine his philosophical position rooted in continental philosophy with "a good story" about his training relationship with his horse Flash. And yet what is missing for me from

Patton's narrative is a deeper reflection on this desire to train, and hence master another being—and on the pleasure of that. Even if we recognize that precision in training involves making the horse "do the right thing," this does not explain why "we" would want to achieve this in the first place. What is the purposefulness of horse/man training? The argument about ennoblement borrowed from horse trainer Vicky Hearne that Haraway brings under the rubric of flourishing and that Patton also refers to is just too close to colonial narratives of improving the native for my own, admittedly paper-thin animal lover's comfort. Of course, Haraway and Patton are no strangers to postcolonial theory. Patton also realizes that "The aesthetico-moral defense of the activities for which animals are trained is corrupt...to the extent that it misrepresents what, anthropomorphically, we might call the 'values' of the animals involved and it projects onto them as natural certain aptitudes and airs that are valued by their all too human trainers" (93).

How does he then get out of the potential accusation of rationalizing certain human preferences and culturally acquired desires for beauty, grace, and skill through training practice? Not very well, I fear, as evidenced in the following declaration: "Disciplinary relations of command and obedience are precisely a means to create and maintain stable and civil relations between different kinds of beings, not only among individuals of the same species, but also between representatives of different species" (95). Conceding, after Nietzsche and Foucault, that all social relations are power relations does not resolve the socio-political quandary that not all social relations are the same; they do not all *mean* the same thing, and are not *necessary* in the same way. For example, how has a decision been reached that training horses is a good thing? I am not particularly convinced by the more spiritualist justification of human-horse training provided by Game as a way of living together more "creatively" (7–8). While the majority of us humans would probably agree that training horses is not morally equivalent to beating or eating horses, I also wonder what criteria underpin Patton's notion of "civility" that structures his declaration and how he has arrived at it. Patton says that we learn from animal training "that hierarchical forms of society between unequals are by no means incompatible with ethical relations and obligation toward other beings" (95). But this argument has to be developed further via the

notion of species singularity, the forgetting of which will only perpetu-
ate the species exceptionalism that both Haraway and Patton are so keen
to avoid. By asking "What is the point of training?" I am not therefore
promoting some kind of Edenic fantasy of free roaming wolves or mares.
I am only suggesting that a clarification is needed with regard to the affective investments of animal lovers and animal studies theorists. The
reflection on the trainer's desire to make the universe supple, to have it
bend under their command, is nevertheless something Haraway and Patton withhold in their affective analyses of human-animal relationships.
Even if we acknowledge, as Patton does, that a training relation is one
possible form of an ethical relation which "enhances the power and the
feeling of power of both horse and rider" (97), we are back in a logical
loop, with the theorist's fantasy and projection covering over the violence
involved in making the world and in making meanings in the world with
and via animals.

What's New Pussycat, or Bioethics Otherwise

Is there a way out? As the discussion above hopefully demonstrates, any
gesture of attempting to propose an ethical framework is always inevitably suspended between anthropocentrism and violence. Yet this recognition should not absolve us of an ethical responsibility to work out better ways of living-with—with humans, other animals, and machines. As
biotechnologies and digital media are constantly challenging our established ideas of what it means to be human and live a human life, they also
command a transformation of the recognized moral frameworks through
which we understand life, as well as a rethinking of who the moral subject is in the current conjuncture. The so-called post-humanist critique
discussed throughout this essay has the potential to call into question the
anthropocentric bias of our established ways of thinking—i.e., the belief
that the human is situated at the top of the "chain of beings" and that this
special positioning entitles him or her to a particular set of consumerist
and exploitative attitudes towards non-humans (mammals, fish, rainfor-
ests, the ecosphere as a whole, etc.). Following Haraway *et al.*, the human
can be understood instead as being part of a complex natural-technical
network and as emerging in a dynamic way out of this network. On this

emergence, the human is presented with an ethical task of having to make decisions, always in an uncertain terrain, about life, in all its different incarnations and enactments.

In the biodigital age, this tentatively differentiated human needs to respond to an expanded scope of obligations, beyond those exerted by singular human others. The field of bioethics thus has to deal not just with questions of the transformation of life on a biological level—via genomics, DNA sequencing, cloning, and so forth—but also with life situated in a broader political context, through questions of the financing of the biotech industry, of the database management of the immigration and asylum systems, of the normativity of cosmetic surgery, of national and cellular surveillance, of biocitizenship, etc. The decision-making processes of those who call themselves human, with all the awareness of the historical and cultural baggage this term carries, and of the temporary and fragile nature of any such identification, are important in any situation when issues of life and its multiple transformations are at stake. Involvement in these processes does not have to amount to the celebration of human superiority though: it should rather be seen as a practical mobilization of the human skills, however compromised and imperfect, of critical reflexivity and practical intervention. Now, the question of whether "animals" or "machines" should also engage in such ethical processes is irrelevant, even if we recognize that the features and behaviors that used to be seen as uniquely human have recently been identified across the species barrier. It is irrelevant because this responsibility only ever refers to "me": a temporarily stabilized singular human who emerges in-relation-with human and non-human others.

The moral quandary of whether "we" should respect parrots, bacteria, cyberdogs, or even iPods that is sometimes raised in the context of interspecies ethics shows a reluctance to submit this "we" category, in all its implied unity and speciesism, to a rigorous critique. Also, in the framework outlined throughout this essay ethics is not so much about respect, because respect assumes that I am already fully constituted as a moral agent before I encounter the other, any other, and then I can give this other my gift of recognition, care, and kindness. Instead, ethics can be thought more productively in terms of phenomenological responsiveness and moral responsibility—a position that assumes that whatever attitude I adopt towards the other, I am already responding to the other's presence and demand.[9] Indeed, sometimes withholding respect might be the most responsible thing to do, depending on the circumstances. Also, it is worth emphasizing again that the notion of the human—who, as soon as she takes up ethical responsibility, she differentiates herself from carrots, machines and the general flow of life—does not disappear altogether in this "alternative" bioethical theory, even if we raise some substantial questions for the humanist, anthropocentric assumptions around many traditional bioethical positions.

Understood in this way, bioethics becomes a supplement to both morality and politics; a prior demand on those of us who call themselves humans to respond to the difference of the world critically and responsibly, without taking recourse all too early to pre-decided half-truths, opinions, beliefs, and political strategies. But it is not something that can be "implemented" once and for all or become a practical tool for resolving specific moral dilemmas over life and death. The kind of alternative bioethics I am attempting to outline here cannot be instantiated in a single "example" because any such example would inevitably take over and even colonize the need for open-ended critical work of bioethics by becoming a measuring stick against which other bioethical cases and dilemmas could be compared.[10] In undertaking this kind of critical-creative work of bioethics, I am much more interested in shifting the parameters of the ethical debate from an individualistic problem-based moral paradigm in which rules can be rationally and strategically worked out on the basis of a previously agreed principle, to a broader political context in which individual decisions are always involved in complex relations of power, economy, and ideology.

By pointing to a place of difference as a productive site of relationality and interspecies kinship, bioethics as an ethics of life the way I envisage it has the capacity to challenge the hierarchical system of descent through which relations between species and life forms have traditionally been thought. At the same time, focusing on the multiple instances in which this difference manifests itself, always differently, is one way of ensuring that we do not collapse various beings and life forms into a seamless flow of life, and then continue philosophizing about it as if nothing had happened. This non-normative, technics-aware bioethics thus needs to seriously consider the polyvalent relations of co-evolution and co-emergence. However, it must also carry a visible trace of reflection on the very process of its creation: from the human vantage point of language, philosophy, and culture. In other words, this technics-aware bioethics entails an injunction to give an account of the violence of thinking ethics, including that of interspecies relations.

Importantly, doubt needs to become the condition and structuring device of such an alternative bioethics. Yet this is not the impartial doubt of the Cartesian ego cogito. Rather it involves the suspension of the cognitive essentialism that knows the nature of interspecies difference in advance, all too early. Even if this sounds like a much more tentative and hesitant ethical proposition than some of those discussed throughout the course of this essay (not to mention many procedural or value-based bioethical theories, where different forms of life are assigned value in advance and are then weighted against each other), it can perhaps speak more convincingly to those of "us" to whom animal love does not come "naturally," as it were. It can also keep a check on those animal studies experts who love their companion species, or even themselves *as* companion species, a little too much. Because the question that is posed to us is not only "What does my pet want?" or even the Cartesian "But as for me, whom am I?" but also, perhaps first of all, "And what if a bacteria responded?"

Notes

1. For a discussion of how the features and behaviors that used to be seen as uniquely human have been identified across the species barrier, see Wolfe 35 and Calarco 3.

2. The figure of the cyborg, borrowed from the tradition of cyberfeminism, has been an important concept in my work. In my *On Spiders, Cyborgs and Being Scared: The Feminine and the Sublime* and *The Cyborg Experiments: Extensions of the Body in the Media Age*, the cyborg served as a hybrid, material figure signaling the human's kinship with other creatures as well as the human's dependency on technology—or what the philosopher Bernard Stiegler has called "originary technicity." Yet the power of this metaphor has perhaps become somewhat exhausted, not only because of the transience of academic fashions for metaphors and concepts. While cyborgs for me have always been technical and processual, I am concerned that my continued use of this

concept may give too much ammunition to the proponents of many "fluid" theories of human-machine couplings, where the overall metaphor of the flow seems to have swept away any discrete beings and entities. But the defense or critique of the cyborg as a singular entity is not my primary aim in this essay. My efforts rather arise out of my dissatisfaction with *some aspects* of the relational theory of becoming which at times leads to an all-too-quick dissolution of differences between beings, species and kinds—hence my return to the human "after the cyborg" here.

3. Haraway engages here with Derrida's essay, "And Say the Animal Responded?," first delivered as a lecture in 1997 and included in *The Animal That Therefore I Am*.

4. The important animal studies texts whose authors have made significant efforts in resituating the traditional debates and discourses on the animal beyond their anthropocentric assumptions and biases but which have nevertheless fallen prey to at least one of the three blind spots listed here include, to name but a few, Adams, Baker, Fudge, and Haraway's *The Companion Species Manifesto*.

5. Some of the ideas included in this paragraph have been borrowed from my review of Haraway's "Dogs R Us?", 129–131.

6. Dogs and other animals do not come to us from some kind of prelapsarian world: they are actors and subjects in the complex technoscientific networks of technocapitalist production. Following Edmund Russell, Haraway recognizes that dogs are "biotechnologies, workers, and agents of technoscientific knowledge production in the regime of lively capital;" they are herders "deliberately selected for their working capacities," sled laborers, workers/competitors in sheep trials, and livestock guardian dogs (56). Like humans and other animate and inanimate world beings, dogs are mutually co-emerging via the interlinked multiple processes of biotechnological production. And yet Haraway also acknowledges that it is humans who "make the deliberate plans to change things" (56), and who thus define the purpose and direction of many of these transformative processes—be it those of guide dogs for the blind or training dogs in competitive agility sports—even if, in order to achieve these objectives, "dogs and people have to train together in subject-changing ways" (57). However, she also argues that people and dogs "emerge as mutually adapted partners in the naturecultures of lively capital," which leads her to postulate that we should think harder about what she terms "encounter value" (62). The latter will also presumably be very different depending on whether we are encountering a dog or a microbe. The existence of such different economies of scale and cuteness is one of the key reasons why the overarching value- and principle-driven interspecies ethics is rather difficult to design.

7.   Commenting on Derrida's ethical thought, Calarco explains that the inevitability of violence in any relation with the Other "should not be taken to mean that such violence is immoral or that all forms of violence are equivalent. Rather, the aim is to undercut completely the possibility of achieving good conscience in regard to questions of nonviolence toward the Other. The ideal of ethical purity is ruled out a priori as structurally impossible" (136).

8.   In *Technics and Time, vol. 1* Bernard Stiegler draws on the paleontological theories of André Leroi-Gourhan to argue that the human is originally prosthetic, i.e. dependent on technical prostheses for his or her emergence and existence. For Stiegler, the drive towards exteriorization, towards tools, artifice and language, is due to a technical tendency which already exists in the older, zoological dynamic. It is due to this tendency that the (not-yet) human stands up and reaches for what is not in him or her: and it is through visual and conceptual reflexivity (seeing herself in the blade of the flint, memorizing the use of the tool) that she emerges as always already related to, and connected with, the alterity that is not part of her. For more on the consequences of this line of thinking for our idea of ethics, see my *Bioethics in the Age of New Media*, 35–63.

9.   Broadly speaking, the philosophical framework for understanding ethics in this way is provided by the work of Emmanuel Levinas and by Derrida's rereading of it. Levinas' ethical theory shifts the focus of attention and concern from myself to the Other and can therefore be read as a blow to human self-centredness. The place I occupy in the world for Levinas is never just mine. Instead, it belongs to the Other, whom I may have oppressed, starved or driven away from my home, my country and my life. His thought provides a justification for caring about the life, any life, of the Other, especially the precarious and destitute lives of all those who lack recognition in the dominant political debates and policies, and those whose biological and political existence is confined to "zones of exception": comatose patients, asylum seekers, refugees, people with non-normative bodies and looks, victims of biotech experimentation. Yet drawing on Levinas in an effort to develop a post-humanist bioethics is not unproblematic as his theory suffers from an anthropological bias, which is evident, for example, in the excessive weighting he gives to human language. His notion of the Other therefore needs to be expanded if, in the digital era, we are not sure any longer whether the Other who is before me is human or machinic, and whether the "fraternity" Levinas talks about extends to all of DNA-kin (chimpanzees, dogs, bacteria). I discuss the viability of Levinas' philosophy for thinking a bioethics of human and non-human relations in *Bioethics in the Age of New Media*.

10.   Having said that, in my various writings I have addressed multiple bioethical scenarios and events which arise in the context of cosmetic surgery, abortion,

cloning, genetic testing, or art practice which uses biomaterial, and have also suggested ways of thinking ethically about all these different cases.

Works Cited

Adams, Carole. *The Sexual Politics of Meat: A Feminist-Vegitarian Critical Theory.* London and New York: Continuum, 1990.

Baker, Steve. *The Postmodern Animal.* London: Reaktion Books, 2000.

Calarco, Matthew. *Zoographies: The Question of the Animal from Heidegger to Derrida.* New York: Columbia University Press, 2008.

Derrida, Jacques. *The Animal That Therefore I Am.* New York: Fordham University Press, 2008.

Fudge, Erica. *Animal.* London: Reaktion Books, 2002.

Game, Anne. "Riding: Embodying the Centaur." *Body and Society* 7.4 (2001): 1–12.

Glendinning, Simon. *In the Name of Phenomenology.* London: Routledge, 2007.

Haraway, Donna. "Becoming-With-Companions: Sharing and Response in Experimental Laboratories." *Animal Encounters.* Ed. Tom Tyler and Manuela Rossini. Leiden: Brill, 2009.

---. *The Companion Species Manifesto: Dogs, People, and Significant Otherness.* Chicago: Prickly Paradigm Press, 2003.

---. *When Species Meet.* Minneapolis: University of Minnesota Press, 2008.

Patton, Paul. "Language, Power, and the Training of Horses." *Zoontologies: The Question of the Animal.* Ed. Cary Wolfe. Minneapolis: University of Minnesota Press, 2003.

Sax, Boria. "Human and Post-Animal: Review of Haraway, Donna J., *When Species Meet.*" H-Nilas, *H-Net Reviews.* April 2008. Web. 30 June 2009. <http://www.h-net.org/reviews/showrev.php?id=14416>.

Stiegler, Bernard. *Technics and Time, 1: The Fault of Epimetheus.* Trans. Richard Beardsworth and George Collins. Stanford: Stanford University Press, 1998.

Wolfe, Cary. "In Search of Post-Humanist Theory: The Second-Order Cybernetics of Maturana and Varela." *The Politics of Systems and Environments,* Part I. Spec. issue of *Cultural Critique* 30 (Spring 1995): 33–70.

Zylinska, Joanna. *Bioethics in the Age of New Media.* Cambridge: The MIT Press, 2009.

---. *The Cyborg Experiments: Extensions of the Body in the Media Age.* London and New York: Continuum, 2002.

---. "Dogs R Us?" Review of *The Companion Species Manifesto,* by Donna Haraway. *parallax* 12.1 (2006): 129–31.

---. *On Spiders, Cyborgs and Being Scared: The Feminine and the Sublime.* Manchester: Manchester University Press, 2001.

Chapter 9

Post-Trauma

Towards a New Definition?

CATHERINE MALABOU

In his article "Descartes and the Post-Traumatic Subject," Slavoj Žižek develops a very insightful critique of the current neurobiological and neuro-psychoanalytic approach of trauma. He challenges the way in which these approaches tend to substitute for the Feudian and Lacanian definitions of psychic wounds.

Žižek's critique may be summarized in the following terms: while developing its own critique of psychoanalysis, namely of Freud and Lacan, neurobiologists would not have been aware of the fact that Lacan, precisely, has already said what they thought he hasn't said. They would thus be ventriloquized by Lacan at the very moment when they thought they were talking from another point of view than that of Lacanian psychoanalysis.

Why is that? How is it possible to repeat Lacan without knowing it? According to Žižek, contemporary approaches to trauma would remain unaware—out of disavowal or of desire—of Lacan's most fundamental statement: *trauma has always already occured*. A specific trauma, such or such empirical shock, may happen only because a more profound and originary trauma, understood as the Real or as the "transcendental" trauma, has always already occured. Trauma had always already happened. Already always already. Lacan had already said always already. The new approach of trauma would only be a confirmation, and not a destitution, of the always already. It would be a mere repetition of what has already occured and been said.

To state that trauma has already occurred means that it cannot occur by chance, that every empirical accident or shock impairs an already or a previously wounded subject. There is an obvious rejection of chance in Freud and Lacan. Beyond the always already principle. Something that Lacan had never said, to the extent that I wanted to give a chance to a thought which would definitely escape the always already's authority, which would give a chance to chance.

"Before I focus on the notion of chance, I want to state that the possibility of such a beyond is opened (this is the central thesis of my book) by current neurobiology and its redefinition of both the unconscious (named neural unconscious or neural psyche) and the trauma, consequently the post-traumatic subjectivity." Neurobiology and neuropsychoanalysis challenge the Freudian conception of the psychic accident understood as a meeting point between two meanings of the event: the event conceived of as an internal immanent determination (*Erlebnis*) and an encounter that occurs from outside (*Ereignis*). In order for an accident to become properly a psychic event, it has to trigger the subject's psychic history and determinism. The "Ereignis" has to unite with the "Erlebnis." The most obvious example of such a definition of the psychic event is the example, often taken by Freud, of the war wound. When a soldier, on the front, gets traumatized by a wound, or fear of the wound, it appears that the current real conflict he is involved in is a repetition of an internal conflict. Shock is always a reminder of a previous shock. Freud would then have then considered PTSD as the expression of the always already character of the conflict or trauma.

Neurobiologists admit on the contrary that severe trauma 1) is fundamentally an "Ereignis," that is something which happens by mere chance from the outside; 2) it thus dismantles the *Ereignis/Erlebnis* distinction to the extent that it severs the subject from her reserves of memory and from the presence of the past. After severe brain damage, which always produces a series of disconnections and holes within the neural network, a new subject emerges with no reference to the past or to her previous identity. A neural disconnection does not trigger any previous conflict. Instead, the post-traumatized subject disconnects the structure of the always already. The post-traumatized subject is the never more of the always already.

We can then state that a neural disconnection cannot belong to either of the three terms that form the Lacanian triad of the Imaginary, the Symbolic, and the Real, to the extent that this triad is rooted in the transcendantal principle of the always already. We propose to entertain a fourth dimension, a dimension that might be called the material. From a neurobiological point of view, the trauma would be taken to be a material, empirical, biological, and meaningless interruption of the trancendental itself. This is why post-traumatic subjects are *living examples of the death drive* and of the dimension *beyond the pleasure principle* that Freud and Lacan both fail to locate or to expose. Beyond the always already principle is the true beyond the pleasure principle.

Žižek affords a certain credulity to these ideas but rejects them out of hand for three main reasons:

1. These statements are seemingly ignorant of the Lacanian distinction between pleasure (*plaisir*) and enjoyment (*jouissance*). Enjoyment in itself is precisely beyond pleasure. It is this painful surplus of pleasure that resists being contained within the framework of the pleasure principle. Enjoyment is the always already confronting us with death, and without which we would be trapped in pleasure only. In other words, neurological trauma cannot be but a form of enjoyment. Lacan has always already said that disconnection, separation from the past, lost of memory, and indifference, are modalities or occurrences of enjoyment. The unconscious is always already ready for its own destruction: "What is beyond the pleasure principle is enjoyment itself, it is drive as such," writes Žižek (136).

2. The second objection concerns destruction itself understood as the presence of what Lacan calls the Thing (*la Chose*). The Thing is the threat of death. Without this threat, which mainly appears to the subject as the threat of castration, any empirical objective danger or hazard would remain meaningless to the psyche. Here comes the always already again: "Castration is not only a threat-horizon, a not yet/always to come, but, simultaneously, something that always already happens: the subject is not

only under a threat of separation, it is the effect of separation (from substance)" (141).

3. This last sentence expresses the main objection: according to Žižek, the subject is, since Descartes, a post-traumatic subject, a subject structured in such a way that it has to constantly erase the traces of its past in order to be a subject. Thus, and once again, the experience of being cut off from oneself is a very old one. Neuriobiology doesn't teach us anything new on that point, it rather confirms the very essence of the subject: "The empty frame of death drive is the formal-transcendental conditions" of subjectivity: "What remains after the violent traumatic intrusion onto a human subject that erases all his substantial content is the pure form of subjectivity, the form that already must have been there" (144). Further: "If one wants to get an idea of cogito at its purest, its 'degree zero,' one has to take into a look at autistic monsters (the new wounded), a gaze that is very painful and disturbing" (146).

From Descartes to Damasio via Lacan, there would, once again, be one and only one principle: *trauma has always already happened.*

To answer these objections one may insist that the motif of chance, thought and elaborated in a certain way, deconstructs the always already, which appears to be a barrier to what it is supposed to be—that is, a barrier to destruction. If destruction has always already happened, if there is something as a transcendental destruction, then destruction is indestructible. This is what, in Freud and in Lacan, remains extremely problematic: destruction remains for them a structure, the repetition of the originary trauma. What if the always already might explode? What if the always already were self-destructive and able to disappear as the so-called fundamental law of the psyche?

In order to address these issues more specifically, let's concentrate on the status of chance in a dream that Freud analyzes in chapter 7 of *The Interpretation of Dreams,* and that Lacan comments in his turn in seminar 11, *The Four Fundamental Concepts of Psychoanalysis,* in chapters 5, "*Tuché* and *Automaton,*" and 6, "The Split between the Eye and the Gaze."

Freud writes:

> A father had been watching beside his child's sick bed for days
> and nights on end. After the child had died, he went into the
> next room to lie down, but left the door open so he could see
> from his bedroom into the room in which the child's body
> was laid out, with tall candles standing round it. An old man
> has been engaged to keep watch over it, and sat beside the
> body murmuring prayers. After a few hours sleep, the father
> had a dream that his child was standing beside his bed, caught
> him by the arm and whispered to him reproachfully: 'Father,
> don't you see I'm burning?' He woke up, noticed a bright glare
> of light from the next room, hurried into it and found that the
> old watchman had dropped out to sleep and that the wrap-
> pings and one of the arms of the beloved child's dead body had
> been burned by a candle that had fallen on them. (5: 547–8)

The issue immediately addressed by Freud is to know whether we can
consider such a dream as a wish-fulfillment. Isn't it on the contrary an
objection, a counter example to the theory of dreams as wish-fulfillment?

Let's consider Lacan's answer to this issue. First of all, after having re-
minded us of this dream, Lacan posits that psychoanalysis is "an encounter, an essential encounter—an appointment to which we are always
called with a real that eludes us" (53). This essential missed encounter,
or misencounter, with the real is the encounter with the trauma. According to Lacan, this dream stages such an encounter. The Freudian question comes back at that point: if this dream stages the encounter with the
trauma, how can we consider it as a wish-fullfillment, as a fullfillment
of a desire?

We need to understand more precisely what the very notion of "encounter with the real" means. The analysis of this formula ("encounter
with the Real"), forms the content of Chapters 5 and 6. This formula is
contradictory to the extent that "encounter" refers to something contingent, accidental, something that may or may not happen, and "real," on
the contrary, designates for Lacan the necessary and determined mechanism of repetition, the always already of the trauma. How then can we
encounter—contingently—the necessity of trauma? Here, the notion of

chance is emerging. How can we encounter—by chance—the necessity of the trauma which has been always already here?

It is on this point that Lacan refers to Aristotle, who distinguishes in his *Physics* two regimes of events or of causality. First *"tuché"*: which means fortune, contingency; then *"automaton,"* the blind necessity of the repetition mechanism, the compulsion to repeat as such. We then have chance on the one hand, determinism on the other. According to Aristotle, everything that comes to pass is due to one of theses two modes of temporality. *Tuché* will decide if you will meet by chance a friend on the agora today. *Automaton* governs the cycle of sunset and sunrise, or the seasons cycle, etc. Lacan comments on these two modes: *"Tuché*, he says, is good or bad fortune" (69). *"Automaton* is the Greek version of the compulsion to repeat" (67). Even if this encounter between two regimes of events and two modes of causality is said to be a missed encounter, it is nonethesless an encounter. Again, how is this possible?

Here begins the analysis of the dream. In this dream, what does belong to *automaton* and what to *tuché*? As Lacan puts it: "Where is the reality in this accident?" (58) and where is the accident in this reality? Obviously, what belongs to *tuché* is the falling of the candle and the burning of the child's arm. This is the reality, Lacan says, but not the real. The Real is the unreal "resurrection" of the child and the words "Father, can't you see I am burning?" And here, Lacan starts to analyze *tuché* as a secondary kind of causality or of reality. The child's burnt arm is not the real accident in this dream, it is not the Real. The Real comes with the speech, the son's address to his father. *Tuché* has no autonomy, it is in fact only a means for the Real or the *automaton* to emerge. There would only be one mode of happening, that of *automaton*, with a disguised version of it, a mask, *tuché*.

Chance, or fortune, is only an appearance, an "as if." What happens "as if" by chance is in fact always the automatism of repetition, the primary trauma: "What is repeated, in fact, is always something that occurs *as if by chance*" (54).

Lacan asks himself what is genuinely burning in the dream: is it the child's arm, or the sentence uttered by the child: "Father, can't you see that I'm burning?" "Does not this sentence, said in relation to fever," asks Lacan, "suggest to you what, in one of my recent lectures, I called the cause of fever?…What encounter can there be with that forever inert being—even now being devoured by the flames—if not the encounter that occurs precisely at the moment when, by accident, as if by chance, the flames come to meet him? Where is the reality in this accident, if not that it repeats something more fatal *by means* of reality, a reality in which the person who was supposed to be watching over the body still remains asleep, even when the father reemerges after having woken up?" (58).

It is clear that if contingent reality is always a means for the Real to come to light, it is then always secondary. When Lacan asks what is the reality in this accident, he means that there is something other, in the accident, than the accident: "Is there no more reality in this message than in the noise by which the father also identifies the strange reality of what is happening in the room next door?" (58).

The contingent external encounter of reality (the candle collapses and inflames the cloth covering the dead child, the smell of the smoke disturbs the father) triggers the true Real, the unbearable fantasy-apparition of the child reproaching his father. Again, what burns are the words, not the arm. "Father, can't you see I'm burning? This sentence is itself a fire-brand—or itself it brings fire where it falls" (69) Further: the veiled meaning is the true reality, that of the "primal scene."

In other words, there is a split between reality and the Real.

Now is the moment for approaching the problem of wish-fulfillment.

Lacan writes: "It is not that, in the dream, the father persuades himself that the son is still alive. But the terrible version of the dead son taking the father by the arm designates a beyond that makes itself heard in the dream. Desire manifests itself in the dream by the loss expressed in an image at the cruel point of the object. It is only in the dream that this truly unique encounter can occur. Only a rite, an endlessly repeated act, can commemorate this…encounter" (59).

This dream would then be a kind of fullfillment to the extent that it would render the encounter with "jouissance," enjoyment, possible. The fullfilment is not always linked with pleasure, says Lacan, but it can be linked with jouissance. We remember that "jouissance" is defined by Žižek as the beyond of the pleasure principle, the excess or surplus of pleasure which transforms itself in a kind of suffering which is the very expression of the death drive. Because we can only encounter "jouissance" in dreams, then this dream is, in its way, a wish-fullfillment.

Is the way in which Lacan distinguishes two kinds of realities in this dream, a true one and a secondary one, not properly inadmissible? Cannot we think that the accident of the candle falling on the child's arm is traumatizing per se, that it does not necessarily trigger the repetition mechanism of a more ancient trauma? This accident would then be as real as the words it provokes.

If there is a beyond the pleasure principle, can we still understand it as a beyond chance, beyond the accident or beyond contingency? This is precisely what is no longer possible. When the victims of traumas are "burning," we certainly don't have a right to ask: where is the reality in these accidents? We certainly don't have a right to suspect contingency for hiding a more profound kind of event, for being the veiled face of the compulsion to repeat. To split reality from the Real, contingency from necessity, the transcendental from the empirical, good or bad fortune (*tuché*), from necessity (*automaton*). Reading this Lacanian interpetation, we cannot help but visualize the psychoanalyst as a fireman looking at the catastrophe and saying: "there must be something more urgent, I am due to take care of a more originary emergency."

The accident never hides anything, never reveals anything but itself. We need to think of a destructive plasticity, that is a capacity to explode, that cannot, by any means, be assimilated by the psyche, even in dreams.

The answer we can give to the second objection, concerning castration as something which has always already occured, is that the threat of castration is what helps Lacan to always see, even if he says the contrary, the Symbolic at work within the Real.

Castration is for Freud the phenomenal form of the threat of death. Because it means separation, it gives death a figurative content. About separation, Lacan declares: "We must recognize in this sentence ['Father can't you see I'm burning ?'] what perpetuates for the father those words forever separated from the dead child that are said to him" (58). We find here the motive of separation. Here, separation, the child's death, the separation from the child is the trauma, the *automaton*. But since this separation can be expressed by another separation, that of words—words separating from the body—then the trauma encounters the symbolic and never escapes it. The real is separated from itself thanks to words, thanks to the symbolic.

What challenges the idea that castration or separation has always already happened is precisely the fact that this always already is the presence of the Symbolic in the Real, consequently also a kind of erasure of the trauma. There is no "pure" Real.

What brain damage allows us to see is that the violence of the traumatizing lesions consists in the way they cut the subject, as we already noticed, from its reserves of memory. The traumatized victims's speech doesn't have any revelatory meaning. Their illness does not constitute a kind of truth with regard to their ancient history. There is no possibility for them of being present to their own fragmentation or to their own wound. In contrast to castration, there is no representation, no phenomenon, no example of separation, which would allow the subject to anticipate, to wait for, to fantasize what can be a break in cerebral connections. One cannot even dream about it. There is no scene for this Thing. No words.

We don't believe in the possibility of responding to the absence of meaning by reintroducing some kind of hidden repetition of the Real. We have to admit on the contrary that something like a total absence of meaning is the meaning of our time.

There is a global uniformity of neuropsychological reactions to traumas, be it political, natural, or pathological traumas. "Žižeks considers this new uniformized face of violence"

> First, there is the brutal external physical violence: terror attacks like 9/11, street violence, rapes, etc., second, natural catastrophes, earthquakes, tsunamis, etc.; then, there is the 'irrational' (meaningless) destruction of the material base of our inner reality (brain tumors, Alzheimer's disease, organic cerebral lesions, PTSD, etc.), which can utterly change, destroy even, the victim's personality. We would not be able to distinguish between natural, political and socio-symbolic violence. We are dealing today with a heterogeneous mixture of nature and politics, in which politics cancels itself as such and takes the appearance of nature, and nature disappears in order to assume the mask of politics. (125)

What Žižek doesn't seem to admit is that a new form of violence is emerging today, one implying a new articulation of the concept of the Real, we might also say the concept of what is burning. A concept that would give chance its chance, a chance that would never be an "as if," an "as if by chance."

Let's turn to the third and last objection. We remember that for Žižek, post-traumatic subjectivity is nothing other than the classical Cartesian form of subjectivity. The subject is an instance capable of erasing all substantial content in order always to be new and present to itself and to the world. This is as true as the whole history of metaphysics.

This might be true, but it is difficult to believe that traumatic erasure can occur without forming each time a new subject, unaware of the previous one. Repetition is plastic, it gives form to what it destroys. We have to think of a form created by destruction, the form of a new person, which is not the transcendatal subject, but what undermines it, as the threat of its explosion. The plasticity of contingency has the power to bestow its own form on the subjects that it shocks. A subject that burns, and that urges us to see, at long last, that it is *really* burning.

⁓

What is a shock? A trauma? Are they the result of a blow, of something that cannot, by any means, be anticipated, something sudden, that comes from outside and knocks us down, whoever we are? Or are they on the contrary always predestined encounters? Something which would force us to erase the "whoever you are" from the previous sentence to the extent that an encounter presupposes a destination, a predestination, something which happens to you, to you proper, and to nobody else ? According to this second approach, a shock or a trauma would always result, as Freud states, from a meeting between the blow itself and a preexisting psychic destiny.

Is this Freudian conception still accurate to characterize current global psychic violence, or don't we have to admit that blows, shocks, strike any of us without making any difference, erasing our personal histories, destroying the very notion of psychic destiny, of childhood, of past, even of the unconscious itself?

For Freud and for Lacan, it seems clear that every external trauma is "sublated," internalized. Even the most violent intrusions of the external real owe their traumatic effect to the resonance they find in primary psychic conflicts.

When it comes to war neuroses, Freud declares in his Introduction to "Psycho-analysis and the War Neuroses," the external accident that causes the trauma is not the genuine cause of it. It acts as a shock or a blow which awakens an old "conflict in the ego." The genuine enemy is always an "internal enemy" (17: 210).

According to Freud, there is only one possible kind of "neurosis etiology": the sexual one. Some passages from "Sexuality" in *The Aetiology Of The Neuroses* and from "My Views on the Part Played by Sexuality" in *The Aetiology Of The Neuroses* are clear in this respect. In the first, Freud states: "The true ætiology of the psychoneuroses does not lie in precipitating causes" (7: 250).

In the second text, Freud sums up his whole theory of infantile trauma and recapitulates all the changes he has brought to it. He says that he was forced to give up the importance of the part played by the "accidental influences" in the causation of trauma (7: 275). Traumas are not caused by effective events or accidents but by phantasms: "Accidental influences derived from experience having receded into the background, the factors of constitution and heredity necessarily gained the upper hand once more" (3: 250).

For Freud, brain injuries and brain lesions, since they are regarded as merely external, cannot have a real causal power. The brain has no responsibility in the course of our psychic life and in the constitution of our subjectivity. The brain is not responsible, which also means that it cannot bring a proper response to the questions of danger, fragility, and exposure in general. It is exposed to accidents but not to the symbolic and or psychic meaning of accidents. Sexuality appears to be first of all, for Freud, not only the "sexual life" but a new specific kind of cause, which alone is able to explain the constitution of our personal identity, our history and our destiny. There is a wide gap between external and internal traumatic events, even if, as we know, the frontier between inside and outside is being constantly redrawn in Freud. Nevertheless, it is clear that none of the determinant events of our psychic life has an organic or physiological cause. In a certain sense, such events never come from outside. There are no sexual accidents properly speaking.

In *Beyond the Pleasure Principle*, Freud goes so far as to state that the emergence of a neurosis and the occurrence of a physical lesion are antithetic and incompatible: "In the case of the ordinary traumatic neuroses two characteristics emerge prominently: first, that the chief weight in their causation seems to rest upon the factor of surprise, of fright; and secondly, that a wound or injury inflicted simultaneously works as a rule *against* the development of a neurosis" (18: 12).

Freud here recognizes the importance of surprise and terror. He seems then to admit the power of chance and the absence of anticipation. However, this power either causes a physical wound or a psychic wound. In the first case, there is a narcissistic bodily investment which takes care of the wound, as if organic injuries were able to cure themselves without any help from a psychic therapy. It is as if physical and psychic wounds have nothing in common unless the first can be translated into the language of the second, to be considered as "symptoms." It means that for Freud, people suffering from brain diseases do not obey psychoanalytic jurisdiction. That is why, perhaps, we do not encounter any kind of despondancy in Freud's clinical studies.

We then emerge with the idea that the psychic life is indestructible:

> The primitive mind is, in the fullest meaning of the word, imperishable. What are called mental diseases inevitably produce an impression in the layman that intellectual and mental life have been destroyed. In reality, the destruction only applies to later acquisitions and developments. The essence of mental disease lies in a return to earlier states of affective life and functioning. An excellent example of the plasticity of mental life is afforded by the state of sleep, which is our goal every night. Since we have learnt to interpret even absurd and confused dreams, we know that whenever we go to sleep we throw out our hard-won morality like a garment, and put it on again next morning. (Freud 24: 285–6)

Even if Lacan displaces many Freudian statements, he also shares many Freudian statements on the indestructibility of psychic life, which is another name for *the always already*. Neurobiology puts the so-called psychic immortality into question. Our socio-political reality imposes multiple versions of external intrusions, traumas, which are just meaningless brutal interruptions that destroy the symbolic texture of the subject's identity and render all kinds of internalization/interiorization impossible as well as the accident's reappropriation or resubjectivation, because some regions of the brain have been destroyed. Nothing, in psychic life, is indestructible.

At some point in his review, Žižek evokes the possibility that neurobiologists would only project their own desire, without mentioning it, in their account of neurobiological victims and meaningless trauma: do they "not forget to include [themselves], [their] own desire, in the observed phenomenon (of autistic subjects)?" (137).

Here comes desire again! But we might of course reverse the objection: does not Žižek omit to include his own desire for the always already? Even if he is one of the most accurate and generous readers of current neurobiology, as it is manifest in his great book, we might interpret here the meaning of such a desire as a fear of the trauma of being definitely separated from Lacan.

Works Cited

Freud, Sigmund. *The Standard Edition of the Complete Psychological Works of Sigmund Freud.* 24 vols. London: Hogarth Press, 1956–74.

Lacan, Jacques. *The Four Fundamental Concepts of Psychoanalysis.* Trans. Alan Sheridan. New York: W.W. Norton, 1978.

Žižek, Slavoj. "Descartes and the Post-Traumatic Subject: On Catherine Malabou's *Les Nouveaux Blessés.*" *Qui Parle.* 17.2 (2009): 123–147.

Chapter 10

Ecologies of War

Dispatch from the Aerial Empire

Mike Hill

*The realities of today's operational environment … is modified
by population explosion, urbanization, globalization,
technology, resource demand, climate change and natural
disasters, and proliferation of weapons of mass destruction.*

– Tactics in Counter Insurgency

SkyOps

The central question of this entry on war—let us recall the genre most
akin to military affairs and call this writing a "dispatch"—is not why we
should put "ecology" under the heading of empire but the reverse: why
use the word ecology as an organizational term by which to connect intra-
governmental violence with so many other forms of "mass destruction"?
Of course, the term empire is itself contested, and in the ecological sense,
I would argue, it has also changed. While still a routine marker for uni-
lateral global supremacy and for capital accumulation within an epoch of
US-inspired neo-liberalism, empire also invites us to rethink geographical expansion from within dimensions that are rather more disorienting
than the traditional limits of the nation-state would allow. This is true in
a spatial sense as well as a temporal one.[1] In this expanded notion of empire, history is witnessing an unprecedented convergence of the once disparate systems of technological and environmental modalities of conflict
listed by US Army Counter Insurgency doctrine (COIN) as comprising
a twenty-first century co-"operational" reality of war. On this order, there

are key words from the epigram above that move the traditionally geo-graphic orientations of empire into what we might call its aerial domains. The term aerial here should signal not only the destructive potential of the atmosphere, catastrophic climate change, and by extension, the com-ing resource wars, but should also pertain to the spatio-informational armament, endless ensembles of antennae, satellitic vision, those super-sites of knowledge transmission, data analysis, and tele-connectivity that re-orient conventional military arts. According to the dynamics of aerial empire, one might say that the battlefield becomes etherized, and war is perpetuated, indeed made immanent to life itself. The key-words from the epigram: "population," "technology," "mass destruction," are tried-and-true war items to be sure, but how to work "climate change" and "natural disasters"—as of 2008, legally defined as essential to US security policy[2]—into a military schema that regards "nature" as a functional part of the atmospherically embedded war machine? How to account not just for sky assassins in the form of unmanned drones but also hurricanes, drought, species mutation, extreme weather, rising tides—forces of ma-chinery and natural elements that work so closely together that they are impossible to divide, let alone objectively suss out from the banal vio-lence of every day life?

There is of course a clear if also dotted line that connects twenty-first century US security policy with global ambition as far back as the Mon-roe Doctrine and up through the Cold War, comprising two centuries and more of overt and covert military presence in key regions of the world. The list of Cold-war era interventions alone—military-sponsored coups, incursions, assassinations, and police acts—are well rehearsed and readily rehearsable: Iran (1953); Guatemala (1954); Dominican Repub-lic (1965); Indonesia (1965); Chile (1973); El Salvador (1980s); Gre-nada (1983); Panama (1989) (Retort 80–88). Before September 2001, there were already 285,000 troops in at least 130 countries (510,927 troops in 151 foreign countries are reported in 2009), and at the peak of the Cold War there were 1,014 foreign US military bases (761 reported in 2008).[3] As is well known, the US sells more than 50 per cent of all weapons on the world market, with the near-failed state of Mexico being our most recent reversal of first-world violence come tragically home.[4] All this said, the admittedly hazy term aerial empire is not meant to diminish concern over the standing record of war proper and its traditional arsenals, nor should we ignore the hypocritical brutishness of so much continued inter-state aggression in the name of democratic freedom. But let me qualify if not excuse such haziness: to the extent that this record of violence is presumed to exist as an effect of (and presumably, in order to fortify) a writerly privilege of objectified safety in the imaginary "green zone" of civil society, and to the extent that civil society is arguably transformed by the reality of permanent and proximate war, a different kind of analysis—we should say a different analytic—of war is right now starting to emerge. What can writing do and not do in relation to war today? To ask the question is to take seriously the US National Security Doctrine (NSS), which in the wake of September 11, 2001, renders the "saying" of anything regarding war as being said by the citizen who is always also the suspect of our amped-up security state. In this peculiar sense, war presents a double bind for the very conceptualization of war from a standpoint that presumes to be critical of it. If, as I want to suggest, war has seeped into civil society relations and critical thinking as such, then it is unsatisfactory or at least highly troublesome to reduce the ecologies of war to a seamless next step in the perpetuation of US imperial dominance, itself never on less stable ground. The same 2009 COIN field manual cited in the epigram above sums up this double-bind by referring to the predominant conception of foreign military occupation as a matter of "armed civil affairs" (*Tactics* C-7). And next to the *National Security Strategy of the United States of America* (NSS), one begins to surmise, apropos the US Patriot Act and the US Northern Command (20,000 domestically deployed rapid-reaction forces focused on the coming internal disturbances), that this phrase also refers to the arming of civility at home.[5] On the one hand, contemporary COIN doctrine openly connects with more than two centuries of US military confrontation with insurgency, from the Whiskey Rebellion (1791–94) in the eastern states, to the eradication of Native Americans in the Western Plains (1785–1890s), and from there, to the Boxer rebellion in China (1898–1901), Poncho Villa in New Mexico (1916), Agusto Sandino in Nicaragua (1927–1933), and so on. On the other hand, COIN also insists that irregular warfare—the twenty-first century resurrection of the non-state combatant, and in response, the self-internalization of war *cum* security within the US body politic—

has become a normative social condition that jettisons the link between justice and peace. The notion of civil society as a peaceable (and let's not forget, highly privileged) zone of communicative reason has become a shibboleth-effect in a context of extra-judicial assassination and unconventional war. In the past, US covert assassination ops focused on state officials and civilians of interest in countries with whom we may (Vietnam) or may not (Latin America) have been overtly at war, but were carried out by CIA-trained local paramilitary groups and police forces. In 2010, there are 13,000 Special Operations commandos deployed worldwide, an unprecedented number that is apposite to a US strategy of targeted killing well beyond the confines of the traditional battle field. And as noted by the *New York Times* in December of 2009: "For the first time in history, a civilian intelligence agency is using robots to carry out a military mission, selecting people for killing in a country where the United States is not officially at war" (Branfman). The country referenced here is Pakistan, but the Global War on Terror authorizes such tactics wherever they are deemed necessary: beyond the Middle East, in the former Russian Republics, Yemen, Somalia, Saudi Arabia, Kenya, and so on. Mechanized assassination further permeates the infusion of violence within the world's peaceable zones of relative safety, a general effect of twenty-first century warfare that is evidenced by the secret practices of overhead, and underwear, bombers alike.[6] In a paradoxical sense, the call for global civil society comes at a historical moment when sociability itself has become a newly invigorated paramilitary Operational Area (AO). Here intra-state violence supercedes, while appearing to compliment, the more primitive mode of making war in a geographically coherent national mode.[7] Put in bumper sticker speak: really, "freedom isn't free."

Thus a continued (rather, a *continuous*) "Revolution in Military Affairs" (RMA), to cite Defense Secretary Robert Gates, ushers in a "*new* reality...for America, and for humanity [insofar as] the lines separating war [and] peace...have become more blurred" (5; emphasis mine). At stake in this blurring between war and peace, which Gates rightly extends to the existence of anything we might go on calling the human, is an innovative set of techno-environmental insecurities that are arguably effacing— at different levels and with different speeds—the coherency of the state and of the state's anthropomorphic referents in any of humanity's ethical guises (read here: left-liberal notions of the human being and right-wing possessive individualism, alike). Twenty-first century war doctrine regards population control, race and ethnic division, the manipulation of computerized knowledge systems, deliberate and non-deliberate manifestations of environmental modification (ENMOD), epidemic disease, and resource scarcity as commonly intertwined within a complex set of super-surfaces that mutate almost too fast to be described (*Tactics* A-4). What is new, a 2009 US Army Strategic Studies Institute paper insists, "is that climate change poses security threats unmatched among environmental phenomena" (Parsons 2). And what is radically new is that climate change represents a relatively untapped means for engaging in war, "a unique and promising opportunity for the United States…to advance its security interests" (Parsons 7). The explicit reference in this citation is to competing US-China interests in Sub-Saharan Africa, the rush to grab oil, natural gas, and other commodities; but think, implicitly, of hurricane Katrina as the preemptive first strike in a planetary civil war that no one has officially declared. In this "new" ecology of war (the scare quotes are meant to mark extremities of chronology, breaks, as well as compressions and expansions in the experience of time), the epistemo-military arts are developing techniques that incorporate a symbiosis of agencies—biological, atmospheric, geological, and mechanical—that from any other perspective than war would be revealed as the suicidal miscellany of a planet abandoned to siege.

This present dispatch thus limits itself to transmitting a set of strategic connections between biotic as well as non-biotic factors of military conflict. These connections are becoming central to a new war doctrine, while they are only beginning, by fits and starts, to forge analogues of philosophical critique that may or may not be able to stand up against it. To continue this forging, we will have to range widely from global tele-surveillance, drone-warfare, and the weaponizing of culture, to other, tactically significant life-and-death scenarios, such as climate change, viral transmission, the US Amy's investment in chaos theory, and the culling of the human species cloaked as humane adaptation (the count of climate refugees is estimated to be 50 million in 2010, 200 million or more by 2050) (Glenn and Gordon 2). These items have not until now been found under the heading of war. But they may be given a certain uneasy futuristic logic given war's new organizational capacities. And if the phrase aerial empire fails to call forth a political formula guaranteed to preserve the cause of human equality, or if this dispatch begs the charge of being mere catastrophe porn, it is because the reality of conflict within which any humane conviction might be proffered is riddled with the same evanescent mini-movements, the same insurgent groupuscles, not simply of this or that "population" but also insurgencies of knowledge and (or, *as*) matter, a movement of movements that criss-cross traditional phyla, and by doing so, exceed the epoch of what Jürgen Habermas wishes to preserve as the "human being *per se*."[8] Consider, it has been 44 years since President Lyndon Johnson's advisory council linked greenhouse gas to "marked climate change." And as of 2009, about $3 billion per year are spent on symposia, conferences, films, TV shows, publications, and the like, on environmental issues. In 2010, there are 80 million references to climate change on the Internet alone (Editorial 24). What to make of such visibility, such ubiquity, and therefore, apparent normalization of planetary risk? Should we assume that the almost sadistic publicity of our precarious life is sufficient alone to generate change; or does the apparent apostasy of scientific truth confirm the existence of a change already in our midst? If as I want to suggest this change has at least already mutated public sphere activity (perhaps not least, in the form we are practicing it now), then we will have to work with a dispatch that retains both a critically modest and germinal status.

Las Vegas in Afghanistan

Every morning in Las Vegas, Steve Smith kisses his wife
and young daughters goodbye, gets in his car, drives
50 minutes down the freeway, past shopping malls
and casinos, and goes to war in Afghanistan.

– Christopher Goodwin, *The Sunday Times*

Clearly, the banalization of war as so much work-a-day clock punching is evident in this epigram from the *Times*. All of middle-class life appears to be here, wife and family at home, the daily drive, reminders to shop (lest the terrorists win), the name Smith, even the division between leisure work implied by the act of reading *The Sunday Times*. But this scene is met with a violent *frisson* of nasty equations that determine the guaranteed loss—casino-like—of bourgeois existence and of our global war gamble alike. Gaining is losing in this epigram: consumption is risk without winning, just as war is nowhere and everywhere at home. What is being depicted in this casually chilling account of the military work-shift is the latest in leading edge war-tech applications, the manning of the MQ-9 Reaper drone, which pipes real-time video images as well as other data at light-speed to the cock-pit key-boards where Officer Smith launches Hellfire missiles on unsuspecting targets worlds away. Let us consider this Reaper-moment as emblematic of at least one—the mechanical or robotic—facet of the aerial empire. This is not only the unmanning of the war machine but is also the unmanning of *man*.

The historical genesis of Unmanned Aerospace Vehicles (UAVs) can be located in the Nazi V-1 and V-2 rocket programs. This technology, spun out in the 1950s with the CIA's development of the drone prototype, was first deployed in 1959 in order to serve the secretive Rockefeller interests (Chase Manhattan and Standard Oil) in Latin America.[9] The Reaper's forerunner, the MQ-1 Predator, was used in Yemen in 1992, and deployed in Bosnia in 1994, where it has returned since. In the twenty-first century, aerospace power, such as the Strike Star program, as well as the Predator, the tiny hand launched Raven, and the larger Shadow, gives the military 24-hour continuous air occupation in Afghan and Pakistani skies—and over unknown countries with whom we are not (overtly) at war—365 days a year, at the stealthy height of 21,000 feet, with a range of 3,700 miles from launch base, and with the immediacy of striking the keyboard and dropping the key-strike.[10] There are currently more than 7,000 UAVs deployed by the US military (not to mention those used by Iran, and Hezbollah—a political movement, not a state). On average 2009 saw about one drone strike a week. These techno-terminators are capable of generating 16,000 hours of video a month, far more than can be digested by the human eye, and are therefore being equipped with new batteries of machine intelligence. Drone vision can see through walls, and create biometric data-pictures that translate daily patterns of life, such as street movement and travel routes, into omni-visible target-rich environments. Defense Secretary Gates wants more UAVs, and has already said that the next generation of fighter planes will be the last manned fighter aircraft (Robertson). An estimated 40 or more countries are currently developing drones in 2010.

At one level, the military drono-sphere is a stealthier and more lethal adaptation of US assassination campaigns that go as far back as the Kennedy administration's endorsement of the coup that lead to the South Vietnamese autocrat Ngo Dinh Diem's demise in 1963. Only in the current instance, with estimates as high as 50 civilians killed for each terrorist leader, remote control warfare trades in higher immediate non-combatant loses.[11] At another level, the dawn of the eternal sortie is not the usual art of war. Even with civilian causalities as high as they are—but how can one distinguish the civilian from the insurgent?—the 600 plus Hellfire missiles dropped by Predators in one year's time are being touted for hitting over 90 per cent of their targets. UAVs are credited with killing more than half of al Qaeda's top 20 leaders. But, paradoxically, by surrendering killing to the finer-tuned war machine, by minimizing the human input necessary to launch the new weapons of war, the drono-sphere at least publicly promises a more humane and also farther-reaching way of killing human beings. In line with the RMA's more general over-haul of contemporary war doctrine, new tactical priority and new financing is being given to UAV and supporting programs.[12] Military experts remark that we are only at the cusp of drone potential, and suggest that the UAV is poised to have the biggest impact in 5,000 years on how war is waged (Robertson, n. 18). Traditional fighting tools, not least of which is the regular, human solider, are being replaced by—or better, are being reabsorbed into—unconventional military hard- and soft-ware that are creating a uniquely twenty-first century war imaginary. This imaginary runs the gamut from Officer Smith's trigger *cum* keyboard, to insect-size swarms of nano-drones, robotic snake surveillance, pain-inducing microwave sky-beams, robotic canines, bio-mass consuming automated ground-war machines (the Energetically Autonomous Tactical Robot, or EATR program), and insect-inspired digital optics.[13] But let us stay within the aero-technical realm, to the extent that staying there is possible, and hone in on the knowledge systems that accompany drone war and are endemic to the RMA, the revolution not only in military—but recalling Secretary Gates—also in human affairs.

Defense Department documents outline certain key temporal adjustments in the future of—or better, the future *as*—war. New satellite technology now focuses on high-density cities and other sites, targeting them full-time as potential locations of "urbaniz[ed] insurgence" (Graham 1). Through the use of UAV video surveillance, either deeply embedded within city architecture or loitering in the atmosphere over potentially insurgent areas, highly sophisticated computer software profiles and comparatively reads normal movement patterns against anomalies of human flow in the micro-geographies of the planet's civilian populations. Pattern recognition capabilities such as this can be used either as a platform for the hellfire missile, or to set aloft "fan-propelled swarms [to] disperse nano-payloads" of various levels of destruction or interference, even before the insurgent act of violence can occur (Graham 3). These new capabilities enable warfare to operate in a way that "compress[es] the kill chain," or by a "first look, first feed, first kill" operation, as the Raytheon Corporation puts it. Kill chain compression accelerates the time it takes to find and kill a target to a point of sight-velocity in which opposition disappears the very moment it is configured. "Before [you] can drop your weapon and run," the R&D publicity reads, "[you're] probably already dead" (4). Preemptive war technology is the tactical application of an overall national strategy. It effaces the enemy at the same moment the enemy is designated as such. More peculiar still, the enemy exists in an autogenic way; that is, as an opponent who is effectively generated within the same social space as friendly military occupation. This slippery zone of friend/foe distinction works according to relationships of violence that—if they can be pictured—are always already armed.[14] The target itself is not seen and then destroyed: seeing is its destruction according to current war R&D. According to the DARPA technologies, the less distinguishable it is from civilian life, the less visible and the less objectifiable, the more effective war becomes. Real-time satellite, CCTV, and drone transmissions compress the duration between violence and representation. There is ideally no peaceable distinction between the time it takes to take a picture and the time it takes to strike.

In this way, machine vision re-works our spatial bearings and enables the weaponization of temporality itself. It is not enough to say that war is made more proximate by the notion that, in the homeland, everyone is at least potentially both suspect and object of terror; nor is it sufficient to argue, as Virilio would have it, that the RMA depends on a "dromo-logical revolution" (as in the Greek *dromos*, 'course of running') by tech-nically increasing the dynamics of speed.[15] What we might call a *drono-logical* revolution works according to the twin mastery of both space and time, with intensities of compression and expansion, as well as degrees of velocity, that vary depending on the objective of whatever application is at hand. To put the RMA completely, twenty-first century war functions according to intensities of both proximity *and* distance, of both speed *and* latency, at specific levels and according to discrete military goals. For example, kill-chain compression makes targeting a nearly instanta-neous act; but it also means that war in terms of beginnings-and-ends is displaced by a time signature evidently stopped in its tracks. Wartime is both reduced *and* extended to the hyper-stasis of an eternal present. Similarly, regarding space, on the one hand drone war makes violence seem virtual and remote. On the other hand, the eternal sortie makes war an utterly proximate activity, disintegrating the distinction between vio-lence and ordinary life, however each side defines the ordinary. To cite a particularly apposite example of the new time and space mastery at the core of the RMA, consider kill-chain compression along with Cyberki-netics Inc.'s "brain-gate" program, which for the first time has enabled human brain-computer interface (BCI) in its most intimate sense.[16] This application was seized upon immediately by the Defense Advanced Re-search Projects Agency (DARPA) in 2002, and by 2009 has been fund-ed by more than $25 million in Department of Defense (DOD) grants. Consistent with the DOD's own war neuromics program, BCI harkens toward a moment when weaponry will be literally hard-wired to the hu-man brain, and when *firing* will designate both a micro-synaptic, spatio-cranial event, and a cyber-kinetic macro-explosion on the geography of a battlefield both virtual *and* real. Warfare is here inserted into a network of electricity and human biomass such that thinking itself, now a kinetic ac-tivity, becomes the most deadly weapon of all. A four-millimeter square silicon brain implant, studded with 100 hair-thin microelectrodes, is at-tached matrix-like via a skull-plug that coverts brain waves into a pattern of optical or other data via computer translation. This is a version of dro-no-sphere activity that has absorbed the human being from yet another angle. And again, we see a drono-spheric application that is predicated on a dynamic of non-linear time made possible by new ways of gathering, computing, reading, and infinitely re-reading, computerized data. Here, synapses fire in an only apparently random molecular order, that is, only apparently random to the human eye, which needs machine translation to form coherent micro-patterns that can be extended to whatever weapons system at light speed: intelligence becomes data; becomes electro-kinesis; becomes war. In this way, BCI is capable of stretching and shrinking, accelerating and freezing, the twenty-first century battlefield into one long moment of the right here and now.

Realized by the symbiotic connection between human and machine, BCI uses just a fraction of the brain's 100 million neurons. Here again we can see the connection between kill-chain "compression"—the elimination of an enemy without the slow subject/object alignment that used to guide face to face human combat in a different rhythm of terrestrial violence—and technologies of knowledge "compression," *per se*. There are other examples, beyond the brain's newfound military plasticity, as well. As part of the new UAV technologies, the emerging science of digitized fractal compression is displacing *merely* mimetic real-time image technology with an entirely different space-time calculus. Whereas an older format of JPEG technology uses bit-maps to break down an object into more or less co-equal translations that parallel each other according to individual squares on corresponding grids (the computer screen's and the camera frame's), fractal media offers a more complex notion of image production. Here the word compression means to rethink, and reinterpret (albeit mathematically) a given scene, rather than to simply distill, unpack, and reproduce it. The fractal *mis-en-scene* as such reads a picture that is both more fabricated and more real, producing different layers of spectator-knowledge depending on the sensitivity of the machine and what algorithms are at hand: heat oriented, chemically differentiated, movement based, and so on.[17] In JPEG technology, the more complex the snapshot of the image, the higher the compression ratio is needed for a reliable replication of the object being viewed. It is a question of knowledge as payload, and only so much data can be "lifted" from a visual field at once. But according to fractal image reproduction, the object (read here: target) is produced beyond the battlefield without needing the physical referent. This version of data compression needs only a fragment of the battle scene and a set of mathematically determined fractal instructions to create a given pattern and zero in on its anomalies. The same algorithmic technology that underwrites BCI and that sorts through the meshwork of fractal data compression are used in 2010 to fine-tune shipping networks, predict life-spans, recall records from emails and social networks, map social movements, and predict weather patterns.

As we have already seen, a complex space and time adjustment is at work in the drono-sphere in that it mobilizes what we might call an eternal latency.[18] BCI and fractal data compression together help bring the war machine into an all-seeing and eternal present. At the macroscopic level, fractal media looks among the myriad chaos of life-and-death scenarios for new patterns yet to go into the tool kit of war. In the same way, at the microscopic level, molecular brain firings and computational readings recombine in war's electric flow. At both levels, these patterns can be stored within a vast data bank so that the machine learns greater and greater subtleties in evaluating the norms and deviations of whatever changing groupuscle or latent micro-movement. Essential to the efficiency of weaponized war media, large or small, twenty-first century compression technology uses computational projection to decrease the amount of data needed to be compressed. It uses math to lighten data's so-called weight. Fractal media, as we have seen, only needs to determine what is *probably* there, in the same way the human eye compensates for blind spots and peripheral vision. Drone war is thus executed, Vegas-like, according to a deadly gaming of the epistemo-military odds. The apparently random events that comprise the patterns of collective human existence are finally given objectifiable if also utterly malleable status according to the new war machine. Rather than being tethered to the old bit-map visual technology, which claims mere representational fidelity, mathematically produced targets enable a sort of hyper-vision that invigorates aleatory events and former epistemic blindness—as well as those sheltered spaces of peace called ordinary life—with unprecedented war potential. Drone hyper-vision sorts and manipulates certain life-rhythms (brain waves, as well as social movements) at the speed of light, and therefore offers a more effective application of war fighting than using plain human sight. And by working the image-data from within the fractal war register, not only is image fidelity displaced with image production, but it also becomes possible—and militarily useful—to locate otherwise invisible targets from multiple perspectives at once. For example, the Reaper is being fitted in 2010 with the $150 million Gorgon Stare system. This apparatus configures the drone with multiple super-powered cameras capable of filming two-and-a-half miles around and from 12 different angles (Schachtman). Even if 12 targets are visualized in 12 different directions, the Stare could simultaneously orient the elimination of each. The Argus program—named after the Greek monster with a hundred eyes—will use 92 cameras at once in its round-the-clock orbits. The eternal orbit of the Reaper is the mechanical embodiment of war by fractal means, which is to say, by mathematical probability, rather than by plain human sight, a temporal and ontological "revolution" to be sure: Las Vegas in Afghanistan, once more. A next generation of UAVs, the British Taranis, will take over completely from the human fighter "pilot," as autonomous craft take off and land, survey an area, and return, without any human input. Provided legislation can be amended, civilian cargo flights could be automated by 2015, ushering in a juridical mutation in the notion of human responsibility, commensurate with a mutation in the human root and branch (Goodwin n. 15).

The advance of drone war (and ESCYBERCOM more generally) presents dynamics that we can apply to the basic war policy questions glossed earlier in reference to the US National Security Strategy (NSS). The oft-used term "shadow wars" in this document have both real and representational applications. With kill-chain (temporal) *and* fractal (spatial) compression/expansion in mind, we should say that the NSS extends war's technical logic into a policy statement that recombines the real and representational targets. In the same way, the compression of battle within the statellitic mode produces singularities of non-linear time and blurs the present and the past into an eternal future of violence. Recalling Gates, this unique time-space signature is concurrent with the way war is "blur[ing]" into peace in the form of "shadow" wars. There are "shadow" wars fought today (in Sudan, Syria, Pakistan, and Mexico) where no offensive power claims a presence, and no one takes credit or blame for whatever victory or loss. And we know US policy allows for unannounced attack (if not extra-judicial assassination) in at least 20 different nations (Hallinann). One of the first declarations of President Obama was to underscore the uniqueness of twenty-first century war—no longer the Global War on Terror (GWOT) but simply the "Long War"—as "increasingly unconventional and transnational" (qtd. in Hsu). When the NSS speaks of a "war without duration," insisting that "campaigns need not be sequential" but instead will adhere to a principle of "direct and continuous action," we are well within the fractal time-space purview of the drono-sphere. This does not simply mean continued investment in the Bush Doctrine of preemptive and permanent war, although the Weinberger and the Powell doctrines, which were designed for large-scale, nationally circumscribed oppositions, and for warfare with clear beginnings and ends, are unlikely to return. Rather, the policy of permanent war—or its paradoxical lengthening by way of compression—brings us to a future, after Bush, of war as unseen and everywhere apparent, up close and distant, sped-up and frozen in time.

But technology, such as BCI and fractal data compression, comprises only one level of the aerial empire. In 1991, Manuel De Landa asked a question about whether expert machines, with their own knowledge banks, could produce robot events sufficiently strong to move the executive capacity of the military technocrat to the computer itself, and thus remove humans from the loop. "Could this [emergent satellite and robotic] technology," De Landa writes, "be the beginning of a new breed of machines, predatory machines, capable of hunting and killing humans on their own?" (*War* 161). De Landa goes on to pose the problem, which has gone without its due response, of "a technology of multi-spectral analysis... [and] the ability to detect the very chemical composition of the objects in a picture" (*War* 181). Here De Landa rightly detects a mixing of life-and-death scenarios at a level beyond mere techno-manipulation, a level where the drone reabsorbs its human operator, and where the question of war enters a uniquely contemporary biosynthetic domain. But before elaborating on weaponized biosynthesis, that is, before moving us back to climate change vis-á-vis history of militarized environmental modification (known since the 1970s UN debates as ENMOD), a response to De Landa's question about the shelf-life of the human being needs to be at least partially sketched.

Excursus on the Human

Mass base members are the true silent supporters of insurgency.
                                    – Tactics in Counterinsurgency

A book released by the Bay Area political collective, Retort, seeks within the "contradictions of military neo-liberalism" a "new political era,"
one that admits, with unusual frankness, that "the reality of permanent
war renders inadequate the notion of 'peace' as an oppositional strategy" (15). In a statement that paraphrases Secretary Gates's insistence
on the blurred divisions of traditional battle, Retort "understand[s] that
peace… [in a twenty-first century setting] is no more than war by other means" (94). On the one hand, the group wishes to retain the term
"Left" as "a placeholder for the last best hope of human kind" (14). On
the other hand, Retort wishes to eschew any semblance of a "Left" "van-
guard ideal[ism]" that would reduce critique to a "primordial form of human bonding" (185). What is to be done, "*humanely*" (emphasis original) they ask. Caught between a current war reality without peace and
the very kind of anthropocentric thinking that a new political era of war
is in the process of displacing, Retort both admits a "prevailing sense of
failure [of the 2003 anti-war movement, and the anti-capitalist Left gen-
erally]" (1), and proclaims, with a hint of mourning, to be "partisans of
wishful thinking" (9). There is a parallel tendency in twenty-first century
war discourse, both within military circles and in opposition to them,
that finds in war a positive if also troubled sort of political potential. This
potential concerns the final voicing of a grand collective silence—the
"mass base"—which, precisely on the order of kill-chain compression,
both intensifies the operational significance of humanity as a tool of war
and simultaneously displaces the category of the human being.[19] Can we
find a positive reactivation of the so-called masses in the vicissitudes of
twenty-first century war discourse, and must the masses be a term set by
historical default to connote human forms of biotic combination to the
exclusion of geological, atmospheric, or climactic processes that exist
outside human control?

Current conceptualizations of the multitude are inadequate for coming
to terms with planetary violence on such an expansive order, and are ar-

guably limited by anthropocentric notions of biopolitics. Antonio Negri and Michael Hardt, for example, embrace an epoch of an emergent warfare state, and argue, as I am, that war has "become the primary organizing principle of society" (12). Because the modern *"warfare"* (as opposed to *"welfare"*) state is "fractured by internal division," "new mechanisms of control… [also promise the] creation of new circuits of cooperation and collaborations," an "unlimited number of encounters within the warfare state network" (xiii). As the crypto-ontological analogue to post-Fordist shifts in economic production ("crypto-" because non-individuated), the multitude here marks a "living alternative that grows within Empire" (xiii). Perhaps the word analogue is slightly unfair, in that it is the central point of the book to mark a historical moment where economic and social relations, like Gates's "blurring" of war and peace, fold over into one another, thus giving affective experience its political due, and replacing the spatially and temporally disciplined notion of the fixed laboring subject with a more appositely fluid understanding of commercial informatics and immaterial (both cognitive and caring) modalities of work. The social order has thus moved from a period of uniform striation (including the striation of the "working class," and its attendant mythos, the dialectic), to a post-unitary formation that "brings death" but also, "paradoxically, must produce life" (13). Thus life exists in the form of a positive biopolitics of mass agency and on behalf of human renewal. There is a certain kinship, traceable through a Deleuzian and Spinozist philosophical register, that connects the multitude to De Landa's interest in the war machine mentioned above, and at further remove, to the fractal vicissitudes of what I have been calling the aerial empire. But it is rather a deficient kinship, which betrays a selective reading of Deleuze. The most questionable aspect of the multitude writ as fractal macro-subject is the equation in Negri and Hardt's book between the mass's adaptation of asymmetrical combat and the prominence of what they call "sympathetic moral feeling." Here the primary agency of "affect" is presented according to the ideals of the Scottish Enlightenment, specifically, the moral philosopher *cum* Godfather of liberal capitalism, Adam Smith (Hardt and Negri 50). That the multitude is finally an anthropological marco-subject is clear in Negri and Hardt's emphasis on the communicative procedures attendant to biopolitical production, grounded as they are said to be in a "common"—though occulted—"desire of the multitude" (51). By contrast, "Adam Smith's invisible hand," De Landa writes correctly, is "at the core of modern linear economics" (*Thousand Years* 42). So, too, is Smith's notion of human reciprocity and historical development, as Marx insists upon in his critique of Smith's teleology of economic progress, a version of affective response that is calculated to flatten experience into a highly atomized and individualist brand of socio-commercial order.[20] The term multitude thus presents us with a scenario that jettisons Habermasian rationalist notions of the human being *per se* but replaces communicative reason with a vitalist—and all too human—affirmation of biopower as working within the networks of human affection that future wars might invigorate and sustain across nationalist lines. But will war sustain the human being as such in a net-centric approach to human relations, and why should it?

A different approach, one consistent with De Landa's pioneering work on machine intelligence, would allow us to account for a fuller spectrum of the non-biotic factors of war that are now only beginning to gain tactical military priority. "Who does the earth think it is?" (Deleuze and Guattari 39) is not a rhetorical question, nor is it posed with the expected organic chauvinism (De Landa's term) that haunts a humanely inspired circumscription of the multitude. To put the question that Negri and Hardt do not answer in a distilled fashion, is it possible to conceive not of a new genealogy of morals but, after De Landa, of their *geology* instead? This question puts paid to the illusion that "structure is the earth's last word" (Deleuze and Guattari 41), even where the structure in question is that last set of frontiers separating the human from the non-human, the biological from the geological strata, and here we can extrapolate, technological from ecological realms. One effect that goes missing in current theorization of the war machine à la Negri and Hardt is the way in which war criss-crosses and remixes organic and geological segmentation, and exceeds the bivocal logics that work within—so as to keep separate—these entirely mutable divisions. This criss-crossing, if we follow a different reading of Deleuze, is predicated an alloplastic rather than a homoplastic conception of agency and historical change (Deleuze and Guattari 60). Alloplasty, in the way it is rendered from this position as the total otherness of time, makes a completely different sense of the terrestriality of war, or rather, of war's persistent flows of *de*-territorialization, in that by loosing the moorings of the human being, we can recognize war's aerial status in the fullest possible sense: the shifting isomorphisms that cut back-and-forth between biotic and non-biotic factors of war.

In giving humanity an intermediary—or better, an *intra*-mediary— function among the mass of agencies that intersect the planet rather than assuming an isolated or purely formal notion of historical change, De Landa elaborates on Deleuze's notion of the abstract machine (Deleuze and Guattari 56), and here develops a conception of temporal process as dependant on the shifts in the machinic phylum. De Landa insists upon the productivity of knowledge on the order of a Spinozist conception of "substance," and embraces both mind *and* matter commonly (as we have seen in brain computer interface) as a heterogeneity of elements whose volatile combinatory arrangements are of more interest than their fixed or molar forms. Yet De Landa's take on multiplicity exceeds the multitude writ as a composite of affectively charged human-centered socio-political events, on the order of a postmodern Adam Smith. The machinic phylum refuses to take at face value, and is indeed designed to remix, the "phenomena of centering, unification, totalization, [and] integration" that are presumed to exist between and within this or that line of biotic or non-biotic (let alone species) difference (Deleuze and Guattari 41). The machinic phylum refers to those instances of change that depend upon "dynamical systems operating far from equilibrium," for example, "the uncontrollable elements of ecosystems, the climate…changing weather patterns" (De Landa, *Thousand Years* 279), as much as the turbulence of war. The machinic phylum designates a moment of change that depends on agencies that initiate "auto-catalytic"—or seemingly accidental—events that in turn have "cross-catalytic" consequences. This chain of tipping-points, call them phylogenic trip-wires, spring further accident inducing consequences that require machine intelligence for human beings to use or understand. Thus again, the accident is only an apparently random event, and can be ordered logically (recall again, BCI and fractal data compression) with certain technological prosthesis. Such phylogenic trip wires would depend on such atmospheric or geological changes that work as non-human replicators, and reconfigure the status of the human as such (De Landa, *Thousand Years* 151). We have seen the machinic phylum's dynamic in the case of the drono-sphere. Here, time and space compressions recombine the visual field of battle according to the fractal mathematics of war. And if we allow for the shift in life-form that is the coming robot-soldier, it becomes clear that the machinic phylum also enables us to re-evaluate the processes of self-organization in other spheres, "living creatures with their inorganic counterparts" (104). In this sense, the human being as such becomes a provisional coagulation of biomass that forms "one of several interlocking chains...within a meshwork of heterogeneous elements" evolving equally by chance as by design. By rejecting a neo-institutionalist approach to the question of the human, and relatedly, to the social or polity, De Landa offers a sufficiently expansive and detailed model by which to rethink the tactical value—beyond the anthropocentric tethers of the multitude—of biology and geography, recombined within, and across, one another. As we shall see, the US Army is working on precisely this kind of bio-geological recombination. By giving climate change strategic significance as a force multiplier, and by researching—indeed at the atmospheric level—the organizational lessons of environmental change, we may now claim both weather and natural resources as unpredictably volatile extensions of aerial imperial war.

ENMOD by Default

We regard the weather as a weapon. Anything one can use to get
his way is a weapon and the weather is as good a one as any
– —Dr. Pierre St. Amand

Well before US Navy researcher Dr. Pierre St. Amand made his statement equating weather and weaponry in 1966, the relationship between warfare and environmental change has been an essential factor in war. Archimedes wanted to use the sun's rays, which could be concentrated off highly polished Grecian shields, to set Roman ships afire. The troops of imperial Rome in turn sowed salt into the fields of Carthage, sterilizing the earth, and producing an early example of eco-nomadism that forced a total migration from the city to avoid starvation.[21] Queen Elizabeth beat Spain on the high seas due in part to a storm. Napoleon Bonaparte lost Russia because of bad weather, and was thereby prompted to ask Urbain

Leverrier, the astronomer who discovered Neptune, to foretell winter storms along shipping and military paths. During the war of 1812, the US Army Surgeon General created a directive to keep climatological records to assist war efforts, creating the first electronically networked weather stations in the US. And during the Buffalo Wars of the 1840s, the US realized that eradicating the buffalo economy would help clear the plains of their human foes and end the indigenous American's way of life (Halacy 31). The US civil war is given credit for expanding the network of weather observing stations. And even though President Lincoln resisted increased funding for the new science of weather forecasting, there were already 500 telegraphic nodes by the outbreak of the war in 1861 (Whitnah 10). The civil war thus set the stage for longer-term increases in congressional funding for weather technologies, and for the US Army signal service to assume responsibility for meteorological knowledge in 1870. By 1881, the National Weather Service (NWS) and the National Oceanic and Atmospheric Organization (NOAA) reorganized climate science outside the military budget, though both the NWS and NOAA are traditionally headed by military officers and remain quasi-military organizations (Fine 211).

World War I, the first total war of the twentieth century, depended upon the use of wind patterns and humidity levels to deliver airborne mustard gas, phosgene, and chlorine. But because wind knowledge was in its infancy, gas warfare had only moderate effectiveness (about four per cent of casualties).[22] The first such attack was made possible by German Nobel Prize scientist Fritz Haber (1868–1934), the inventor of chemical fertilizer, and only later the father of chemical warfare. By World War II, environmental variables and the art of war were fully and officially intertwined. By 1956, the giant brain of the US-Army financed Electronic Numerical Integrator and Computer (ENIAC) was announced, creating new possibilities not only for calculating bomb trajectories and kill ratios but also for providing the computational power necessary to produce the kind of mathematically based, multi-layered atmospheric forecasting that Professor Bjerknes and the Bergen school of proto-meteorology could only speculate about at the turn of the nineteenth century. Spurred on by the Russian Sputnik, the US Naval Research Laboratory took the first official steps to put a weather satellite into the earth's atmosphere. With support from the US military's Research and Development Corporation (RAND), and with participation from 8 federal agencies including the Army, Navy, and Air Force, 1966 saw the world's first operational weather satellite system. At this moment, climate and war went global in a scientific sense, and the atmosphere could be observed every 12 hours from a single orbiting machine.[23] Between 1967 and 1972, the tactic of environmental modification (ENMOD) was fashioned in a sustained and developed way. Attempting to extend the monsoon season in Southeast Asia, the US military dispersed several tons of silver iodide from its C-130s and F-4 Phantoms in order to produce heavy rain over the centuries old Ho Chi Minh trail. Operation Popeye, as the program was known, ran ENMOD missions over neutral Cambodia and Laos (in violation of international law), as well as in North and South Vietnam. Popeye was active to the tune of 2,600 flights, 47,000 units of cloud seeding material, and a cost of $21.6 million.[24] Not to be outdone by the Romans in Carthage, the DOD also attempted ENMOD missions against Cuba in 1969 and 1970. The goal was to cause clouds to drop their rain before reaching the island, producing a genocidal crisis of starvation and drought.[25]

Thus the earliest historical examples of unconventional warfare—whether accidental or deliberate—were climatological in nature. And as this history has not been fully written, we can offer here a set of working distinctions, useful for making some final points about the aerial empire, between the manner in which weather has been called upon during the Cold War to enhance the military arsenal, and beyond that, the manner in which climate change is altering the dynamics of war doctrine in a multi-polar post-Cold War epoch. To bring the list of past ENMOD activities mentioned above into a contemporary context, we must distinguish between the instrumental uses of climate change and a new science of environmental security that both seizes upon the event-opportunities of the coming eco-catastrophes, and translates the aleatory dynamics that produce atmospheric and geographical extremes into an emergent war analytic. To understand the current stakes of climate change as a military force multiplier, we must make the distinction—crucial for understanding what I called above the shelf life of the human being—between EN-MOD by design, which is the pre-planned fabrication of climate change à la Popeye; and ENMOD by default, which is the turning of environmental crises into an autogenic form of weaponry that works its violence not only against but also eventually without the need for human beings.

In the mid-1970s, the Soviet Union, who had its own long standing ENMOD programs, publicized previous US activities in Indochina. Since 1977, then, the final version of the treaty defines ENMOD to encompass:

> any technique for changing—through the deliberate manipulation of natural processes—the dynamics, composition or structure of the earth, including the biota, lithosphere, hydrosphere, and atmosphere, or of outer space, so as to cause effects such as earthquakes and tsunamis, an upset in the ecological balance of a region, or changes in weather patterns (clouds, precipitation, cyclones of various types and tornado storms), in the state of the ozone layer or atmosphere, in climate patterns or in ocean currents.

However, the conditions under which this treaty was ratified, a major point of contention between the opposing Cold War blocks, was the US insistence that "each State Party to the Convention undertakes not to engage in military or any other hostile use of environmental modification techniques *having widespread, long-lasting or severe effects* as the means of destruction, damage or injury to another State Party" (emphasis mine). By attaching the definition of "severe" to the time-space caveats of "widespread and long-lasting," the DOD aligned US delegates to the UN introduced a provision that would allow for a future deployment of environmental war. They managed to put key loopholes around the most important variables in war: as we have seen above in the context of emergent war technology, the control of space and time. These variables began to be re-introduced in a serious way as recently as 1996. In a paper, collectively authored by 7 Air Force Officers, called "Weather as Force Multiplier: Owning the Weather in 2025," the idea of "full spectrum conflict" presents weather manipulation as a "more important weapon than the [atomic] bomb" (House 5). "Air Force 2025" measures hurricane energy in terms of bomb capacity, noting that a worthwhile "tropical storm is equal 10,000 one megaton hydrogen bombs" [House 18]). The 45,000 lightning strikes that hit the planet daily are said to contain "electro-potential…with offensive military benefit" that might be induced by "atmospherically buoyant...microscopic" computer drones, designed to seed the sky with the chemistry necessary for "aimed and timed lightening strikes" (House 27). The connection between this version of electropotential and brain wave interface is not an immediate one, since the latter interface, insofar as it absorbs the human in the war machine, is more akin to ENMOD by default. With specific focus on the ionosphere (the atmospheric layer 1200 miles above earth where radio waves are reflected as a natural mirror), AF 2025 also evokes the High-frequency Active Auroral Research Program (HAARP). Established in 1992 and based in Gokona Alaska, HAARP is an array of 180 tower transmitters, 72 feet in height mounted on thermopiles spaced 80 feet apart in a 12 by 15 rectangular grid.[26] Put simply, HAARP is an ionospheric heater designed to excite low atmospheric particles, the largest such machine ever built.[27]

Thus ENMOD by design is by no means off the military table (and note: the American Meteorological Society now endorses an ENMOD approach to curb global warming), but it is not as fully apparent in (publicly assessable) doctrinal discussion in the way that ENMOD by default currently is ("Re-engineering" 7). The time-and-space caveats attached to the 1977 UN ENMOD convention have taken on unprecedented significance given the current climate change reality, which is no longer overtly dodged by the current US ruling apparatus (military, government, corporate). Rather, climate change is embraced as a target enhancing operational environment, the purest form of ENMOD by default. This adaptation to, indeed embracing of, planetary risk makes military strategy out of a forgone conclusion of anthropogenic climate catastrophe. However, anthropogenesis—a crucial qualification—does not at all translate to the preservation of the human being. Consistent with both military technology and national security policy, ENMOD by default disintegrates the efficacy as much of human will as of the human being as such. Humanity may appear to determine war in the aerial empire, but we are by no means in control of the new dynamics of planetary violence. At 350 ppm, we are at—and are surpassing—a level of "dangerous anthropogenic interference" (DAI), with CO_2 levels to approach 450 parts per million by 2012 (Kolber 42).[28] (China's toleration proves higher, at 550 ppm and even 750 ppm.) Ice caps are melting, sea levels rising, faster than the conservative International Panel on Climate Change (IPCC) predicted in 2007. At the current pace of extinction more than half the earth's animal species will be gone by the end of the century, and according to a 2009 MIT Integrated Global Systems model, it will be too late to stem eco-catastrophe much sooner than predicted. IPCC panel head Rejendra Pachauri cites 2012, the expiration date of the US rebuked Kyoto Protocol, as the planet's next tipping-point (qtd. in Vanderheiden xi). The same 2009 Strategic Studies Institute (SSI) document that we cited by way of introducing drono-spheric SkyOps several moves above also displaces the human-centered notion of ENMOD by deliberate design à la Operation Popeye with a far more complicated (if not also suicidal) strategy of ENMOD by default: adaptation to, as much as mobilization of, the destructive power unleashed by coal-produced CO_2 gases. Here the term climate change moves the problem of ecology from the limited context of anthropogenesis toward a more perversely expansive morphogenic realm of agitated particles, chance compounds, and aleatory aggregates that are given human purpose only in the wake of this or that event of mass crisis. The ecology of war is seen here as a way of fighting so-called cross-border wars that are not merely *trans*-national (as across national lines) but are also *infra*-national (as within nations) because war is phylogenic now. Climate change becomes an accelerant and a multiplier of military force (*TSC* 4) that eventually turns on its masters.

We have seen the mutation of space and acceleration of time as noted in the SSI climate change materials already at work in brain-machine interface technologies (BMI), and in the drono-sphere, examined above. Here, recall, we found a set of innovative war applications that fused machinery and meat. Let's also emphasize that, given the blurriness of contemporary security doctrine and the twenty-first century war machine, we also detected an elaborate data-driven war analytic that no longer cares to divide war from peace, foe from friend, risk from security, alterity from homeland, state power from civility, and so on and so forth with the traditional divisions of Western modernity. The notion of climate change as a form of tactical enhancement may also be applied to the way in which fractals and chaos are being considered with renewed pervasiveness in emergent military systems. A 1996 Navel War College paper, "Chaos Theory: the Essentials of Military Applications," provides a theoretical foreshadowing of drone technology, using chaos analysis in a precisely analogous way that De Landa's uses the term machinic phylum. In the temporal sense, chaos is defined, apropos James Gleick's well-known work, as "behavior that is *not periodic,* [but is] *apparently random*, where the *system response is still recurrent* (the pendulum still swings back and forth) but *no longer in a predictable way*" (James 14; emphasis original).[29] By the chance synchronizing of aleatory time signatures that both cut across and recombine biotic and non-biotic strata (for example, climate change and human beings), computer technology produces similar mutations of space. Like fractal media, chaos theory allows us to identify " *transitions* between various dynamics, that are common to many systems" (14). But again these dynamics cannot be visualized in an intelligibly useful way without the mathematical reading ability brought about by electronic machine vision. Algorithms turn chaos into otherwise invisible new phylogenic lines. Consistent with fractal media, the chance event is seized upon to coordinate unforeseen alignments between unlike entities, as drone vision produces a probable calculus—Las Vegas style—of a virtual battlefield that we cannot simply model in advance. "Chaotic flow generates time intervals with no periodicity of apparent pattern" (15), which is the operational equivalent of security predicated on proximate and perpetual war. And most importantly for understanding the relations of violence in the aerial imperium, the intra-systemic dynamics of chaos gain military application by modeling weapons on climate at several levels. Climate change is conceived of in the literal sense with ENMOD by design. In turn, ENMOD by default eventuates in a stage of war that transcends humanity's capacity to control what we might as well summarize as an atmospheric army about to go rogue. Chaos theory seeks military benefit by reorganizing war according to the asymmetrical systems of "weather dynamics and clouds." And on the order of the machinic phylum, twenty-first century war is predicated on non-linear similar turbulence events, wind patterns, storm systems, lightening-bombs, ecological weapons, that are literally tipped by mechanical "swarms where battlefields are filled with new clouds that carry lethal capabilities" (James 79).

Climate change is a new—and will become the predominant—means of waging if not also of modeling war. The atmosphere has now become a weapon both by design and by default. And to the same extent, related technologies such as BCI and fractal media efface and reabsorb the human being. This effacement/reabsorption happens, in the first instance, as the war machine has wedged a new machinic phylum across carbon- and non-carbon based life forms; secondly, and more dramatically, this process of effacement/absorption happens in the sense that humanity has stacked the odds against its long-term survival. The victory for this or that side of the global human population is no longer a presumptive goal in the context of an aerial imperium. As mentioned above once be- fore, there are 50 million environmental refugees in 2010, and according to UN estimates there will be more than 200 million by 2050, marking an epoch of population culling if not also a set of re-divisions within the human species (Glenn and Gordon 2). In the eco-suicidal register that is coterminous with ENMOD by default, humanity itself becomes a side, a losing side, within a meshwork of trans-biotic agency that wins by en- veloping its human other. Rather than being apparent as a category that might be divisible into simply national oppositions, so-called transna- tional war means that the human being is becoming barely traceable as a fading bio-political ideal. With the 1925 Geneva protocols against chemi- cal warfare in mind, the International Committee of the Red Cross "urges [us] to…remember our common humanity" (International Committee of the Red Cross 3). Within the aerial empire, remembering humanity may be all we are going to have.

Notes

1. For the economic side of this debate, see Harvey and Wood.

2. The Fiscal Year 2008 National Defense Authorization Act, Public Law 110- 181, section 951, amends 10 U.S. Code § 118 to require that the next national security strategy and national defense strategy include guidance for military planners on the risks of climate change, and that the next quadrennial defense review examine capabilities the armed forces will need to respond to climate change.

3. On the physical reality of US militarism in the form of foreign bases, see Johnson.

4. Not surprisingly, in 2010 Mexico adopted an Israeli supplied drone war program to battle its own drug cartel insurgence. See "Mexico deploys Israeli UAVs in War on Drug Cartels."

5. On the Northern Command, see "Pentagon to Detail Plan to Bolster Security."

6. For an excellent example of the colonial revolutionary warrior in US history, see Ewald.

7. The important question of the failed state cannot be addressed in this short space. But see Hitchcock.

8. For Habermas, the "human being *per se*" furnished the political self-understanding of the bourgeois public sphere. See 29 ff.

9. On the Helio Courier, see Colby and Dennett 69, 282.

10. UAV specifications in this section are taken from House, et. al. On drone specs, see De Luce.

11. By some estimates US air strikes in the "long war" have killed 85 per cent women and children. See Engelhardt.

12. See Drew.

13. On the EATR program, see Byrne.

14. On "autogenic war," see Hill.

15. See Virilio 73 ff.

16. See Martin.

17. See Davis.

18. On the latency and image, see Parks 137.

19. I have explored the changes around the concept of humanity and contemporary war doctrine in a special issue of *Differences* called "The Future of the Human." See my "'Terrorists Are Human Beings': Mapping the US Army's 'Human Terrain Systems' Program."

20. Adam Smith is an apt figure in post-structuralist variations on the Marxist tradition. See Louis Althusser's discussion of Marx's reading of Smith. See also my "The Crowded Text: E.P. Thompson, Adam Smith, and the Object of Eighteenth-century Writing."

21. See Russell.

22. See Haber.

23. See Fishman and Kalish.

24. For a detailed account of American environmental war efforts and their effects in Indochina, see Stockholm International Peace Research Institute.

25. This assault on Cuba occurred according to former DOD consultant Lowell Ponte. Pentagon sources deny such operations. See the *International Herald Tribune.*

26. See H.A.A.R.P.

27. See Shachtman and Chossudovsky.

28. See also Hunt.

29. The *locus classicus* for this text and other chaos-oriented war doctrine is James Gleick's bestseller, *Chaos: Making a New Science.*

Works Cited

Althusser, Louis. *Reading Capital.* London: Verso, 1999.

Branfman, Fred. "Mass Assassinations Lie at the Heart of America's Military Strategy in the Muslim World." *Alternet.* Web. 24 August 2010. <http://www.alternet.org/story/147944/>.

Byrne, John. "Military Death Cyborg Synergy Come True." *Rawstrory.* Web. 7 July 2009. <http://rawstory.com/blog/2009/07/new-military-robots-could-feed-on-corpses>.

Chossudovsky, Michel. "Weather Warfare." *Ecologist* May 2008: 14–15.

Colby, Gerard and Charlotte Dennett. *Thy Will Be Done: The Conquest of the Amazon.* New York: HarperCollins, 1996.

Davis, Frederic E. "My Main Squeeze: Fractal Compression." *Wired.* Web. <http://www.wired.com/wired/archive/1.05/fractal_pr.html>.

De Landa, Manuel. *War in the Age of Intelligent Machines.* New York: Zone Books, 1991.

---. *A Thousand Years of Non-linear History.* New York: Zone Books, 1997.

De Luce, Dan. "No Let-up in US Drone War in Pakistan." *Commondreams.org.* Web. 21 July 2009. <http://www.commondreams.org/headline/2009/07/21-6>.

Deleuze, Gilles and Felix Guattari. *A Thousand Plateaus: Capitalism and Schizophrenia.* Trans. Brian Massumi. Minneapolis: University of Minnesota Press, 1987.

Drew, Christopher. "Military Budget Reflects a Shift in US Strategy." *The New York Times* 7 April 2009. Web.< http://www.nytimes.com/2009/04/07/us/politics/07/defense.html>.

Ewald, Captain Johan. *Diary of the American War.* New Haven: Yale University Press, 1979.

Editorial. *New Scientist.* July 15, 2009.

Engelhardt, Tom. "Killing Civilians," *Tomgram.* Web. 24 April 2009. <http://www.tomdispatch.com/post/print/175063/Tomgram%253A%>.

ENMOD. *The Convention on the Prohibition of Military or any Other Hostile use of Environmental Modification Techniques.* Web. <http://www.sunshine-project.org/enmod/primer.html>.

Fine, Gary Alan. Authors of the Storm: Meteorologists and the Culture of Prediction. Chicago: University of Chicago Press, 2007.

Fishman, Jack and Robert Kalish. *The Weather Revolution.* New York: Plenum Press, 1994.

Gates, Robert. "US Global Leadership Campaign." 15 July 2008. Web. <http://www.defenselink.mil/faq/comment.html>.

Gleick, James. *Chaos: Making a New Science.* New York: Penguin, 1987.

Glenn, Jerome C. and Theodore J. Gordon. *2007 State of the Future.* Washington, DC: World Federation of the United Nations Associations and American Council for the United Nations University, 2007.

Goodwin, Christopher. "Hunting Down the Taliban in Nevada." *The Sunday Times* 22 Mar. 2009. Web. <http://www.timesonline.co.uk/tol/life_and_style/men/article5944961.ece>.

Graham, Stephen. "US Military vs. Global South Cities." *Z Magazine.* 20 July 2005. Web. <www.zmag.org/content/showarticle.cfm?S>.

Haber, Ludwig Fritz. *The Poisonous Cloud: Chemical Warfare in the First World War.* London: Oxford University Press, 1986.

Habermas, Jurgen. *The Structural Transformation of the Public Sphere.* Cambridge: MIT Press, 1989.

Halacy, D.S. *The Weather Changers.* New York: Harper and Row, 1968.

Hallinann, Conn. "Who are the Shadow Warriors? Countries are getting Hit by Major Military Attacks, and No One is Taking Credit." *Foreign Policy in Focus.* 28 May 2009. Web. <http://labs.daylife.com/journalist/conn_hallinan__foreign_policy_in_focus>.

Hardt, Michael and Antonio Negri, *The Multitude: War and Democracy in the Age of Empire.* New York: Penguin, 2004.

Harvey, David. *The New Imperialism.* Oxford: Oxford University Press, 2003.

Hill, Mike. "The Crowded Text: E.P. Thompson, Adam Smith, and the Object of Eighteenth-century Writing." *English Literary History* 69.2 (Summer 2002).

---. "'Terrorists Are Human Beings': Mapping the US Army's 'Human Terrain Systems' Program," *The Future of the Human*, special issue of *Differences: A Journal of Feminist Cultural Studies* 20.2–5 (2009).

Hitchcock, Peter. "The Failed State and the State of Failure." *Mediations* 23.2 (Spring 2008): 70–87.

House, Col. Tamzy J. et al. *Weather as a Force Multiplier: Air Force 2025*. August 1996. Web. <www.au.af.mil/au/2025>.

Hsu, Spencer S. "Obama Integrates Security Councils." *The Washington Post* 27 May 2009. Web. <http:www.washingtonpost.com/wp-dyn/content/article/2009/05>.

Hunt, Julian. "China's Growing Pains." *New Scientist* 18 Aug. 2009: 22–23.

International Committee of the Red Cross. "Preventing the Use of Biological and Chemical Weapons: 80 Years On." 6 Oct. 2005. Web. <http:/www.icrc.org/web/eng/seteeng0.nsf/htmlall/gas-protocol100605>.

International Herald Tribune. 29 June 29 1976: 2.

James, Major Glen E. *Chaos Theory: The Essentials for Military Applications*. Navel War College: Newport Paper Number Ten, 1996.

Johnson, Chalmers. "America's Unwelcome Advances." *Mother Jones* 22 Aug. 2008. Web. <http::/www.motherjones.com/print/15574>.

---. *The Sorrows of Empire*. New York: Metropolitan Books, 2004.

Kolbert, Elizabeth. "The Catastrophist." *The New Yorker* 29 June 2009: 42.

Martin, Richard. "Mind Control," *Wired* 13 March 2005. Web. <http://www.wired.com/wired/archive/13.03/brain_pr.html>.

"Mexico deploys Israeli UAVs in War on Drug Cartels." *Homeland Security Newswire*. 26 Aug. 2010. Web.<http://homelandsecuritynewswire.com/mexico-deploys-israeli-uavs-war-drug-cartels>.

National Security Strategy of the United States of America. Falls Village, CT: Winterhouse Edition, 2002.

Parks, Lisa. "Planet Patrol: Satellite Image, Acts of Knowledge, and Global Security." *Rethinking Global Security*. Ed. Andrew Martin and Patrice Petro. New Brunswick: Rutgers University Press, 2006.

Parsons, Rymn J. *Taking up the Security Challenge of Climate Change.* Leavenworth, KS: Strategic Studies Institute, 2009.

"Pentagon to Detail Plan to Bolster Security," *The Washington Post.* Web. <http://www.msnbc.msn.com/id/27989275>.

"Re-engineering the Earth." Editorial. *New Scientist* 29 July 2009: 7.

Retort. *Afflicted Powers: Capital and Spectacle in a New Age of War.* London: Verso, 2005.

Robertson, Nic. "How Robot Drones are Revolutionizing the Face of war." *CNN.* 26 July 2009. Web.<http://www.cnn.com/2009/WORLD/americas/07/23/wus.warfare.remote.uav/>.

Russell, Ruth. "The Nature of Military Impacts on the Environment." *Sierra Club, Air, Water, Earth, Fire.* San Francisco: Sierra Club Special Publication, 1974.

Shachtman, Noah. "Air Force to Unleash 'Gorgon Stare.'" *Wired* 19 Feb. 2009. Web. <http://www.wired.com/dangeroom/2009/02/gorgon-stare/#more>.

---. "Strange New Air Force Facility Energizes Ionosphere." *Wired* 20 July 2009. Web. <http://www.wired.com/print/seccurity/magazine/17-08/mf_haarp/>.

Stockholm International Peace Research Institute. *Ecological Consequences of the Second Indochina War.* Stockholm: SIPRI, 1976.

United States Army. *Tactics in Counter Insurgency CFM 3-24.2.* Department of the Army: 2009.

Vanderheiden, Steve. Ed. *Political Theory and Global Climate Change.* Cambridge: MIT Press, 2008.

Virilio, Paul. *Speed and Politics.* Los Angeles: Semiotext[e], 2006.

Whitnah, Donald R. *A History of the United States Weather Bureau.* Urbana: University of Illinois Press, 1961.

Wood, Ellen Meiksins. *Empire of Capital.* London: Verso, 2003.

Chapter 11

Notes Toward a Post-Carbon Philosophy

"It's the Economy, Stupid"

Martin McQuillan

One more try to save the discourse of a "world" that
we no longer speak, or that we still speak, sometimes
all the more garrulously, as in an emigrant colony

           – Jacques Derrida, *"Economies of the Crisis"*

Post-Carbon Philosophy

This is an essay about philosophy, its task and object, after the end of a carbon economy. This topic is not wild science fiction; according to most estimates we (collectively as a planet) have reached or surpassed the moment of peak oil (the point at which world reserves begin to dwindle). Effectively the post-carbon epoch has already begun, since it is now a task of the critical imagination to envisage a world beyond the fractal distillation of petroleum. The task of thinking a post-carbon world also revolves around the difficulty of thinking 'a world' at this moment, that is to say, a world made global by what we have been taught to term mondelization or more strictly mondelatinization (a globalization based on western hegemony and privilege).[1] The place of philosophy, as a western model of thought, is no doubt vexed in this situation, given that all of the terms of globalization such as "economy," "law," "sovereignty," "world," and so on are all philosophical terms and are all metaphysical through and through. However, given where this task of thinking is beginning from and the resources it has to hand we will have to pick up the philosophical heritage that confronts us and come to terms with the obvious and inevitable difficulty of becoming part of the history of the object that one wishes to describe through this philosophical vocabulary. If it is true that we are entering an epoch of new materialities for which we as yet have no descriptive framework then philosophy must respond to this situation. The question of matter after all is also a philosophical concept. The empirical and all empiricisms are, as Derrida notes as early as "Violence and Metaphysics," philosophical gestures that embed themselves within the history of philosophy. His reading of Levinas in this essay is to suggest the ways in which Levinas demonstrates that all empiricism is metaphysical, and a constant philosophical thematization "of the infinite exteriority of the other." Levinas in contrast understands the empirical not as a positivism but as an experience of difference and of the other. "Empiricism," claims Derrida, "always has been determined by philosophy, from Plato to Husserl as nonphilosophy: as the philosophical pretention to nonphilosophy" (152). That is as philosophy's way of affecting to speak in a non-philosophical way. However, nothing can more profoundly conjure the need for philosophy than this denial of philosophy by philosophy. Within the metaphysical schema that is nonphilosophy, the irruption of the wholly other solicits philosophy (i.e. the logos) as its own origin, end, and other. There is no escape from philosophy as far as empiricism is concerned; there will only ever be a thinking about the empirical that is philosophical. It is this radicalization of empiricism that deconstruction proposes as a breathless, inspiring journey for philosophy in the later years of the twentieth century; as Derrida states in the opening paragraphs of the essay on Levinas, it is the closure of philosophy by nonphilosophy that gives thought a future: "it may even be that these questions are not philosophical, are not philosophy's questions. Nevertheless, these should be the only questions today capable of founding the community, within the world, of those who are still called philosophers; and called such in remembrance, at very least, of the fact that these questions must be examined unrelentingly" (79). So, the question of the materiality of a post-carbon economy may not be a question that philosophy has the resources to answer but which must nevertheless be thought about and so determined in a philosophical manner. It may be the case that long before peak oil we reached the point of peak philosophy, with Hegel or Marx, Nietzsche, or Heidegger and what remains is a post-philosophical speculative economy, which in some necessary way sits on considerable philosophical and metaphysical reserves. This thought will be of use to us in the coming pages; just as I am at pains in this opening paragraph to point out that one cannot seek to swap climate change denial for the denial of philosophy.

It will then be difficult to imagine the new materialities of the age of climate change without philosophy and in fact the persistent theme of matter in the discourse on environmentalism will undoubtedly compel us towards philosophy. It may be the case that philosophy will tell us that all and every environmentalism is a metaphysics grounded on an unquestioned empiricism based upon an unsustainable distinction between nature and culture. The task of a deconstruction of the question of the environmental then might be a rethinking of the experience of the environment, and the environment as experience, as an encounter with an irreducible presence and perception of a phenomenality that is also an experience of the other, the wholly other, and of difference. It is this wholly other, the other that separates Derrida from Levinas, that must be attended to as the new materiality of an epoch of climate change and post-carbon economy. However, in this essay I will not be attending to the environmental effects as such of carbon. In a certain sense it is nonsense to speak of a post-carbon materiality since even if hydrocarbon fuels were to be outlawed tomorrow, carbon and its allotropes would remain, as they were in Plato's time, the fourth most abundant element in the universe. Therefore, whenever I speak of a 'post-carbon philosophy' the question in hand does not strictly concern the depletion of a material itself. Rather, the task for thinking relates to the sort of world, being in the world, and thought concerning the world that an economy and culture based on the exploitation of hydrocarbons has given rise to, and what its prospects might be as this economy and culture inevitably weans itself off of petroleum and onto some other alternative energy source, while living with the inheritance of a century of intensive hydrocarbon use. In the end, the culture and economy of post-carbon-modernity might not look that different from the one that we occupy today. Undoubtedly, carbon-fuelled capital will not easily give up its privileges in favour of so-called sustainable living, and will seek to replace the risks of a carbon-based economy with those of a nuclear-based economy. The new materialities and bio-diversity challenges of the post-carbon age may quickly begin to look exactly the same as those of the present moment, the here and now proposing its own future. The shape of things to come is not the object of our speculation here. Rather, in this text I would like to consider the question of speculation itself.

Philosophy will not name an alternative energy source, and this is a question that philosophy cannot answer and may not be a philosophical question. Philosophy, on the other hand, offers a model of crisis. It is at its most eloquent when talking about limits, ends and telos, and about the inability of theory or the humanities or the human sciences to ground themselves in institutions and actions, and concerning the incommensurability between what we still call "politics," "ethics," "economy," and the global mutations today and the deconstruction of those mutations. If we are to understand what is most singular about our present time it will emerge from this philosophical reflection. However, the challenge for philosophy is not to draw down upon this template but to name and situate the most acute moment of the here and now as a crisis that distinguishes it from all previous crises. It is in understanding how the present crisis (of the globalization of neoliberalism, climate change, peak oil, and bio-diversity extinction), differs from all other crises (in the history of western colonialism, say) that philosophy might begin to think philosophically about this moment. Equally, there may well be no universal experience of this moment that would enable philosophy to act in a philosophical manner with respect to it. Given the diverse experiences of what it might mean for different parts of the world to be in this situation there may not be either a common horizon or discourse capable of offering an assured competence to frame and explain the crisis. In this sense, the philosophical concept of crisis that holds in the tradition after Valéry and Husserl would be faced with an inability to phenomenalize and ontologize a determinable universal experience of the crisis. Philosophy then sits on the cusp between being drawn to the crisis as the only means of determining it and having its own constitutive divisibility demonstrated by its inability to address the crisis through the redundancy of its own model of crisis.[2]

It may be the case that the crisis of peak oil and simultaneous irreversible climate change is only a concentration and reiteration of previous liminal cases in the history of the exploitation of planetary resources by the west. For example, kerosene derived from coal and petroleum replaced whale oil as the source of illumination in America and Europe. The whaling industry had been in decline for a decade due to diminishing sperm whale populations and the destruction of the Northern whaling fleet during the civil war, when hydrocarbon illuminants were introduced out of necessity and innovation leading to gaslight homes and cities and a new phase of development in modernity. However, to say that our present crisis today is not unique does not mean that it is not singular. The task for thinking about the present crisis might be to understand the idea of the crisis today, the understanding that this is a crisis, that it corresponds to an idea or model of a crisis, provided for us by, say, philosophy and is theatricalized in contemporary discourse as such. The status of the idea that the world is in crisis as doxa might be one of the defining features of this crisis, the very thing that makes it like no other moment. The singularity of our present crisis might be defined by the resources spent in the mediatisation of the idea that the world is in crisis, by the competing political interests of the day (the advocates, the activists, the sceptics, the deniers, and the lobbyists) through all the channels of contemporary communication. On the one hand, within such rhetorical exchanges, the naming or denial of a crisis always serves a political interest. On the other hand, to identify an event as a crisis is always to ontologize it and to submit it to the model of the crisis that would explain it and domesticate it. Perhaps, we might say that today is not a crisis at all but rather the latest instance of a long history of planetary exploitation by capital, this instance being no more critical than any other in a long history. The naming of a crisis in the present works to mask that history and to neutralize it, giving it form and therefore a program and calculability.

For either side of the present debate on climate change, say, to name only one of the threats to planetary life today, to name this process and event as a crisis would be to appropriate it for the present and for a metaphysics of presence. In giving the event of climate change a form and a certain calculability one has begun to neutralize the effects of its unknowable future and to erase the experience of alterity at the heart of an encounter with the wholly other. To name it as a crisis is to subject it to the temporality of "the crisis," namely that it will one day come to an end and a state of normativity will be restored. One side of the debate would say that "normality" (whatever normal might mean on a planet that has weathered at least five major ice ages) can be resumed by cutting carbon emissions and introducing "sustainable" energy consumption. The other side says the present is in fact normal and no change in climate is in process. Either way, each side depends upon the idea of a normative climate derived from the idea that a change in climatic conditions would constitute a crisis for the human race. A crisis that would no longer allow mankind to run a system of resource exploitation that has sustained its development for the last two hundred years. In other words, what is at stake in the climate change debate is the very future of a world economy and the normative, or, ideal conditions for its operation. That is to say, the debate is predicated on an essentially conservative notion of how to sustain the ideal or normative. In fact, the event and singularity of climate change is constituted in the concept that it is already irreversible. The singularity of climate change as a crisis might be that it is not subject to the temporality of the crisis and that it might be a crisis without resolution and so demonstrate itself not to be a crisis at all but a constant state. In this sense crisis becomes a permanent condition or at least the resolution of this crisis is the construction of a new idea of the normative. In this way, climate change must change the very idea of a crisis by which we seek to determine it. At the same time, climate change becomes part of the latest chapter in the history of the idea of crisis and continues to be appropriated by it and subsumed to the model it undermines.

On the issue of irreversible climate change and peak oil, I find myself to be surprisingly sceptical. Given that hydrocarbon consumption is already in decline and without fresh initiatives (although there are many mountain tops to be dynamited and much oil shale to be extracted yet) even the most optimistic forecasts suggest that petroleum consumption will have dwindled to almost nothing in my life time, why should we then be overly concerned by targets for climate emissions set for fifty years into the future? I do not doubt the damage that will be caused to, say, the polar ice caps during those fifty years and the resultant biodiversity loss. However, such targets seem to me to be aimed at 'eking out' the remains of carbon emission rather than addressing the more fundamental underlying causes of climate change. This "eking out" is also a transition phase for global capital as it acquires a new carbonless fuel. In fact, while it may take a million years for the planet to correct the damage inflicted in the next fifty, surely this realignment of the environment will take place in the absence of continued fossil fuel consumption. That is to say, that irreversible climate change is not necessarily irreversible, just that it is irreversible in the lifetime of global capital that as a planetary life form is something of a Johnny-come-lately. In this way, the discourse on climate change on all sides retains the vestiges of an irreducible humanism and the parochialism of western metaphysics. It would not be enough, it seems to me, for philosophy to accept the discourse and axiomatics of climate change advocates, even if it were possible to accept the science without reservation. Rather, this discourse in its present state is open to question, is fragile and perfectible, or even deconstructable (as Derrida reminds us of the abolitionist discourse on the death penalty[3]) because it more often than not limits the idea of planetary life to the present conditions of a western-lead globalization and so inadvertently positions climate change as the latest accident to befall the western subject. In this way, climate change is the latest phase of the crisis of European humanity. Accordingly, it calls for a response from western humanity, one that will require the response of science, philosophy, and the human sciences (including economics). However, as an encounter with the wholly other of planetary life beyond the limits of western humanism, the event of climate change will transform, mutate, and challenge the protocols of European humanity's intellectual apparatus. Climate change accordingly is a challenge to reason and so to philosophy as the custodian of western reason. If one were to question or attempt to exceed this as the locus of the present discourse of crisis, one might quickly find oneself in a position where terms like "crisis" and "irreversible" were no longer appropriate.

As soon as we have determined a moment of crisis, with the temporality of a crisis and the calculability of a crisis, then we have entered the realm of economy. The response to a crisis is always economic in every sense of that word. Just as we bring a crisis "in house" by naming it as such, one must always ask what is the quickest and most efficient way of bringing a crisis to an end. Equally, in the final analysis, we are often told a planetary crisis will be a question of economics. However, just as one must question reason as the axiom of crisis, then we must question whether economics can continue to stand as a strictly determinable region of competence in the face of such a crisis. One would have to ask if economics can offer a competent realm of judgment, decision, and will to respond to the demands of the incalculable. It is not that economics does not have a response to the incalculable, but rather that a response directed here cannot be purely or strictly economical. This is where philosophy makes a return in the economy of crisis management.

There is a clear and legible connection between what the oil industry calls "speculation" and the speculative philosophical enterprise. I would like to suggest that speculating for oil has been the basis of industrial modernity and the western economy for the last two hundred years (whether that oil was derived from the exploitation of hydrocarbons or whales is a moot point, even though the use of oil as a fuel dates, according to Herodotus, to Babylon 4,000 years ago). As that which fuels the engine of the economy, that which makes the economy as such possible, the search for oil is an investment in a venture with the hope of gain but with the risk of loss. The speculative structure of oil exploitation follows from and is now itself the basis for the structure of all investment in stock, property, and the fictional products of capital today. As with speculative philosophy, it involves the conjecture or theorization of a future event in the absence of the firm evidence of a present. It is this speculative structure that opens the future as a thinking of risk and as thinking as risk, that closely ties philosophy to the carbon economy. The question of the post-carbon economy is therefore clearly a matter of concern for philosophy. I have been careful to speak here from the beginning of a "post-carbon economy" (although we might also say "post-carbon-economies" since there will undoubtedly be more than one). While oil is a material thing, the stuff itself as it were, the price of oil is a question of economy, a matter of relation, and is irreducibly conceptual. My concern in this text is to think through the prospects for an economy and culture (if that is not a tautology) based upon the pricing of hydrocarbons as fuel. This question may come down to one that concerns the future of speculation itself, as much as it does a speculation on the future. I would like to offer a hypothesis here, even a speculation, apropos of today, that will need to be put at risk and tested, namely that whenever we speak of so-called "environmental catastrophe" the business of "financial crisis" is never far behind. In fact, a strong formulation of the hypothesis might be that the two are intimately connected, and that their relation always follows from a structure of speculation. In this sense, philosophy is what is put at risk and must put itself at risk by the conjuncture of the two.

Oil Reserves

The western-lead global economy is predicated on the value of oil. At the end of the Second World War, the Bretton Woods monetary conferences created the World Bank, the International Monetary Fund, and established a new international monetary system of competitive disinflation relative to the US dollar by tying the gold standard to the dollar. This system worked well for a while and enabled the post-war reconstruction of western Europe and Japan, and put in place the inaugural openings of the General Agreement on Tariffs and Trade which form the basis of the global economy today. However, the Bretton Woods Gold Exchange system began to break down in the mid-sixties under the pressures of the excessive costs of the Vietnam War and the resurgence of the European and south Asian manufacturing base as exporters of global trade. By November 1967 as the value of the dollar began to look increasingly precarious, withdrawals of gold bullion from the US Treasury were becoming excessive (as national governments, notably De Gaulle's France, redeemed their dollar holdings against bullion stocks as agreed at Bretton Woods). When sterling was devalued in 1967, Bretton Woods was doomed; the dollar came under further pressure to devalue itself against gold in order to protect the value of Federal reserves against redemption of dollars by foreign governments. The plot of Ian Fleming's 1959 *Goldfinger* (adapted as a film in 1964) can only be understood in relation to the Bretton Woods concords. The threat to render the Federal gold reserve inaccessible after exploding a radioactive bomb, would have meant national governments could only redeem their reserve dollars against Ulrich Goldfinger's own gold reserve (said to be the second largest in the world) thus pushing up the value of his gold and mortgaging the US economy to Goldfinger's personal enterprises. Consequently, James Bond, agent for the sick man of Europe, temporarily rescues not only the post-war, cold war status quo of the Bretton Woods agreement but secures the future of western leadership in a global economy. Rather than risk the depletion of the US gold reserve and the collapse of the US credit rating in 1971 President Nixon abandoned the dollar-gold link dissolving the terms of Bretton Woods in favour of a system of free floating currencies, with the international banks and the markets determining the value of the dollar. This combined with the ongoing costs of Vietnam lead to inflationary pressures and wage-price freezes in the American national economy. OPEC discussed the value of pricing oil in several currencies to spread the risks of the volatile American domestic scene. However, in 1974, Nixon moved to do a deal with Saudi Arabia only to price oil in dollars when the Saudis, unknown to the rest of OPEC and the US's western allies, secretly purchased $2.5 billion in US Treasury bills with their surplus oil funds (equivalent to 70% of all Saudi assets), once more ensuring the position of the dollar as the international reserve currency and initiating the phase of American global hegemony based on petrodollar recycling, swapping the gold standard for the standard of oil, so-called "black gold." As shocks in the price of oil followed political and supply instabilities, so the need for national governments to acquire US dollars ensued. On the one hand, dollars flow into oil supplying countries far beyond the needs of domestic investment. These surplus dollars are stored in banks in New York and London to retain their value as dollars. On the other hand, oil-importing countries need to buy dollars to meet the rising price of oil. In the 1970s developing nations in Africa borrowed dollars from international banks sitting on surplus petrol dollars, creating debts to be repaid entirely in dollars and at the then-high levels of interest rates based on inflationary pressures in the western national economies. In this way, the emergent, post-colonial African continent was impoverished and a cycle of crippling debt initiated. The IMF set up by Bretton Woods was used to enforce debt repayment to the international banks through the implementation of 'austerity' programmes that also opened up developing countries to western private companies. As surplus petrol dollars flow in from OPEC countries and are leant out again as Eurodollar bonds or loans, the Federal Reserve is in a unique position with respect to creating credit and expanding the money supply.[4] It is this situation that enables the United States to sustain improbable budget deficits and latterly allowed the bail out of Wall Street after the 2007 banking crisis. However, in a post-cold war, multi-polar era, after peak oil, the position of the dollar as world reserve currency is once more in question. Previous attempts to rebalance the world economy now have genuine impetus from the need to address the imbalance of current accounts between the US and China, Chinese currency manipulation, and the emergence of the Euro as an alternative or additional reserve currency. Further, the cost in blood and treasure of physically securing the oil supply through military means may prove unsustainable for the US (the cost of bailing out the banks, $660 billion, was the same as the US annual military budget for 2007). In a post-carbon economy, it might not be the best position to be sitting on a mountain of petrodollars.

There is then a great deal at stake in the question of a post-carbon economy, beyond the actual "irreversible" damage done to the earth's climate by carbon emissions. Oil is presently the essential fuel of the global economy and oil trades are the basic enablers of manufacturing infrastructure in every industrial nation, of global transportation, and the primary energy source for 40 percent of the industrial economy. Oil trades in dollars have been the basis for American economic, cultural, and military hegemony since the 1970s, and the liquidity that ensures the development of the western-lead global economy. A post-carbon economy presents a considerable challenge to the present geo-political dispensation and, co-terminus to this, the current conditions of capital. It is for these reasons that we might say that the response to climate change as a staging post in the on-going crisis of European humanity, revolves around more than a purely scientific solution that will bring the crisis to a dénouement to enable a return to western-capital normativity, and everything that depends upon it.

Modern as the phenomenon might be and while philosophy has a great deal to say about "energy," for example, if I might be allowed to paraphrase one of Derrida's more familiar hyperboles: no philosopher as a philosopher has ever taken seriously the question of oil. Oil and carbon emission has a massive readability today and may define the most acute moment of the paroxysm that makes the present crisis like no other. This is not to say that there have not previously been bouts of financial uncertainty and environmental disasters precipitated by oil. In fact, the history of oil production might be nothing other than a chain of such instances.

Rather, the most decisive index of the present moment is the toxic combination of climate change caused by carbon emission, the urgency for global capital of the risks of peak oil, and the central role played by oil trades in the global economy. We might go so far as to say on this later point that the entire practice of the western economy, that is the so-called global economy, depends upon oil. That is to say, that while the idea of the world market and of the "free exchange" of goods has a philosophical heritage running through early modern humanism and enlightenment thought, our present understanding of all exchange, debt, and faith runs through oil. To speak of a post-carbon economy might in fact be to say something quite radical, given that our present situation is so intensively related to the price of oil. To think an industrialized economy without the price of oil may on the one hand simply be a question of swapping one transcendental signifier for another, as gold was replaced by oil, so oil might be replaced by a trade in plutonium recycling. On the other hand, an opportunity exists here to understand economy as an experience of difference and as an encounter with the wholly other. This would require an other understanding of economy, one that was not dedicated to the utilization of wealth (what we now call a "restricted economy") but one in which we began to understand the complexities of a sovereign economic term such as gold or oil, not in its loss of meaning but in relation to its possible loss of meaning (what Derrida, after Bataille, after Hegel calls a "general economy").[5] In this sense, a "post-carbon economy," presents an opportunity for a consideration of economy not to be limited to the circulation of strictly commercial values, the meaning and established value of objects such as gold, oil, and plutonium or so-called "carbon swaps." Rather than a phenomenology of values as a restricted economy, we might begin to understand what exceeds the production, consumption, and destruction of value within the circuit of exchange. What Bataille might call "energy" beyond the energy of oil. This would not be a reserve of meaning within economy but an aneconomic writing of economy that is legible because its concepts move outside of the symmetrical exchanges from which they are identified and which according to a certain logic of recuperation they continue to occupy. This task of paleonymy as deconstruction is not one that philosophy will undertake on its own but one that will be played out in the irreversible mutations that take place in the global economy as a consequence of climate change, one which philosophy, opened by the materialism of nonphilosophy, will merely be at the forefront of reporting. It returns us to a familiar problem with which we began: having exhausted the oil reserve and the language of philosophy, the unfinished project of Modernity must continue to inscribe within its frames and language of intelligibility (i.e. philosophy) that which nevertheless exceeds the oppositions of concepts governed by its doxical logic. It is not that nineteenth and twentieth-century thought is incapable of responding to the new crisis of climate change but that climate change is a product of such thought as its latest episode and challenge. On the other hand, such a reading of economy seeks to understand or think what is unthinkable for philosophy, its economic blind spot.

The reserves of deconstruction suggest writing in general as a slick economy without oil reserve. Derrida's text on Bataille and economy was first published in *L'arc* in May 1967, well into de Gaulle's diplomatic and economic attack on Bretton Woods and American expropriation of the European economy through dollar investment. His seminar on counterfeit money was given in the academic year 1977–78, between the two shocks in the price of oil in 1974 and 1979, when, as Muriel Spark puts it her 1976 novel *The Takeover*, "a complete mutation of our means of nourishment had already come into being where the concept of money and property were concerned, a complete mutation not merely to be defined as a collapse of the capitalist system, or a global recession, but a sea-change in the nature of reality as could not have been envisaged by Karl Marx or Sigmund Freud" (127). Spark's fiction identifies here a "mutation" more significant than the local weather of a global recession or the collapse of western capitalism. She recognizes precisely the deportation of value itself from the symmetrical alternatives of exchange within a restricted economy of meaning. This is not a deconstruction brought about by philosophy but a critical climate change in the entire environment of meaning that shifts and re-settles of its own accord. For sure, capitalism survived the oil crisis of the early 1970s but as result there was an irreversible change and redistribution in the meaning of meaning itself. A clear line can be drawn from the substitution of gold for oil in 1971 to the credit bubble of 2007 and the transformations in capitalism (around futures and credit transfer derivatives) and the global economy (around the planetary production and consumption of natural resources). The question of the price of oil, and so of the petrodollar and the pricing of the global economy, must always be a question of the phenomenon of credit. The monetary crisis of 2007, the so-called "credit crunch," was a matter of the credit-worthiness and the credibility of the value of assets. Oil futures and the future of oil are a question of credit and so of faith: belief in the conventional authority of the market and the credibility of the economy, economists, and politicians. The authority of the market is constituted by the accreditation, both in the literal sense of capitalization and credit-worthiness in future exchanges but also in the sense of legitimation as an effect of belief or credulity. The authority of a fiction of economy such as a global financial and industrial system based on the future pricing of petroleum depends upon a planetary act of faith that far exceeds the credibility required to believe in climate change. It should not be surprising that the current financial crisis is a crisis of credit, a monetary crisis based upon the exchange of credit itself independent of physical assets, a dematerialization of money and value that requires a leap of faith and which in the absence of tangible proof tests that credibility to the limit: a sea change in the very idea of reality.

Carbon is the element that oils faith in the global economy. It is inextricably bound to the history of a formation of a world that is essentially Abrahamic and European. It is over the question of the propriety of oil that the geopolitical now plays out all the contests between Europe and its others, and between the religions of the book.[6] The price of oil is the liquidity that fuels what Derrida called in 1994, "the world war" between all the people of the book, whose preeminent figure is "the appropriation of Jerusalem" (*Spectres* 52). Faith in the book and faith in oil are the two pillars of globalization and the temple of capitalism. In the complex history of the development of industrial capital and industrial Capitals, the city, polis and metropolis, oil powers the transformation of monetary forms from the pre-modern faith in metals to the belief in credit exchanges and credit-worthiness of the name as signature or future position. In this history of Modernity, oil is surely then closely linked to literature, not only as the energy source that fuels the illumination of literary production, but as the alternative, yet intimately related, site of an idea of credit, debt, and belief that runs across the modern period. Oil itself is not the stuff of literature, although certain exceptional cases might be identified. For example, Melville's *Moby Dick* in 1851 is a text on the cusp of a transition from whale oil to hydrocarbons; modern literature would be unthinkable without the automobile, the aeroplane or gas lighting, from *The Great Gatsby* and *Mrs. Dalloway* to *Sherlock Holmes*. Zola's *Germinal* is one of many texts on the subject of carbon extraction, and Dickens' *Hard Times* is notable for its description of Coketown: better examples could no doubt be multiplied. On the other hand, film is the stuff of oil, and cinema is only a special case within the history of modern literature.

Post-Carbon Culturology

As Mac and Oldsen walk across a sunset beach in Bill Forsyth's *Local Hero*, the American petroleum negotiator asks his Scottish guide, "Can you imagine a world without oil?" Between them they make a list of the potential losses to modernity: "No automobiles, no paint or polish, no ink and nylon, no detergents, no Perspex, no polythene, no dry cleaning fluid and no waterproof coats." Mac stops Oldsen incredulously—"they make dry cleaning fluid out of oil?" They should also have added to this list "no film and no cinema." Acetate film or "safety film" replaced the combustible Nitrocellulose in the 1950s, and has in turn been superseded by polyester of PET film. *Local Hero* (1983) is a slick and economic film about the optimism of the North Sea oil rush in the 1970s. Environmental catastrophe is assured as the Knox Oil and Gas Company from Texas seek to transform a Scottish beauty spot into an oil refinery for the exploitation of North Sea oil reserves. However, the wily locals welcome this, understanding that striking oil will transform their lives from subsistence farming to considerable affluence. In the best traditions of Ealing comedy, Forsyth's villagers and their black African missionary minister, Murdo MacPherson, seek to extract the maximum value for their land from the American corporation that imagines that it is exploiting the locals. Nothing was known of the effects of climate change when this film was made. Instead, we have a comedy of aneconomic, colonial reversal and exchange, in which the Texan company (founded by a Scot, with a Calvinist work ethic no doubt) returns to appropriate the Scottish mainland, only to be exploited in return by subjects on the peripherary of an

American empire compelled to seek ever further afield for carbon stocks to fuel its industrial economy after US domestic peak oil. A series of visual parallels and exchanges are set up between the streets of Houston, a city arising from the desert and designed for the automobile, and Ferness [pronounced 'Fairness'] Bay, a fishing village with a sandy bay and rolling green hills, interrupted only by the leitmotif of a solitary motor cycle that appears every time Mac and Oldsen attempt to cross the street. NATO jets also disturb the bucolic scene, combining the advances of oil consumption with the defence of capitalism against the Soviet threat, reminding us of the strategic importance of the Scottish coastline and the north Atlantic oil reserves during the Cold War.

The development at Ferness Bay we are told will make the village the "petro-chemical capital of the western world" and will last a 1,000 years "even through the next Ice Age," which is a telling sign of the status of climate science at this time. Ricky Fulton playing the Knox Oil research scientist working on the project tells his colleague that the predicted Ice Age can be averted by diverting the Gulf Stream and melting the Arctic Circle, "but they won't listen, they want to freeze." There are no concerns here about global warming; rather the wild west of a black gold rush is returned from Texas to Scotland as the frontier of 'European' development and expansion, praising the oil industry as "some business…the only business." MacIntosh, the negotiator sent by Knox Oil to seal the deal, is of Jewish Hungarian stock but is mistaken by the lucky and cheerful Felix Happer (Burt Lancaster), CEO of Knox Oil and Gas, for a Scot. MacIntosh falls in love with the village, becoming more Scot than the Scots, and is one of the few sad to see it being bought out by his own company. Having agreed to set up a trust fund for the villagers, giving them faith in the project by allowing them a share of the profits, he offers to exchange his life in Texas with Gordon Urquart (the villagers' lead negotiator, hotelier, accountant, and mini-bus driver played by Dominic Lawson). He offers "thirty thousand dollars in mixed securities" and his Porsche ("nothing to pay on it, it's pure ownership") for the hotel and Urquart's wife Stella. However, the future of Ferness as a trading place is put on hold with the arrival of Felix Happer from Texas.

Happer is an obsessive amateur astronomer and is drawn to Scotland by MacIntosh's description of the aurora borealis. Happer has a messianic zeal for comets; "look to the heavens for a sign" he instructs MacIntosh before leaving for Scotland. He arrives in the village just as the acquisition has hit a snag. The beach where oil tankers would dock is owned by a beachcomber, Ben Knox, and has been owned by the Knox family for years (Happer's father having bought out the original oil-exploring Mr. Knox while retaining the company name). Several attempts are made to persuade Ben to sell his beach but he declines, explaining that the beach has provided the village economy for years, with between four and five hundred people earning a living through the extraction of chemicals from seaweed: "then the trade routes opened up to the East and farewell Ferness. The business went but the beach is still here. If you got the place, it would be goodbye beach forever." Mac is sidelined as Happer and Ben share their interest in astronomy. Happer abandons his plans to site an oil refinery on the beach in favor of something all together more refined— The Happer Institute for marine research and astronomical observation. Mac returns to Texas; justice has been done in Ferness, a local economy has been created once more around the beach and the proposed Happer Institute but the villagers will no longer be millionaires, as environmental damage has been replaced by marine research. However, it is not clear who the eponymous Local Hero is: the popular Mac, who offered millions of dollars to the villagers; Gordon Urquart, who negotiated on their behalf; the charismatic Soviet fisherman Victor, who visits Ferness to review his portfolio of investments with Urquart; Marina, the research assistant and mermaid (with webbed-feet) who proposes the research institute to Oldsen; or Ben Knox, whose refusal to sell the beach scuppers the oil refinery.

Few radical claims can be made for Forsyth's gentle comedy, but it might be worth noting some features of the film as a study in an economy without oil reserve. Whenever we confront the thematics and axiomatics of oil, there is always a mismatch in exchange values, and always the testing of faith. Mac initially hopes to exploit the locals, they in turn exploit him, Mac and Gordon's negotiations over the trust fund leads to a faith in one another and a proposed if unequal exchange and a wife swap, Ben offers to sell the beach to Mac if he can guess how many grains of sand he is holding but Mac refuses the deal thinking he is being cheated, and ultimately Ben refuses to put a price on the natural resource of the beach. However, this is a film about oil in which no oil appears; all of the comedy is fuelled by speculation concerning the value of the oil, as are the plastic positions adopted by those in pursuit of the movement from oil extraction to plastic and credit cards. When negotiations are ongoing with Mac over the trust fund, Gordon Urquart addresses the villagers from the Reverend MacPherson's pulpit asking them to have faith in him. Faith requires an economic gesture to invest belief in something without tangible evidence and the faith in the value of oil requires a speculative investment in economy without guarantee or reserve.

Local Hero represents an optimistic moment in the history of oil and its relation to money. Paul Thomas Anderson's 2007 *There Will be Blood* is another oil film that pushes the question of oil and faith to its limits. Once again this text works through a series of theo-thanato-econo-carbo exchanges and substitutions that test the faith of those involved in them. Daniel Plainview (played mesmerically by Daniel Day Lewis) is a silver miner who accidently strikes oil in 1898 during the exploration of California. By 1911 he has become an oil speculator seeking further openings in the state. He is told of substantial reserves under farmland owned by the Sunday family and having bought this information for $100 from the runaway son Paul, he visits the Sunday ranch. There he encounters Paul's father Abel and Paul's twin brother Eli (both brothers are played by Paul Dano). Paul's good news proves correct but Eli strikes a harder bargain and asks for $10,000 to fund the Church of the Third Revelation. However, Abel has a misplaced faith in the seeming Plainview and sells his birth right for a bargain price. Eli was the biblical last judge of Israel before the rule of kings, whose lineage was cursed for defilement of the temple. The filmic Eli's judgment comes into conflict with this Daniel-come-to-judgment on the Sunday oil fields, a veritable den in which it is increasingly difficult to tell who is lying and who is the lion, even when motives are barely disguised in plain view.

Daniel Plainview refuses to bless the first oil well, which he christens "Mary" after the Sunday's youngest daughter who is beaten by her father. He promises her "no more beatings" but the remainder of the film is little more than a chain of beatings in a tale of errant filiations and false fraternity. Daniel beats and humiliates Eli in public in a fight over a supposed loan to the Church; on discovery that the trusted Noah is not his long lost half-brother but a stranger who merely robbed him of his story, Daniel kills Noah and buries his body. However, having been witnessed in the act, Daniel must be baptized in the Church of the Third Revelation as the price of forgiveness for would-be fratricide and in exchange for a piece of land that will enable him to build a pipeline to the Californian coast. During his baptism, Eli humiliates and beats Daniel to exorcise his demons. Oil or the price of oil proves thicker than the blood of the lamb or the blood of the competing families. Eli leaves the community to go on a missionary trip to Las Vegas, while the repentant Daniel is reunited with his son HW who he sent away after losing his hearing in an industrial accident at the Mary well. Years later in 1927 we discover the now alcoholic Plainview in his oil man's mansion confronting his adopted son over his true parentage, stating "You have none of me in you ... I took you for no reason other than I needed a sweet face to buy land." HW communicates through sign language, renouncing any claim on a Plainview inheritance in order to marry his childhood sweetheart Mary Sunday, set up his own business, and practice the religion of the Third Revelation.

After all these signs and revelations, dissolved and resolved partnerships, the film overheats and reaches a tipping point in its final extraordinary scene. In 1927 Plainview lies plain drunk in the bowling alley he has had constructed in his mansion. He is visited by Eli who has become an evangelical radio host and pastor of a far larger church in Vegas. He offers to broker a deal with Daniel for the remaining land owned by the Bandy family over which the pipeline runs; the grandson of the Bandy family requires capital to leave the farm and move to Hollywood "to be in the movies." Daniel agrees to the deal only if Eli will admit that he is "a false prophet and God is a superstition." It emerges that Eli is bankrupt and in desperation agrees to Daniel's contract, and a third revelation of humiliation and beating ensues as the bowling alley substitutes for the previous scenes of the oil well and the church. Eli repeatedly calls out Daniel's words: "say it like you mean it, say it like it's your sermon." However, the broken Eli has put his faith in another false promise as Daniel tells him he has already drained all the oil from the Bandy land. He counsels the miserable Eli who admits that he is a sinner and his disappointment in the Lord who "failed to alert me to the recent panic in our economy...these mysteries he presents." Plainview chases him around the bowling alley striking him repeatedly with a skittle, sparing nothing over Eli's pleas that they are brothers by marriage. He rants "It was Paul who was the chosen brother, you are just after birth…I am the third revelation…I told you I would eat you up." The biblical Eli was the last keeper of the Ark of the Covenant who is told that his sons will die on the same day. With Eli's broken body and Daniel's broken promises littering the scene, Plainview tells his astonished butler "I am finished" as the credits roll.

Anderson's film is made in the full knowledge of the risks of oil production and consumption, as part of an epistemological climate change concerning global warming by 2008. This narrative contract with the viewer of who is also aware of the risks of global warming, is the third revelation of the film: neither the old testament of a covenant with the oil men as part of the manifest destiny of American expansionism, nor the good news of salvation from domestic Peak Oil by the arrival of the new resources in the lands of the Abrahamic tradition, but the apocalypse, namely that oil and the price of oil will bring about the end of everything. There are no comic villagers here with a touching faith in the developmental possibilities of oil exploration, only the singular promise of the sons of Eli that "there will be blood." There should be little doubt about the status of carbon in the world that Anderson's film addresses through the representation of its oily past. Globalization is a theo-thanato-carbo-economy in which all the spectres of the religious and the political, old and new, circulate in a death drive towards depletion and extinction. From the military enforcement of the value of the petrodollar in the Persian Gulf to the devastation of marine life in the Gulf of Mexico, where oil is concerned, as Plainview tells Eli at his baptism, "universal salvation is a lie." Instead the speculative structure of a carbon economy is, like philosophy, always a death drive. A drive towards extraction, consumption, burning off, calculating and fixing the price that must be paid. Similarly, philosophy drives to know and for absolute knowledge to posses the object of its inquiry. However, there is always a price to be paid for absolute knowledge and for speculating on oil. In the hydrocarbon cycle we are left with carbon deposits, traces in the atmosphere that are the cause of global warming and which threaten planetary life for years to come. Philosophical and textual production leaves other traces in carbon-based graphite and ink, which similarly escape the restrictions of circulation and exchange. Writing philosophy about carbon, like making film about oil, is one of those tasks that must inevitably inhabit the positions of the theo-thanato-carbo-economy but somehow render those positions plastic by reading the deposits emitted by the economy in order to rearrange them according to a new logic and criteriology. One must think about carbon and use carbon to do so in order that carbon and thinking about carbon might have a future. Dealing in carbon futures will be the coming task of all materialisms, theologies, politics, and ethics on a planet attempting to keep a world economy above water as the polar ice caps melt.

Post-Carbon Coda

This text has begun to open up a number of questions for thinking the present and future of a "European" culture and economy based on the consumption of oil. It has identified the interrelation of the present economic and environmental crises and suggested a role for philosophy in framing our understanding of these events. It has also proposed a history of oil pricing that demonstrates that its supposedly robust materiality is conceptual through and through. Finally, it has considered the relation of carbon consumption to the dematerialization of money and to faith, credit, debt, and literature (the later pointing towards alternative forms of exchange that disrupt established economies). At each of these steps, an attempt has been made to submit the experience of oil to a thinking of difference and to understanding the risk of climate change as an encounter with a wholly other (planetary life itself) that is also unlocking the reserves of difference within the human. It has proposed a hypothesis for future consideration: the inextricable link between financial crisis and environmental damage. The testing and demonstration of this hypothesis will require a larger work of comparison and analysis that will involve an expanded deconstruction of political economy, political theology, and the unavoidable question of what theory today calls bio-power. This speculation will require time and will give time, the time of a speculation proposed against redemption at a future date, in a race to keep the lights on as one writes in the shadow of oil depletion, a waning telos for a resource that will have been and which will never come again. It is a task of the carbonic economy that will be complicit with the very thing it provokes, ensuring its guilt of the exact thing it believes itself to be innocent of. Perhaps, there will be no thought on carbon without carbon. Perhaps philosophy since Plato will have only ever been a carbon-based form and the end of philosophy will have been the end of carbon. There will always be a price to be paid for such speculations with all hands to the pump in an epoch of what Tom Cohen calls "irreversible critical climate change."

Notes

1. See Jacques Derrida's "Faith and Knowledge: Two Sources of Religion at 'the Limits of Reason Alone'" in *Acts of Religion.*

2. Many of my comments here reprise Derrida's reflection on the idea of crisis in the text "Economies of the Crisis."

3. For example, see Derrida and Roudinescou 152.

4. For a fuller, if partisan, discussion of the petrodollar see Clark.

5. See Derrida's "From Restricted to General Economy: A Hegelianism without Reserve."

6. For a curious take on the messianic merits of oil exploration based on biblical promise, visit www.zionoil.com, a Wall Street listed company dedicated to speculating on oil reserves in the Holy Land.

Works Cited

Clark, William R. *Petrodollar Warfare: Oil, Iraq, and the Future of the Dollar.* Gabriola Island: New Society Publishers, 2005.

Derrida, Jacques. *Acts of Religion.* Ed. Gil Anidjar. New York: Routledge, 2002.

---. "Economies of the Crisis." *Negotiations: Interventions and Interviews, 1971–2001.* Trans. Elizabeth Rottenberg. Stanford: Stanford University Press, 2002.

---. "From Restricted to General Economy: A Hegelianism Without Reserve." *Writing and Difference.* Trans. Alan Bass. London: Routledge, 1978. 251–277.

---. *Given Time: I. Counterfeit Money.* Trans. Peggy Kamuf. Chicago: University of Chicago Press, 1992.

---. "Violence and Metaphysics: An Essay on the Thought of Emmanuel Levinas." *Writing and Difference.* Trans. Alan Bass. London: Routledge, 1978. 79–153.

Derrida, Jacques and Elizabeth Roudinescou. *For What Tomorrow... A Dialogue.* Trans. Jeff Fort. Stanford: Stanford University Press, 2004.

Fleming, Ian. *Goldfinger.* London: Jonathan Cape, 1959.

Local Hero. Dir. Bill Forsyth. Warner Bros., 1983. Film.

Spark, Muriel. *The Takeover.* London: Macmillan, 1976.

There Will Be Blood. Dir. Paul Thomas Anderson. Miramax, 2007. Film.

Chapter 12

Health

No Prescription, Not Now

EDUARDO CADAVA AND TOM COHEN

Yes, there is hope, infinite hope. But not for us.

– Franz Kafka

There are reasons why one might find in America itself a cipher today for extraordinary mutations and blinds. It is not just the accelerated undoing of empire, "democracy," global finance, and planetary resources under the silent droning of a captured telecracy. If America in this sense may seem the quiet epicenter of an epoch-defining ill or blind, if one's approach to it can only seem pharmacological, this makes its unfinished narrative of "health care" reform a sometime allegory of other ills without known prescriptions. Update: As the narrative of Obama's presidency continues to unfold in unpredictable ways, it remains embedded in the transformational time of an "America" in which certain episodes appear as ciphers. The contemporaneous blog that follows attempts to read one such cipher: the allegory of "health care." Captured upon entry by the credit and financial "crisis," Obama took office not only with enormous symbolic elation—among other things, breaking the racial code—but inheriting the catastrophic damages of the "Bush" parenthesis that have led commentators to suggest that Bin Laden succeeded in drawing "America" into a self-bankrupting and self-betraying spiral. There are too many names for the contemporary scene: the unraveling of an empire, the complete takeover by the feudal corporate order, the mediacratic trances that already imply a post-democratic era, capitalism in its hyper-autophagic financialization mode, and the shadow of all the climate unravellings, the scarcity of oil or water, that are repeatedly and functionally denied. Obama increasingly inhabits a curi-

ous disjuncture between the rhetoric of the possible he marketed and the ir-reversible facts he faces, with each one signaling its own form of irreversibility. This is why, at least for now, we can only read the process of an illness in snip-pets, reportage, the flux of contemporary symptoms. From today's perspective (January 2011, exactly one year after the following remarks were written), "Obamacare" has passed but remains a miasma: the signature victory has been demonized and defaced successfully, the trade-offs and lobbyist adjust-ments have done nothing to address its core issue (budgetary collapse), and the bill risks Republican defunding. This episode and palimpsest opens onto other logics that have yet to be played out. (January, 2011)[1]

~

As we write [January 2010], the monstrous compromise that recently has emerged as the signature of health care reform in the United States is still tortuously winding its way through Congress, even as its fate re-mains uncertain. Having moved from great expectations to a motley mix of payoffs and paybacks, the reform effort was struck another body blow in January with the election of Scott Brown to fill Ted Kennedy's sena-torial seat in Massachusetts, depriving the democrats of their filibuster-proof majority. This surprise Republican victory left many predicting that the whole reform effort is dead in the water, or that it will be cut down even further. Given that the health care and insurance industries have had their way, first through their hold on key senators, then through this electoral upset, it is well worth adding the event that makes the fu-ture here perfectly clear: the recent Supreme Court decision to regard corporations as persons and to remove all restrictions on monies flow-ing into campaigns in the name of "freedom of speech." This decision will only facilitate and reinforce the lobbying efforts that have corrupted and crippled the entire health care debate. Against this background, however, we at least would like to offer a still-to-be-finished symptomatology of some of these developments in a dossier for future readers under the title "stories from a zombie democracy," from, that is, a democracy that in-creasingly has handed over its agency to the telecratic tentacles of capital in general. In particular, we wish to delineate the symptoms represented and embodied not only in the rhetorical strategies that have formed the basis of the health care debate but also in the political and social configuration of America's political and national body.

Broken Promises

In order to begin, we would like to evoke a hoped-for future that could not, and cannot, be realized, and for what can be said to be structural reasons. For indeed there was a possible hope—if not an opening—that, with the election of Barack Obama, another face of the "United States" might appear. If this hope could be realized, it would mark, in the chant that energized and articulated it, a "change" we could "believe in," a formulation that suggests that what was at stake was a political scenario that simultaneously was *a metaphysical text*.

But we still can imagine the alternative events, even if this imagined scenario remains a fantasy, and especially when it attaches itself to the figure of Obama alone. We can never remind ourselves enough that Obama himself is simply an effect, the symptomatic embodiment of the desires of a heterogeneous collective grown weary not only of the excesses of the Bush Administration but also of a hyper-capitalist system whose madness is legible in its desire to define, absorb, and determine everything, beginning with the ethical sphere. Nevertheless, the fantasy is compelling: entering office with the specter of economic catastrophe and a stated mandate for "change," "Obama" takes advantage of this shift in circumstances and, rather than only making a few minor face-lifting improvements, rather than pursuing the same politics or economic policies in a more appealing mode, lets more Wall Street firms collapse and therefore breaks the grip of a zombie Ponzi scheme encircling the planet. This act would not only interrupt the Ponzi scheme of deferred "credit" on which the global economy had relied (including the immense and incalculable debt to imaginary future generations), but also the more devastating Ponzi scheme of credibility and reference itself. Indeed, the latter effectively had dissimulated and nearly erased the specter of global climate change and mutating material conditions for "life as we know it" and thereby permitted (and still permits) the withdrawal of resources such as water, oil, species, land, and so on, from generations still to come.

But against this backdrop—and the set of catastrophes that he inherited—Obama works to interrupt the disastrous inertia of America's suicidal drive. This impulse was unleashed and intensified by the Bush Administration, and is just one element of a suicidal impulse that increasingly determines our species and that goes hand-in-hand with the aggression that is widely carried out against the weak within an ensemble of political, cultural, religious, and economic considerations. It has led ("post-9/11") to a loss of wealth, the loss of "democracy" under the pretext of expanding it, the justification of wars that, ostensibly about the spread of democracy and human rights, increasingly sought to concentrate natural resources and capitalist riches in the hands of a small and privileged part of the human world, and the confirmation of the ongoing, but unacknowledged, racism and neglect that was displayed openly after Katrina. The consequences of Obama's activism would have been a manageable depression in which the financial system would have had to reorganize, oil prices would require an energy consumption pullback, and the opening for a mass infrastructure work project and health care assignation would begin processually to undo the corporate stranglehold and thereby rewrite the national contract in relation to its founding promises.

Crises

If we have begun with this imagined scenario, it is not only to emphasize its distance from what has transpired in the months that have passed since Obama's Inauguration on January 20th, 2009, but also to suggest that the theater of "health care" in America, taken up by Obama as a sure-fire winner, must be read against parallel American crises. Among these—taken up by Obama alongside (and at the same time as) the issue of health care—is "climate change." On the surface, it would seem to be the opposite: a global long-term argument that only takes away from the most urgent and "short-term" present, hurts jobs and companies, and so on. This change in climate cannot be represented or fully comprehended, and can only mean giving things up, including an "Americanness" of sorts (an "Americanness" supported by the fact that, although the United States includes only 5% of the world's population, it consumes 25% of its energy). The legislative initiatives were begun simultaneously and both appear now largely deferred and dead, even as Obama limps to Copenhagen with an unenforceable fig-leaf equal to half of what the scientists consider the inarguable limits to stave off future disaster. One can ascribe all of this to the "short time" cycles of American mediatric reality, or to the determined interests and markets that have decided that all of this is irrelevant to the hyper-rich and to the corporate economy, which would regardless retain their power and survivability.

In striving to return each fallen Humpty Dumpty back to its perch (the economy, Afghanistan and Iraq, Guantanamo, international and diplomatic relations, and so on), Obama misread his moment—and, in so doing, also hastened the very "long-term" catastrophics that he has understood and named clearly. He turned immediately to a managerial restoration mode that relied mostly on financial advisers with ties to Wall Street and the Clinton Administration and that, in the aftermath of the bailout logic of the Bush regime, made the stimulus package the defining initiative of his first 100 days. The battle over the stimulus package, however—which led to a stimulus that was significantly smaller than what was required—set at least one of the stages for the ensuing debate over health care, since its effect on the national debt now is said to constrain what is possible on the health care front.

This is why Obama's health care initiative must be viewed from within this broader *relapse*. According to some, Obama has wanted to embody a presidential style very different than that of Bush: unlike Bush, he would not rush to seize power or enforce his will, he would refuse to exploit a crisis for political gain, he would be rational and calm, a flawless manager rather than a rash and arrogant decider. He would give to his Congress the power to formulate a health care plan that would be universal, or at least accessible and optimally cost reductive, but, by the time the smoke would clear, a bouillabaisse of cut deals and loopholes—arguing that, if reform is anti-market, it is anti-individual—would be shaped and shaven by the corporate industry through senatorial hacks. The debate quickly morphed into a political meme, an emotive or marketing opportunity for the Fox News mode of incessant attack, keyword implants, caricature, and disinformation, all of which aimed at the *delegitimation* of Obama. In this context, Obama becomes less our hoped-for transformer than a tragic figure in the making.

It is essential to trace the means and effects of this effort to unsettle Obama's credibility. How is it, for example, that those who would be most helped by health care reform (the one-time white working class) appear to go against their own vital interests to, among other things, uphold a meme of Americanism versus the foreign (France, Britain, Canada, "socialism," and so on) in the interest of corporate acceleration? How is it that America leaves a significant portion of its population uncovered by health care or lets the insurance industry wield brutal license to use absurd technicalities to cut off people from their plans, even as the spiral of profits—autotelic, and mirroring Wall Street—guarantees a crash resulting from medical expenditures in the next several years? It is tempting to read all the contradictions and aporias at work here, including the subtle racial politics they assume. We would need a long review of America's falling education, its faith-based politics, its open oligarchism and mediatic spells. But as Obama took up this "fight," he became the Hamlet manager of America's post-imperial stupor, resulting in a Potemkin plan that itself is on the verge of being scuttled. What interests us is the allegorical text that seems to be unfolding here.

Rhetorical Implosions

As we already have suggested, the health care debate as a cultural moment appears as a symptomology of a broader set of ills, the ox-wailing of a sick obese animal stuck in the oily swamp of its own making. The health care initiative is a symptomology for a deeper ill, or *mal*, the illness that is reflected in the zombified system that now defines "America" in ways that go beyond the declining empire syndrome. Here we will read just three of the ideological and rhetorical weapons mobilized and directed against health care reform: the *public option, death panels*, and *abortion*:

1) "Public option"—this trope has garnered all the fear and manipulation of the corporate and rightwing rhetorical machine. Initially formulated as the lynchpin of the government's health care reform program, the public option not only would provide insurance to those presently without it, but also would by itself be able to pre-empt the catastrophic medical costs that are projected to sink the economy even further in the next few years. Without this option, millions of consumers will be steered to

insurance companies without any checks on premiums or costs. The American Medical Association accordingly is dead-set against it, pharmaceutical companies reject it out of hand, and the largest insurance companies will not consider it. A clear target, how was it so beautifully and effectively assaulted?

The "public option"—the sole effort to counter health industry monopolies—would be spun so that the word "public" would be heard as "socialism" (a nescient code term from twentieth-century imaginaries and binaries), and "option" would be translated into the sign of government dictatorship, since, as the argument goes, the public option implies a government takeover of American health care. First chiasmus. This latter deflection cannot be dissociated from the rhetorical fringe in which Obama is then cast not only as Kenyan, alien, or illegitimate (think "Bush"), but further—according to, among others, the increasingly popular and rightwing extremist, Glenn Beck—as simultaneously a Stalin and a Hitler. Second chiasmus. As Slavoj Žižek recently has suggested, what is legible in this sequence is "the material force of the ideological notion of 'free choice' within capitalist democracy." Indeed, the Republican Party and the medical lobby (the latter much stronger than even the defense lobby) then convince a large percentage of the public that a "public option"—and even more a system of universal health care—would threaten *freedom of choice* in all matters concerning health and medical treatments (since nearly everyone would be *required* to purchase health insurance). If the simple evocation of this potential threat makes all recourse to contrary evidence entirely ineffective, it is because we are here at the neuralgic point, the first ideologeme, of the American emotive reflex: freedom of choice. The concept of "freedom of choice" is not only at the heart of a certain concept of "American-ness," which is why Obama also can be accused of being non-American, but also the hinge of the campaign against him, since his election is what represented this ostensible choice most clearly. Third chiasmus.

If this ideological battle were to be overcome, the Obama Administration would have to persuade its citizens that, in order to exercise the freedom of choice, a complex network of economic conditions, social and legal regulations, and even, we would say, ethical rules, have to be in place (as the consummate "American" writer, Ralph Waldo Emerson, would put it: "'Tis fine to speculate and elect our course, if we must accept an irresistible dictation"). In today's America, however, this is an impossible lesson to convey, given the absence of any sense of "common good" and the destructive battle lines of a post-democratic telecracy. What instead is reinforced is the ideologeme of "free choice" and all of its concomitant concepts: the self, consciousness, intention, reason, the responsible subject, and, as we have said, "America" itself. Further reinforcing this meme, opponents of health care reform have launched protest movements in the name of free choice that warned of death panels, raised the specter of Nazi Germany, and portrayed the bill as a major step down the road to Communism.

2) "Death Panels": Enter the an-erotic nymph of the satyr-play of the zombie-Imperium, Sarah Palin, who, in a statement on her *Facebook* page in August 2009, first launched the rhetorical grenade of the "death panel" threat into the health care debate. Even though the draft health care bill explicitly states that the proposal "shall not include any recommendation to ration health care, raise revenues or Medicare beneficiary premiums... increase Medicare beneficiary cost sharing (including deductibles, coinsurance, and copayments), or otherwise restrict benefits or modify eligibility criteria," Palin initiated her *Mediscare* tactic with the following set of remarks: "And who will suffer the most when they ration care? The sick, the elderly, and the disabled, of course. The America I know and love is not one in which my parents or my baby with Down Syndrome will have to stand in front of Obama's 'death panel' so his bureaucrats can decide, based on a subjective judgment of their 'level of productivity in society,' whether they are worthy of health care. Such a system is downright evil." A serial liar, Palin continues to insist on the existence of such panels and finds her political prospects shoot up, even after several fact-checking organizations have declared her claim an outright lie.

These two little words in fact have helped derail the town hall meetings that initially were designed to promote rational discussion of health care, a dialogue between lawmakers and their constituents, by stirring up such unruly dissent that legislators have been shouted down by their own constituents.

Palin's fevered warning led to cries of "euthanasia" from angry citizens at health care town hall meetings all across the country, and even led one person to ask: "Adolf Hitler called his program the 'Final Solution.' What will we call ours?" Raising the specter of "death panels"—the Obama plan was later said to be modeled on the order personally written and signed by Hitler in 1939, which set up the Tiergarten 4 board which Hitler mandated to cut health costs by denying health care to those whose lives Hitler and the board determined were not worth living—Palin's inflammatory claim was a shout of "fire" in a crowded theater, a meme grenade rolled down the aisle. Exhibiting the lurid imagination of someone looking for a fight, Palin and others served up a rhetorical orgy of fantasized violence and imagined revolution that, proceeding via opportunistic, conspiracy theories, would stop at nothing to destroy Obama's presidency. What needs to be stressed here is the *branding* and marketing that, together, suggest why the health care debate is less about health care than it is about more deep-seated ills.

In the aftermath of Palin's claim, the bizarre Nazi-Communist-Stalin accusations directed against Obama by the so-called "tea partiers" (drawing on the origins of American revolt from the British) were soon joined to the "rigged town-meetings," where mob-mentality was staged to intimidate politicians and to dominate the media stage decisively. Indeed, while Palin and her collaborators conjured "death panels" that would triage grandma and interrupt the American fantasy of escaping death altogether, of the eternal now of consumption, such panels already could be said to exist, to be enacted and enforced, in what the insurance industry now practices when it rejects and denies insurance claims on the basis of pre-existing conditions (including, among so many others, cancer, diabetes, spousal abuse, pregnancy, and infant obesity).

More interestingly, the insight that the figure of "death panels" conceals hovers within the imaginary fusion of "Hitler" Obama with "Stalin" Obama, the Negro-fascist nightmare of an older white America emanating from the populist-fascist working class that continues to have its strings pulled by insurance industry magnates and the likes of Fox News. Those most likely to benefit from even the mild reforms appear co-opted by the corporate telecratic circuits to exclude racial others once designated as even more dispossessed than they are (and, in the case of illegal immigrants, as un-American). But the insight remains: by invoking the imaginary of the wars of the twentieth century, of the "good" America against its evil twins, a slippage occurs that extends beyond the current issues into the allegorical zones already mentioned (with the specter of "climate change" re-reading all from elsewhere, outside, the future, and the present at war with itself). Rather than "winning" these wars and instituting an era of free-market democratic triumph, these efforts only reveal the contradictions that structure this particular historical moment, and not only this one. As Agamben has noted, a trace of the "Nazi" project lingers, virally, in the biopolitical orders of the post-global order— or in the afterlife of an era of democracy that is still mimicking its own greatest propaganda hits of the past. The fusion of the Chinese ("communist") with the Western ("democratic") hypermarket models parallels the drift toward authoritarian rules that Bush presaged (not least the state of hyper-surveillance and de-politicization of the citizen, a permanent or normative "state of emergency" without end) and which the coming logics of climate change (resource wars, underclass triage, extinction events) irreversibly underwrite today. In doing this, they mirror the impossible conditions of the health care debate. This is why, we might say, the true death panels are the networks that seek to consolidate capital's reign over America and beyond, and do so once again—as in the case with the "public option"—by suggesting a government takeover of "choice," in this instance the choices the elderly and chronically-ill would otherwise have in regard to their care and treatment.

3) "Abortion": Abortion emerged as a major hurdle in the push for healthcare reform legislation, with an amendment from pro-life Democrats to bar federal funds from helping to pay for abortions. Although they claimed that the new health care plan would require Americans to "subsidize abortion with their hard-earned tax dollars," there are presently no provisions within any version of the health care plan that would permit full abortion coverage. In fact, there is an amendment in a key version of the House plan that specifically seeks to ensure that federal funds are not used to subsidize abortion coverage.

The efforts of the pro-life contingent can be read in the same light as the "death panel" attacks, since, like Palin, it mobilizes the same emerging theo-tropic violence that—recoiling as well before climate science as a conspiracy of the left and assaulting "evolution" in American schools— works to confuse and manipulate the debate toward its own political ends. These memes merge, not as equivocations about ending fetal-life through state funding (since any possibility that the government could help fund abortions already has been removed from the reform bill), but because, in the contemporary American context, everything depends on a *contract*. Not with a "Constitution" that theoretically made everyone "free" (despite the rhetoric of the tea-baggers), but with a contract that assumes that what they are ontologically—"man," "Christian," "American," "free agent"—is guaranteed as property, undefiled by monkey ancestors, geological time, or anthropic (and racial) privilege.

Rather than be concerned with the unborn (after all, future generations are here collectively being sacrificed by ignoring imminent climate disasters and by impeding progress on the health care front), the *symbolic of abortion* lies in its positive assertion of a human life, made in God's image, and of the right of this "life" to come into the world once it is conceived—where it can then be triaged, or denied medical care with a pre-existing condition (such as "chubby baby syndrome"). Thus the rhetoric of "pro-life" harbors a necrophantic kernel, the nihilist core and disappearing point of that last extincting trace of the trailing American cloud: the desubjectivized consumer that cannot imagine anything beyond an endless reproduction that, in the "future," would similarly be guaranteed. In this scenario, the middle class increasingly becomes the vanishing point of America's emerging transformation into a feudal corporate oligarchy that, in Paul Krugman's term, inevitably will experience its great "unraveling."

With arguments that mirror each other, everything in the abortion debate results from the exigencies of political and rhetorical framing. For example, the labels "pro-choice" and "pro-life" both presume the values of liberty and freedom, even as they each suggest that the opposition must be "*anti*-choice" or "*anti*-life" (alternatively "pro-*coercion*" or "pro-*death*"). Such arguments dissimulate the underlying issue of *which* choice or life is being considered and *whose* choice or *what kind* of life is deemed most important. This is why the constituency that is angered by any hint that its privacy and capacity for choice will be diminished (by a government takeover of health care, for example) is often the same constituency that opposes the pro-choice argument for the privacy of the decision for or against abortion.

The chiasmic reversals that are legible here take on an even more vertiginous and unsteady form when we register that it has become increasingly difficult to fix and define a discourse of life itself, since we generally think of those who favor increased reproductive freedoms as "pro-choice" and those who oppose them as "pro-life" (why is it, for example, that so many pro-life activists support the death penalty and war, and, as we are noting, are against a health care initiative that could save innumerable lives and indeed make many other lives more livable?). What seems lost in this game of spin and emotional blackmail is the simple fact that the matter of abortion is itself a health care issue, since the possibility of abortion is linked not simply to death but also to life. Indeed, the initiative of health reform has begun in the recognition that our obligation is as much to make lives livable as it is to life itself, and to a life that we know is from the beginning already touched by death.

Three Symptoms

We cut short this quick symptomatology to return to the real patient, America itself, and to the allegorical real that traverses this shadow play that pretends to address the patient's ill by restoring the country's dependency on the insurance lobby and corporations. As we already have noted, the latter represents a different sort of body, a non-subjective "legal" citizen, but one that, as the United States Supreme Court now has declared, has the rights of a subject to make unlimited political contributions, and brings the Wizard from behind the screen. If tempophagy is what one might call the active consumption of "time" in an accelerated turning back that feeds on itself, we conclude with a series of three symptoms that begin to enter legibility in spectral fashion, as the confusing life-support of a post-Imperium zombie "democracy" made even more legible by the recent health care debate:

1) What is most legible in the current debate—and especially in the ongoing diminishment of health reform in general—is that America herself is increasingly entering the zone of the uninsured, self-curtailed by its "pre-existing condition" in the still-expanding implications of what we telegraphically can name the "Bush catastrophe" and of being "America"

in a palpably post-democratic era. America finds itself entirely unprovided for in a world that it has both helped shape and destroy.

2) Without any remedy, the import of the zombie trope returns (zombie banks, zombie politics, and a host of zombie films that make light of the question: vampire or zombie?, the two "public options" we have left for us today). For what "Obama" (as the name of a network of mediated relations) performs across the boards is a naming of the "dilemma" and then a recoil, a refold, a reinscription into the same order we were to have left behind—a reflex to restitute the façade of the familiar, to restore the discredited institution in order to simulate minimal functionality. Even if this script was handed to Obama by the Bush Administration, it doesn't matter, since he remains unable to break its spell in the mediacracy that has supplanted the pretense of "democracy." As with Bush, this tactic appears less a defense against catastrophic logics than a contrived deferral and acceleration of them, a Ponzi scheme in re-animation mode. Increasingly losing his credibility, Obama mimes the evacuation of credit from within an accelerated system anticipating intervention from without (whether this intervention is to arrive in the form of technological solutions, rapture, or the debt and deprivations of the unborn on a dying earth).

Whether what we still call Capital has, as some imagine, an illimitable capacity to manufacture such relapses is hard to discern. If the current system accelerates in relative inertia, this would mean, according to calculations, not just the usual litany of climate catastrophics and their related consequences, but a virtual splitting of populations-to-come into the gated communities of the hyper-wealthy and everyone else—a virtual species split, which links the "survivor" of tomorrow to the eugenics of the "Nazi" phantom, albeit in accordance with wealth rather than with race, at least officially. From this perspective, which always has been that of the corporate right in America, there simply is no point in juggling health care to include everyone. Such a pretense would have to disappear at some point regardless.

3) The health care debate plays to the current symptomatology of an "America" paralyzed internally by a sort of numb panic and tempophagy. What the gods would destroy, they first drug and stupefy (lead-poisoning in Rome would not in any way compare to what is in today's acquifers,

e.g. cocaine, anti-depressants, hypertoxins). It may be that Obama knows this and is merely managing things to an honorable appearing sleep, differently than "Bush," who had stuck all the needles and IVs in the patient to keep her ignorant and distracted, using "9/11" as a narcotic and plotting resource acquisitions for the elite decades hence (we might recall here the innovation of the film *2012*, where the moneyed elite keep the information of a megadisaster to themselves as they plot their exclusive escape). Beneath the reflecting surfaces in this labyrinth are the metaphysics and econometrics of pharmaceuticals and drugs. So pervasive is this in "America" today that it links wars and global politics, failing neighbor states with new shadow narco-states, deals cut with the pharmaceuticals that also accept the toxification of current generations *en masse* (of which traces abound, now, in the river systems) and mediacratic spells that reinforce this intoxication in a way that, as we have tried to suggest, hopes to make true and lasting health reform in the United States a thing of hope rather than of reality. This is why, if "there is hope, infinite hope," it is increasingly "not for us."

In an environment in which "hope" has wrought so much peril—co-opted as it has been by the telecracy as a meme of delay and a façade for re-inscription—would it not be best to retire "hope" in its current forms? Is it possible to inaugurate a politics finally *without hope*? This is perhaps an impossible hope, but the one that seems most commensurate to what the recent health care debates have exposed and left for us to read. In the end, perhaps we can only hope that our being without prescription or remedy may reap us a benefit that we cannot yet see.

Notes

1. This essay forms a sort of "pharmacopolitical blog" on an episode from recent, or current, Americanology—and poses the question of illness, of a state of being without "prescription" for that ill or its contemporary spells. Such "texts" today, whether that of the Gulf oil spill or Bernie Madoff's adventures, arise and disappear from view, as their logics and lines of contamination (or force) continue to permeate the still-unfolding. To this extent, the episode of "Obamacare" cresting in early 2010 is such a thread. A version of this article appeared in *Hurly Burly, The International Lacanian Journal of Psychoanalysis*, 3 April 2010. http://www.amp-nls.org/en/template.php?sec=publications&file=publications/hurly_burly/003.html.

Notes on Contributors

Eduardo Cadava teaches in the Department of English at Princeton University, where he also is an Associate Member of the Department of Comparative Literature, the School of Architecture, and the Center for African American Studies. He is the author of *Words of Light: Theses on the Photography of History* and *Emerson and the Climates of History*, and co-editor of *Who Comes After the Subject?*, *Cities Without Citizens*, and a special issue of the *South Atlantic Quarterly* entitled *And Justice for All?: The Claims of Human Rights*. He is currently finishing a collection of essays on the ethics and politics of mourning entitled *Of Mourning* and a small book on the relation between music and techniques of reproduction, memorization, and writing entitled *Music on Bones*. He also is co-directing a multi-year project entitled "The Itinerant Languages of Photography" that includes scholars, artists, and curators from various countries, but mostly from Latin America.

Timothy Clark is Professor of English at the University of Durham and a specialist in the fields of modern literary theory and continental philosophy (especially the work of Martin Heidegger and Jacques Derrida), also in Romanticism (especially P.B. Shelley) and ecocriticism. He has published many articles in literary and philosophical journals and published seven monographs, including recently *Martin Heidegger, Routledge Critical Thinkers Series*, 2nd ed. (Routledge, 2011), *The Poetics of Singularity: The Counter-Culturalist Turn in Heidegger, Derrida, Blanchot and the later Gadamer* (Edinburgh UP, 2005), *The Cambridge Introduction to Literature and the Environment* (2011). He is currently working on a monograph provisionally entitled Green Deconstruction, forthcoming in this OHP series.

Tom Cohen is Professor of English and co-director of the *Institute on Critical Climate Change* at the University at Albany. He is the author of *Anti-Mimesis, Ideology and Inscription,* and *Hitchcock's Cryptonymies v. 1 &*

2. His most recent title, co-authored with Claire Colebrook and J. Hillis Miller, is *Theory and the Disappearing Future: On de Man, On Benjamin* (Routledge, 2011).

Claire Colebrook is Edwin Erle Sparks Professor of English at Penn State University. She has written books on Deleuze, literary history, gender, literary criticism, and contemporary European philosophy.

Catherine Malabou is currently Professor of Philosophy at Paris X Nanterre and will join the University of Kingston (CRMEP) next fall. Her most recent book, *Changing Difference, Feminism and Philosophy*, will come out with Polity Press in June 2011.

Robert Markley is the W. D. and Sara E. Trowbridge Professor of Literary Studies at the University of Illinois and Editor of the interdisciplinary journal, *The Eighteenth Century: Theory and Interpretation*. His books include *The Far East and the English Imagination, 1600–1740* (Cambridge, 2006) and *Dying Planet: Mars in Science and the Imagination* (Duke, 2005). He is completing a book on literature and science during the Little Ice Age.

J. Hillis Miller is UCI Distinguished Research Professor at the University of California at Irvine. He has published many books and essays on 19th and 20th century literature and on literary theory. His most recent books are *For Derrida* (Fordham, 2009) and *The Medium is the Maker: Browning, Freud, Derrida, and the New Telepathic Ecotechnologies* (Sussex Academic Press, 2009). His *The Conflagration of Community: Fiction Before and After Auschwitz* will appear in 2011 from the University of Chicago Press. A book co-authored with Claire Colebrook and Tom Cohen, *Theory and the Disappearing Future: On de Man, On Benjamin*, appeared in 2011 from Routledge. Miller is a Fellow of the American Academy of Arts and Sciences and a member of the American Philosophical Society. He received the MLA Lifetime Scholarly Achievement Award in 2005.

Jason Groves is a Ph.D. candidate at Yale University where he is completing a dissertation, entitled *Erratic Blocks: Fictions of Movement from Goethe to Benjamin*, which deals with attempts in literature, geology, and biomechanics to conceptualize erraticity. His engagement with critical climate change in the humanities spans several years and includes contributions to *The Global South* and *Impasses in the Post-Global*.

Mike Hill is an Associate Professor and Department Chair of English at the University at Albany, SUNY. His books are *After Whiteness: Unmaking an American Majority* (NYU: 2004); *Masses, Classes, and the Public Sphere*, contrib. ed (Verso: 2000); and *Whiteness: A Critical Reader* (1997). He is currently finishing a book on the moral and philosophical writing of Adam Smith, and has an additional project under way on twenty-first century warfare for the University of Minnesota Press.

Martin McQuillan is Professor of Literary Theory and Cultural Analysis at Kingston University. London, where he is also Dean of Arts and Social Sciences and Director of The London Graduate School. His most recent monographs are *Deconstruction after 9/11* (2009) and *Roland Barthes, or, the Profession of Cultural Studies* (2011).

Justin Read is Associate Professor in the Department of Romance Languages and Literatures at the University at Buffalo (SUNY). His research interests include the urbanization and modernization of the Americas since 1880. His first book, *Modern Poetics and Hemispheric American Cultural Studies*, was published by Palgrave in 2009. Read's articles have appeared in the *Journal of Latin American Cultural Studies*, *Revista de Estudios Hispánicos*, *Journal of Architecture*, and *Modernism/Modernity*, among others. Read is co-founder of the UB Research Group in Cultural Studies of Space.

Bernard Stiegler is Director of the Institut de recherché et d'innovation (IRI) and founder of Ars Industrialis and the Ecole de Philosophe d'Epineuil-le-Fleuriel. Among his recent works in translation are *The Decadence of Industrial Democracies: Disbelief and Discredit, 1* (2011), *Taking Care of Youth and the Generations* (2010), *For a New Critique of Political Economy* (2010), and *Acting Out* (2009).

Joanna Zylinska is a cultural theorist writing on new technologies and new media, ethics and art. She is a Reader in New Media and Communications at Goldsmiths, University of London. The author of three books—*Bioethics in the Age of New Media* (MIT Press, 2009), *The Ethics* *of Cultural Studies* (Continuum, 2005) and *On Spiders, Cyborgs and Being Scared: the Feminine and the Sublime* (Manchester University Press, 2001)—she is currently writing a new monograph on the idea of mediation, *Life after New Media* (with Sarah Kember) for the MIT Press, and working on a translation of Stanislaw Lem's major philosophical treatise, *Summa Technologiae*. She is one of the Editors of *Culture Machine,* an international open-access journal of culture and theory. Zylinska combines her philosophical writings with photographic art practice.

Printed in Great Britain
by Amazon